# The Man Who Saved New York

# The Man Who Saved New York

## Hugh Carey and the
## Great Fiscal Crisis of 1975

Seymour P. Lachman

and

Robert Polner

excelsior editions
State University of New York Press
Albany, New York

Cover photo of Hugh Carey courtesy of the New York State Archives.

Published by State University of New York Press, Albany

For information, contact State University of New York Press, Albany, NY
www.sunypress.edu

Excelsior Editions is an imprint of State University of New York Press

Production by Ryan Morris
Marketing by Michael Campochiaro

**Library of Congress Cataloging-in-Publication Data**

Lachman, Seymour.
    The man who saved New York : Hugh Carey and the great fiscal crisis of 1975 / Seymour P. Lachman and Robert Polner.
        p. cm.
    Includes bibliographical references and index.
    ISBN 978-1-4384-3453-7 (hardcover : alk. paper)
    1. Finance, Public—New York (State)—New York.   2. Municipal Assistance Corporation for the City of New York.   3. Emergency Financial Control Board. 4. Carey, Hugh L.   I. Polner, Rob.   II. Title.

HJ9289.N4L33 2010
974.7'043092—dc22
[B]                                                                          2010018903

10 9 8 7 6 5 4 3 2 1

# Contents

# Acknowledgments

This book would not have been possible without the editing and research assistance generously provided by Murray Polner. The authors are also grateful to Richard Guarasci, the president of Wagner College of Staten Island, New York, the college's Hugh L. Carey Institute for Government Reform, and the Institute's executive assistant, Susan Rosenberg.

Our thanks go out to former Governor Hugh L. Carey for the many extensive interviews he provided, and to the following people, who offered their own recollections, insights and assistance:

Warren Anderson; George Arzt; Ken Auletta; Joseph Bellacosa; Stephen Berger; Jim Brigham; David Burke; Christopher Carey; Dennis Carey; Edward C. Carey; Michael Carey; Francis X. Clines; John Connorton Jr.; Jerry Cummins; William Cunningham; John Dyson; William Ellinghaus; Herman D. Farrell Jr.; Dall Forsythe; Sid Frigand; David Garth; Paul Gioia; Peter Goldmark Jr.; Jeff Greenfield; Linda Greenhouse; Judah Gribetz; John Keenan; Edward I. Koch; Jerome Kretchmer; Melvin Laird; Franz Leichter; Albert Lewis; Michael Long; S. Michael Nadel; Manfred Ohrenstein; Carol Opton; Richard Ravitch; Tom Regan; Merrill Ring; Felix Rohatyn; Howard Rubenstein; Menachem Shayovich; William F. Snyder; Clarence Sundram; Al Viani; James Vlasto; Paul Volcker; and Steve Weisman.

Finally, the authors wish to extend our appreciation to the many librarians who helped us along the way, as well as their archives—as follows: the Special Collections Division, Georgetown University, home of the A. S. Coan Papers, and librarian Ted Jackson; the Gerald R. Ford Library, University of Michigan, and librarian Stacy Davis; Bailey Library, Hendrix College, and librarian Judy Robinson; Special Collections Division, Hugh L. Carey Congressional Papers, St. John's University, and librarian Dr. Blythe E. Roveland-Brenton; Baruch College Archives, home of the Jack Bigel Collection and the Municipal Assistance Corporation Archives, and librarian Sandra Roff; the Carl Albert Center Archives, University of Oklahoma, and librarian Jackie Slater; the C. W. Post library; the Rare Book and Manuscript library, Columbia University, and librarian Carrie Hintz; the Great Neck,

New York, Library and its always helpful reference librarians; the New York State Library and Katherine Storms, senior librarian; and the New York State Archives and Christine Ward, assistant commissioner.

In the end, though, any deficiencies or errors in this book are the authors' alone.

# Introduction

Late one afternoon in May, 1980, Governor Hugh L. Carey and an assistant counsel were returning to his office after a public event marking the fifth anniversary of the court consent decree to close the Willowbrook Development Center in Staten Island, New York, a nightmarish institution for the developmentally disabled. Carey's aide, Clarence Sundram, knew that throughout his political career in Washington and Albany, the governor had dedicated himself to the needs of the disabled. As their car carried them back toward Manhattan, Carey turned to face Sundram, saying that while people would probably credit him first and foremost with rescuing the city and the state from the brink of bankruptcy during the great New York City fiscal crisis of 1975, he personally was proudest of signing the legal agreement that began the process of finally placing Willowbrook's poorly served residents in small neighborhood group homes and day care sites around the state. It was a long-overdue step that set a humane standard for the treatment of the retarded.

For any politician, merely rescuing New York from the cliff's edge of economic collapse would have been accomplishment enough. But Carey, frequently mistaken during his extensive career for a traditional Irish-American machine politician, harbored a principled and progressive sense of public responsibility and purpose. Unlike many contemporary politicians who inflate a kernel of achievement into an exaggerated resume while relying on armies of consultants, speechwriters, and pollsters, Carey led a substantial life. He grew up during the Great Depression, fought in World War II and helped liberate a Nazi death camp, and ran for Congress. His first campaign came the same year in which another liberal Irish Catholic, John Kennedy, captured the White House, and with the active help of his huge family—he and his wife, Helen, raised fourteen children—Carey defeated the popular Republican incumbent in his conservative Brooklyn, New York, district. He survived five more tough campaigns as he worked his way up the hierarchy of the House of Representatives to a seat on the powerful, tax-writing Ways and Means Committee. Confident in himself, and ambitious for more prominence, he ran for governor of New York in 1974; tripped up the Democratic nominee,

1

Howard Samuels; and went on to sweep virtually every county in the state in the general election, in which he defeated Republican governor Malcolm Wilson and ended sixteen consecutive years of GOP dominance in New York State. Carey's contributions in his two terms as governor came to encompass the first significant attempt to reform the state court system in decades; the cleanup of Love Canal, a milestone in the unfolding national focus on the environment; and the rehabilitation of New York City's deteriorated and graffiti-strewn subway fleet, among other notable accomplishments. He was, and remains, one of New York State's most effective yet least appreciated governors.

Our book seeks to set the record straight, placing the greatest emphasis on the 1975 fiscal crisis, which, at one hair-raising juncture, came within hours of causing America's largest city, and financial capital, to declare itself insolvent. Such an admission of gross political and governmental failure could have touched off social and economic distress and upheaval on a wide scale, not only within the city of nearly eight million people, but across a recession-mired nation already demoralized by the recently concluded Watergate scandal and Vietnam war, a $30-billion-a-year misadventure. If what Carey came to label forcefully as "unthinkable"—a New York City bankruptcy—did occur, many world leaders feared nothing less than a disruption of the international banking system and the global economy.

It's also our hope that this book will help readers, including current and future policy makers and politicians, to recognize the enormous dangers of unrestrained public spending in deference to favored constituencies, election considerations, special interests, or outmoded habits and traditions. While many mechanisms for improved fiscal stewardship of New York—city and state—function to this day, including some imposed during Carey's tenure, they are in danger of losing their force and meaning and may be more easily evaded as government veterans of 1975 retire or die and as institutional memory fades. So it was during the fiscal crisis of the mid-1970s, which unfolded four decades after the Great Depression, and so it could well be the case again, now thirty-five years since the 1975 shocker. Indeed, the global economic slowdown of 2008 brought about a painful awareness that most households, companies, and governments harbor too much debt, thanks, in part, to the deregulated banking system, years of loose credit, and political and public complacency.

Commissioned by the Hugh L. Carey Institute for Government Reform, a center established in 2007 at Wagner College in Staten Island, *The Man Who Saved New York* is an unauthorized account portraying many vivid aspects of Carey's youth, military service, and political career against the backdrop of a changing and challenged city, state, and nation. While we do not pretend that the book represents the last word on Hugh Carey, our research was helped in particular by ten extensive interviews with him, as well as with dozens of friends, observers, members of his family, and a gifted group of former aides, such as Stephen Berger, David Burke, John Dyson, David Garth, Peter Goldmark, Judah Gribetz, S, Michael Nadel, Carol Opton, Richard Ravitch, Tom Regan, Felix Rohatyn, Clarence Sundram and others, in both prominent and supporting roles, who Carey inspired to conduct some of the finest work of their careers, setting a modern standard for excellence in state government recruitment and results. That Carey's administration was virtually free of corruption scandals and patronage marks another feat in the checkered history of New York and other ethically challenged state governments.

In any narrative about the fiscal crisis, Carey, we found, belongs at the center, though most historical and analytical accounts of the period have not put him there. Indeed, the initial signs of the maelstrom stirred when he first arrived in Albany, New York, in January, 1975. By the end of that seminal year, with the crucial help of many in his administration and several business executives as well, he had braved a ferocious storm for which there were no parallels in American history except perhaps the Great Depression, and he surprised many by becoming a leader of resolute action and an astute, effective, and eloquent statesman.

When he was a boy growing up during the 1930s, Hugh Carey's parents, like many descendents of Irish immigrants to America, deeply admired President Franklin D. Roosevelt, who championed the destitute masses and favored them with jobs, emergency food, and hope when, in New York, even the vaunted Tammany Hall political machine could no longer offer people a reliable hedge against impoverishment. As an adult, working with his brothers in the petroleum business as their father had done, Carey was swept up by all the euphoria surrounding John F. Kennedy's presidential campaign. The winds of liberalism and political change that were stirring in the early 1960s helped Carey unseat the undefeated conservative New York congressman Francis Dorn. At the time, the novice politician and his wife were raising their growing family, and their sons and daughters donned handmade costumes, sang, and pitched in to win the hearts, and votes, of many Dorn supporters. In the best tradition of the Kennedy years, Carey, who with his square build, bushy eyebrows, and disapproving stare resembled an Irish cop, cultivated lasting friendships in Washington with many of its most formidable leaders. He also acted to assist the powerless, such as the developmentally disabled, forging the first trade school for the deaf, in Rochester, New York. During his fourteen years in Washington, Carey promoted federal funding of educational opportunities for all, balancing political confrontation and compromise as the pivotal backer of the landmark U.S. Education Act of 1965. This was perhaps his most important and enduring congressional success, as it marked the first time the federal government provided significant funding for schools, both public and parochial.

An engaging storyteller, with a flair for spontaneous and exuberant performance, Carey did not, all the same, choose at any point to write his own book about his life and career; his zone of comfort and proven strengths lay squarely within the realm of the spoken word. It was also the case that some of Carey's gubernatorial advisers were unusually adept at managing the media and getting their own voices across in the press; Carey rarely got in their way, once explaining (to Felix Rohatyn), "When you're right, I get all the credit, but when you're wrong, I get only half the blame." Carey, too, tended to be self-effacing in formal appearances, and he relied heavily on David Burke and Judah Gribetz, among other behind-the-scenes actors, to help translate his free-flowing instincts and opinions into public statements and political action.

Yet it was Carey who, jeopardizing his own political popularity, enlisted the state government in a string of calculated financial and political risks on imperiled New York City's behalf; compelled an often implacable Mayor Abe Beame to slash and reorder city spending; placed the city's financial house under stern state supervision; and somehow prevailed on a reluctant President Gerald Ford and recalcitrant Congress to buoy up the city in late 1975 with billions of dollars in desperately needed seasonal treasury loans.

In the crusade to keep the city from defaulting on its debts to bond-holders and other current obligations, Carey sought to temper the indignant demands of the nation's top banks headquartered in Manhattan, who, he well knew, had long indulged the city's insatiable appetite for borrowing and wielded enormous clout. He secured the crucial help, too, of the city's municipal labor unions, whose leaders bought potentially worthless bonds to keep the city from defaulting and their labor contracts from becoming null and void. And he resisted the voices, whether Democrat or Republican, left or right, of those who for ideological reasons supported or at least were not as distressed as Carey by the prospect of a New York City bankruptcy.

When the city finally balanced its budget according to a federal timetable, it was able to receive, from President Jimmy Carter, guaranteed federal backing for additional borrowing in the municipal bond market. It thus was able to secure continued access to the credit market—the assurance of financing—to pay off its mountainous debts, and won a chance to rebuild its frayed civic fabric under state-imposed constraints, however slowly and painfully.

Carey's politics throughout his political career remained those of a pragmatist. Drawing on the memory of his late father's struggles with credi-tors during the depths of the 1930s, he fostered the conditions and climate in which traditional adversaries could cooperate across lines of suspicion, or at the very least make grudging tradeoffs to keep New York City from going under. All parties in the difficult negotiations recognized that if the city's operations came to a standstill, everyone would have been hurt, and anyone who refused to cooperate with the governor's program would be saddled with the blame.

Less well known, but equally important, was the Carey administration's effort, in the wake of securing seasonal loans from the Ford administration, to keep four large public authorities of New York State from collapsing. Had these troubled statewide agencies' relationship with the municipal credit market been severed, as it very nearly was in 1976, when all New York–labeled debt paper, city and state, was considered risky and suspect, then the municipal credit market might have turned away from doing business with the entire apparatus of state government. Then, New York State would not have been able to allocate annually scheduled aid to all of its localities, and all the local units of government, including the recently assisted New York City, would have almost certainly collapsed.

The country at the outset of Carey's two terms was nearing the end of a liberalism once assiduously cultivated by FDR, Kennedy, and Lyndon B. Johnson. It was the start of a conservative reaction that would sweep the nation, culminating in the 1980 election of Ronald Reagan, more than two years before Carey left Albany. Labor's membership outside of municipal unions had begun to slip nationwide, while corporate power was on the verge of exponential growth. New York City's middle and working classes and unions had in fact flourished in the post–World War II liberal era, but by the mid-1970s, the prosperity they advanced and participated in was under siege from all sides. Factories were departing for domestic and foreign sites that offered tax cuts, cheaper wages, and union-free shops. Rail yards and ports were closing. Vast droves of New Yorkers were fleeing the five boroughs for the neighboring suburbs and the fast-growing, federally subsidized Sunbelt states. The New York City fiscal crisis of 1975 crept up as many Americans felt hostile toward a metropolis with a huge municipal workforce. As it unfolded on the state, national, and international stage, it marked a major turning point in the country's political direction.

For this reason and others, Carey's task of fending off the disaster was more fraught and difficult than imaginable. His ultimate success was nothing short of remarkable, as it was a feat that arose from his experience in Congress, his grasp of business matters, an admirable mix of skilled, independent-minded advisers, and relentless efforts to convert traditional adversaries—labor and business, Republicans and Democrats, upstate and big-city state legislators—into supporters in the cause of saving a great and troubled metropolis.

When he left office at the end of 1982, with anti-tax fury and Reaganomics the new political forces in the country, he left his city and state in a far better place than he had found it.

*Seymour P. Lachman*
*Robert Polner*

# 1

# The Life Stinks Club

*The future governor grows up.*

On a sparkling winter day in Manhattan, Hugh Carey sat at his kitchen table and reminisced, the steam from a water tower on a landing outside the picture window behind him swirling and vanishing. Unhurried now after six terms in Congress and two as governor of New York, long separated from the trappings of power—advance men, the Executive Mansion, government transport, and state troopers—he brought back to life nine decades of his past, with winding and evocative stories strung together with precise details, caustic asides, and wry, sometime self-deprecating wit. ("I am overcome by the magnificence of my verbosity," he intoned after a morning of sinuous story telling.) The third of six Carey sons brought up in Brooklyn, New York, Carey recalled how he was doomed to be treated as little more than a nuisance by his two older brothers, to whom he looked up and sought to impress, and virtually ignored by his younger ones. His face still fine-featured and his eyes penetrating, he waxed as loquacious and word-playful as ever as he described the rigorous habit-clad sisters of the Roman Catholic church who schooled him in such things as math and morality at his parochial school, his mother's administrative work for a world-famous former investigative reporter, and his father's pride-filled determination during the Great Depression to avoid bankruptcy for the petroleum distribution business he had cofounded. Hugh Carey's combat experience in the Army during World War II, and his encounter with a Nazi slave-labor camp, left their indelible marks before he approached the bare-knuckle arena of New York politics for the first time in 1960 and defeated a popular, seemingly well-ensconced Republican congressman in a conservative district.

Over ten interviews in 2008 and 2009, Carey talked, too, of his improbable rise to become one of the most influential members of Congress, his underdog campaign for the Democratic nomination for governor, and of course his epic confrontation, in 1975, with New York City's mountain of debts and desperate shortage of cash or credit with which to meet its expenses—that is, the looming municipal bankruptcy that caught the newly elected chief executive of the state, and just about everyone else, by surprise, and threatened not only his constituents throughout the state but also those of innumerable other states, cities, and school districts, as well as the national recovery efforts led by President Gerald R. Ford. In the view of several world leaders then, nothing less than the stability of their domestic economy and the international banking system were at stake in the great New York City fiscal maelstrom of that year, something no mayor or governor of a large city or state in the country had ever confronted except perhaps during the Great Depression.

It was a rare fearlessness and effectiveness that Carey exhibited in these and many other instances, for which he was not then and has not since been particularly well recognized.

Except, perhaps, nearly midway into his second and last term as governor, when, at one of the closing acts of a stage performance by reporters at an annual press association charity dinner in Manhattan's Hilton Hotel, one of the singers belted out a new fourth stanza for Frank Sinatra's "My Way" that tweaked Carey for his politically self-damaging—some had even called it politically suicidal—refusal to support the return of the death penalty in New York State. Regardless of their individual views on the subject of capital punishment, hundreds of journalists and public relations pros in the audience—a usually skeptical, even jaded bunch—rose and began applauding Carey, who vetoed the first of many death penalty bills to cross his desk in May, 1977, in defiance of conventional political calculation, his less-than certain prospects for reelection at the time, and hardened public sensibilities about rising crime and mayhem. The governor rose from his seat briefly to acknowledge the sustained applause.

"People were applauding a public official for taking a position of conscience," wrote the liberal New York Times columnist Sydney Schanberg, who was present in the ballroom that evening in the spring of 1980. "I've never seen this kind of genuine, spontaneous reaction to an issue and to the man identified with it."[1]

And then there was Willowbrook, the state institution for the retarded, whose wretched conditions had been rationalized and tolerated for years by local, state, and national elected officials. The care of the developmentally disabled was an issue Carey had long been associated with in Congress. Working closely with aides such as chief counsel Judah Gribetz and budget director Peter Goldmark Jr., Carey moved promptly at the beginning of 1975 to end a lawsuit against the state that had been pressed for years by aggrieved parents and child welfare groups. Acknowledging decades of official complicity, Carey signed the judicial consent decree that provided for shuttering the notorious Willowbrook facility in the center of Staten Island, New York, and the removal—to more humane, community-centered facilities—of its maltreated patients. The decree also set the stage for the reform of poorly run psychiatric facilities around the state. While Carey realized, not five years later, that people one day probably would remember him for having organized the rescue of New York City during the 1975 fiscal crisis, the one deed of which he was proudest was what he did when faced with the national shame that was Willowbrook.[2]

Carey was a governor "who never got enough credit for what he did," said Felix Rohatyn, who Carey recruited to state government from the world of finance at the top of the city's slippery slide toward bankruptcy, and who himself got a good deal of well-deserved acclaim for his role in reversing the crisis (a crisis that in short order came close to sinking the entire state government). Ultimately, a wide array of players who were normally rivals if not outright ideological enemies—the major labor unions, the nation's big banks, and both political parties at every level of government—made common cause under Carey's banner of leadership and contributed to the rescue of the nation's largest and most maligned metropolis, or made temporary sacrifices and took immediate risks in order to avoid blame for the downfall of America's financial and cultural capital were it to occur. Rohatyn described Carey as "the greatest person I ever worked with in a crisis situation because he had a sense of humor, he was brilliantly intelligent, he was courageous, and he had something that I think, as I read it, President Franklin D. Roosevelt had, which is: If you do something and it doesn't work, you do something else."[3]

Hugh Leo Carey was born on April 11, 1919, the carrot-topped, fair-skinned child of a business-minded Irish-American family in Brooklyn's Park Slope, a historic neighborhood of churches, family-run shops, attached homes with pocket-sized yards, and tree-lined streets. A child of the Great Depression, his character was conditioned not only by the location and era of his birth and the strong Irish-Catholic atmosphere within which he was raised, but also by his place in the order of the six Carey children, all boys and all of them born at home, as was fairly common in those years between the two world wars, when New York was a vibrant, working-class city of teeming, deep-water ports, smoke-belching factories, and tenements crammed with new immigrants. Brooklyn was an inexhaustible patchwork of insular ethnic neighborhoods connected by trolleys, subways, and ferries to Manhattan, far from the power, prestige, and wealth situated in the city's international crossroads of commerce and banking. Carey's neighborhood was a tightly knit world with narrow limits, where parishes and priests were especially influential, local politicians were major figures, and, as in the stable rural villages of long-ago Ireland, children conducted themselves dutifully under the stern watch of their elders. As any child knew, those who respected the hierarchical roles and interplay of the community would be rewarded, and their lot, and that of their family, would likely improve over time.

Still, young Hugh was not one to be controlled, and felt compelled to take occasional physical risks, some foolish, one of them almost fatal. Like any child, he needed to win the respect and attention of his older siblings with feats of daring, not to mention his teachers and parents, too. Of his many caretakers (his paternal grandparents resided on the top floor of the family's three-story home, and many relatives lived nearby), Carey's most important influences were his parochial school instructors and, of course, his mother and father, who never lacked for rules and standards for the boy—nor were they too easy to trick or impress.

By the age of three, Hugh began to develop a reputation for accidents; his parents lovingly tagged him with a Gaelic appellation for left-footed and clumsy after he fell down the back steps and fractured his right leg. Instead of anesthesia, he was handed a stuffed horse in Holy Family Hospital. Told to clutch it hard, he bit off its head, so great was the pain, as his break was tended to and his leg braced.[4]

Those first years of life included regular trips to a free community health station, a public facility provided by the Irish-built Tammany Hall political machine and City Hall. But for the more serious medical issues that complicated his early development, his mother called upon Dr. McGilligan, the family doctor. It was Dr. McGilligan who diagnosed one of Hugh's illnesses as whooping cough, which, in rare cases, can lead to bacterial pneumonia or even seizures. He warned, "You've got to get this boy to the seashore or he's not going to make it." Terrifying words, indeed. His parents cranked up their roadster and made the twenty-six-mile trip by car and ferry to Long Beach, New York, along the Atlantic Ocean shore on Long Island. There, they looked for a summer home and somehow pulled together the cash and loans to make a down payment on a drafty, wood-paneled bungalow on Pine Street, which became the family vacation home for years to come.

Hugh's pertussis faded in the salt air and his energy returned, but he would never be physically very robust as a kid, nor did he have much appetite for athletics, unlike his older brothers. He turned instead to reading. Sitting at home in Park Slope while the other children played box ball, stick ball, or Ring-a-levio, he gorged himself on any book he could find, eventually tackling tales about scientific breakthroughs, health, and discovery. He thrilled, too, to the popular *Penrod* series of novels by Booth Tarkington, classic period tales of an all-American boyhood in which mischievous boys contrived inventive ways to challenge the "oppressive" authority of their elders. His family fancied he'd be a priest, bishop, or scholar, but not long after recovering from his bout with whooping cough, and given his propensity to find trouble in the farthest corners, he was drawn anew to idle hazards. Probing the mechanism of a kerosene space heater in the anteroom off the kitchen one day, he accidentally set the room ablaze.

Despite his interest in books, Hugh had an abiding terror of starting parochial school. The school stood a mere three hundred yards from his home—St. Augustine's Academy, staffed by the Sisters of St. Joseph. He had never mingled much with other children and was frightened by exaggerated depictions of schoolhouse life mischievously served up by his brothers, who emphasized the terrible strictness of its habit-clad nuns and its administrators. In the mind of a nearly seven-year-old boy practically paralyzed by his trepidations, the principal, Sister James Josephine, seemed especially forbidding, with her shadowy eyes, sharp nose, and pointed chin, though in reality she was a kind and decent educator who came to look favorably upon Hugh. "I began to depict in my own mind a place of confinement, where I'd be among children I never met, kids I never knew—an alien, foreign atmosphere," Carey remembered. All the anxious fears would soon be allayed, however, and by the sixth grade the shy and awkward boy had blossomed into an academic standout, an achievement brought home to him when the older sister of one Janet Gallagher—Janet was the queen of the school spelling bee, and Hugh her closest academic rival—introduced herself on the way home from school one day and, after making sure he was in fact Hugh Carey, slapped him across the face. No matter. Hugh had already been recognized for his success, and had even been selected to serve as an altar boy, hardly an insignificant honor among his peers. He became well versed in the functions and language—Latin—of the Mass. Indeed, the memorable incident with Janet Gallagher only underscored his nascent scholarly prowess.

Another incident, however, awakened him to his mortality. At a weekend retreat organized by his mother for the school's altar boys and their instructors and priests, Hugh's strong desire to do everything at least as well as his two older brothers—Denis Jr., or Joe, as he was nicknamed, and Ed ("God help you if you're the third brother," Hugh sighed many years later)—led him to swim too far out in rough surf. He nearly drowned. "Trying to be with the big boys, I had to dog paddle and was hit by waves," he said. The sandy bottom was out of reach of his flailing feet, the sky no longer visible. "By instinct, I recited a prayer in this moment of my anticipated death, and calm came over me. For some reason, I was ready to forfeit my life, even at that age. But then hands grabbed me and I was rescued."

Hugh reached the eighth grade in one piece and started receiving instruction for the state Regents examinations. His most important influence other than his parents was Sister Mary Maurice, and it was she who telephoned the Carey home several weeks after he braved the benchmark test. The young scholar and all-around good boy, a favorite of his instructors, remembered that he among his family members answered the call that day. "Hugh," Sister Mary Maurice said, barely able to contain her excitement, "the Regents grades are not out yet, but you can tell your parents that you received the highest marks ever scored in my class—99.875—and I believe it's the best grade in the entire borough!"

At St. Augustine's High School, Carey was named class president and even the student coach of the freshman basketball team, two of the highest honors a newcomer could expect. He bonded in his second year with two kids, Jake Lennon and Charlie Zimmer. They became the big-eared, wide-eyed adolescent's ambassadors to the finer things in life, offering vital instruction on where the nearest girls' schools were located, how delicious a 3.2 beer could be, and other lures. Carey grew indifferent to scholarship. He flunked geometry. But he was learning other things.

His home life provided anchorage. Hugh's father Denis, or DJ, was a second-generation Irish-American, the only living son of a laborer, Michael, and a house worker, Delia. Michael and Delia Carey hailed from County Galway and made their way to America in the late nineteenth century in a huge wave of Irish immigration. Each went through the processing portals for new arrivals that existed at Battery Park at the southern tip of Manhattan, before Ellis Island was established in 1892 to receive the torrent of Europeans fleeing poverty and persecution. After Delia set foot first on the alien shores of lower Manhattan, she found work as a maid in a Brooklyn convent. Since Michael didn't have enough money to book passage with her, he traveled at the same time to Liverpool, England, and found work as a brick carrier. In one story told to the family, he plunged three stories and broke his leg under a broken scaffold, yet continued to toil on his bad leg. Later in life, when the Carey boys knew him as "Big Red Mike," he suffered what he referred to as a Liverpool Limp. "It conditioned his attitude toward the British," Carey recalled.

Though greeted with strong anti-Catholic prejudice in America, life was not as bad as it had been under the English, and, given their history of struggling against oppression, Irish immigrants were naturals at organizing themselves at the local level for greater economic and political security and to try to influence American foreign policy vis-à-vis Great Britain. By 1900 in New York City, Irishmen were firmly in charge of the political show. The first New York governor of Irish descent was Martin H. Glynn, who served in 1913–14 after his promotion from lieutenant governor to complete the term of an impeached chief executive. In 1918, the city's burgeoning Irish community helped elect the state's second Irish Catholic governor, Alfred E. Smith, a Tammany regular who had risen from the immigrant streets of the Lower East Side to a seat in the state legislature. Hugh Carey would be the third.

Carey's grandparents raised two daughters and two sons in Park Slope. The older boy, a gifted athlete, died tragically as a teen from a misdiagnosed case of peritonitis. The younger one, Denis J. Carey—Hugh's father—attended Public School No. 9 in the same neighborhood; his formal education ended in the ninth grade. Once out of school, he worked any job he could find to help support his parents and sisters. Energetic and resourceful, he worked as an oil hostler at the Tidewater Oil depot near the family home, servicing trucks and rail engines at the end of their run. With a friend, he established a motor fuel distribution business in the 1920s, calling it Eagle Petroleum. Once he had married and his sons were arriving, he spent his days and nights focused, even fixated, on building up the company. At home, the Careys didn't subscribe to popular general-interest publications such as the *Saturday Evening Post* or *Colliers*, but to the *National Petroleum News* and *Journal of Commerce*. Home was office, and office was home, Hugh remembered. The nightly dining room table talk was peppered with stories of fuel deliveries, tank trucks, expenditures, and revenues, and when the Great Depression arrived and deepened in the 1930s, the living-room discourse was edgier, revealing the pressures and tactics exerted by Eagle's creditors.

The story of how Carey's parents met is intertwined with Denis Carey's desire to succeed in the oil business, in an era when the automobile was becoming more familiar and kerosene-fueled heaters would give way to basement oil-burning boilers and furnaces. Margaret Collins—Hugh's mother—was the youngest of five children and the daughter of immigrants from County Tyrone, Ireland, and when she married DJ Carey she not only became his wife but also his unofficial lifetime associate and assistant throughout his business career. At Erasmus Hall High School, a public school in Flatbush, she did so well that she continued her education in stenography and typing and became a valued employee at the Battery Place home-office of the American Steel Barrel Company, as the assistant to the owner, Elizabeth Cochran Seaman, otherwise known, nationally and inter-nationally, as Nellie Bly, the untiring adventurer, daredevil, social reformer, and pioneering woman reporter who covered World War I, defended poor and exploited children and women, and who, at her death in 1922, was described by the *New York Journal* as "the Best Reporter in America" for her exposé on the appalling way the mentally disturbed were treated in state insane asylums. While working for the *New York World*, Bly had posed as a mental patient at the Woman's Lunatic Asylum on Blackwell's Island in New York City, later called Welfare Island and now Roosevelt Island, and wrote about her experiences in *Ten Days in a Madhouse*, published in 1887, which detailed the degrading and tragic indifference she observed first-hand, scenes similar to those which Hugh would find at Willowbrook almost ninety years later.

As a prominent businessperson in her own right, Bly would regularly depart for globe-trotting jaunts, entrusting "Miss Collins" to serve in her stead at the American Steel Barrel headquarters in lower Manhattan. Soon, Collins became so integral to the day-to-day functioning of the company that its owners named their petite fifteen-gallon barrel after her—the "Collins Barrel"—one of which Carey and his brothers were delighted to see washed up on the shores of Long Island when Hugh was still in parochial school.

With petroleum use increasing, steel barrels were in demand. The more fifty-five-gallon steel barrels a striver like Denis "DJ" Carey could get his hands on, the more fuel he could decant from railroad tanker cars and deliver to corner filling stations. So DJ decided to see if he could get to know the reserved but sociable Margaret Collins; he arranged to invite her to a formal evening ball. Denis's business was going well, growing so reliably that within a matter of four or five years it would monopolize the back page of the indispensable Red Book directory with a prominent display advertisement. As fate, or luck, would have it, Bly's assistant agreed to go on a date with the confident Denis. In the full measure of time, their attraction grew, and the "the oil man" and "the barrel lady" eventually married.

Carey's parents started out as newlyweds in downtown Brooklyn. Gradually, they slowly moved up the avenues and acquired social status. The most prosperous proceeded "up the hill," reaching out of the lower strata toward Third, Fourth, and the even more socially elevated Fifth Avenue, with its stately homes filled with fine silverware, grand pianos, and lace curtains. From roughly the time their boys were out of diapers, the business-minded couple, who ultimately resided on Park Place—but not the crest, Prospect Park West—dreamed of starting a series of modest petroleum delivery businesses for the boys to one day operate. Margaret, with her serious disposition and withering and wise delivery, commanded her children's march toward straight A's (or nearly so) on their report cards, while insisting that they maintain a respectful presence before their elders. But it was his father who, Hugh remembered, looked out one sunny Saturday over their dining room table as the kids' pored over their homework, and commented on the attractiveness of a tin container marked Peerless Pepper.

"That's a good name for a company," he mused. "Peerless."

Eventually, the Peerless Oil Company was born, to be followed by the Remington Oil Company, named in honor of the Remington typewriter Hugh's mother used to type up the business records. The Peerless and Remington companies advanced from their beginnings at the dining room table, led by eldest brother Ed. At first, Ed worked closely with his father and brothers, but, inclined more to giving orders than taking them, he broke off to form his own series of oil companies, for which Hugh worked. By the late 1950s, Ed was on his way to becoming one of the richest individuals in America, and by 1960 was in a position to help Hugh launch his political career.

But Edward M. Carey's phenomenal success was unimaginable when the Great Depression descended, bringing traumatic and demoralizing years that weighed heavily on Denis and Margaret Carey, their business, and the family. Margaret struggled to keep up appearances of middle-class prosperity, never letting her husband leave the house without a derby, smartly atilt on top of his head, and a pristine starched white shirt. As the family's finances tightened, she also took to inserting cardboard cutouts in the worn-out shoes worn by her sons, as there was never enough money for new shoes. She sent the children to school after serving them a watery gruel for breakfast; the days of waking up to the smell of bacon sizzling on the stove, were, if not completely over, then quite out of the ordinary.

Denis Carey's Eagle Petroleum faced crushing and eventually insurmountable obstacles when the stock market crashed. As American laissez-faire capitalism teetered on the brink of collapse, Denis's modest enterprise suffered a staggering blow—the denial of credit by the giant oil companies with which he did business. Eagle functioned by decanting fuel from freight cars into fifty-five-gallon steel barrels and loading the barrels onto its delivery trucks and delivering them to gas stations. It depended on thirty days' credit from the sellers, roughly the amount of time the corner stations (Eagle's customers) needed to pump enough gas to pay for the bulk fuel deliveries.

Eagle's wings were clipped by the monopolistic bond forged by the Seaboard Midland Railroad Company and Standard Oil, both owned by John D. Rockefeller. Trampling over all small competitors in their path, in ways documented earlier in the century by progressivism's fearless muckraker, Ida Tarbell, the behemoths simply stopped extending credit to tiny, local distributors like Eagle, which lacked cash up front to pay for its principal product. When the Rockefellers, through their corporations, determined that they would not accept credit as payment, it was only matter of months before they controlled the petroleum industry to an even greater extent, and Denis J. Carey's trucks were driven away empty from rail depots of Queens and Brooklyn. His company survived in name only under a pile of debts and creditors' demands for repayment.

In spite of it all, the Carey family managed to remain somewhat better off than most of the city's desperate unemployed, keeping their heads above water with the modest rents Denis Carey collected each month on a few small parcels of land he'd bought when he was better off (the telephone company rented one of the properties to store its poles). But Eagle's creditors kept the pressure on, for Hugh's father refused to enter a claim of bankruptcy to preserve the few remaining assets of Eagle Petroleum. Long after it stopped doing business, Denis still showed little patience when friends suggested he get out from under his company's debts by declaring it insolvent. Bankruptcy was a condition he viewed as shameful, akin to reneging on a promise or shirking responsibilities to one's loved ones and community. "It just was anathema to my father," Hugh said years later. "He considered bankruptcy a stigma, or, simply, a disgrace to the family name."

Hugh always remembered the days his father avoided debt collectors seeking to dun him with a demand for payment or slap him with a summons to appear in court because he was among the rare few who had not declared bankruptcy. His father delighted in dodging pursuers staking him out outside the family home; he darted away and caused them to give chase. Once, he tossed a Spaldeen over the heads of Hugh and some of his brothers and scaled the backyard fence behind their home, ostensibly to retrieve the prized pinkish rubber ball. He then ducked into the butcher shop adjoining the rear of the property and slipped out and away onto a busy street through a side door. "The point was always to remain solvent, a relatively unusual condition in those days, and avoid the creditors until he could make payments, which he eventually did," recalled Hugh.

As for those who owed Denis J. Carey money in those days, he let them slide, or accepted payments-in-kind; one year, the family's living room was crammed with lampshades from a destitute light merchant. More substantively, the Careys were assisted and encouraged by Franklin Roosevelt's panoply of New Deal programs, particularly the Homeowners Loan Corporation, which in the early 1930s kept the Careys and many other families out of foreclosure by easing their mortgage payments through advantageous refinancing opportunities supported by the government.

The elder Carey nonetheless endured many difficult months of fitful casting about for money and work during the New Deal period before he landed a salesman's position with the Dutch-English Shell Oil Company, whose bright yellow-and-red logo was then making its way into New York City. For Denis, the job represented a joyless step down from his more successful years as an independent entrepreneur, and an unsympathetic boss did not make things easier. Even the company car he was assigned, a two-passenger vehicle with a rumble seat, decoratively painted in Shell's bright colors (the car the family drove to Long Beach in search of a cure for Hugh's whooping cough), caused him distress, since he had commanded far finer automobiles. So he avoided parking the Shell advertisement in front of his home, and he moved on from Shell as soon as he could.

"I remember waking up one night and listening while my mother and father sat down and composed a letter," recalled Hugh. By then, his father had worked for about year and received a better job offer from the rival Sinclair Oil Company. He liked Sinclair because it was associated with Harry Sinclair, a self-made oil mogul and, equally to his father's liking, the owner of a baseball team and thoroughbred race horses. The resignation letter Margaret typed as Denis narrated it was addressed to a man named Preu—pronounced *Proy*—who lorded over DJ and meted out small indignities. "Dear Mr. Preu," Denis began. His forced and greatly exaggerated politeness was apparent to the rapt Hugh, listening from his bed. "I enjoyed being in your employment for the following reasons . . ."

Denis was hired by Sinclair Oil, and things began to get much better by the late 1930s as the Depression loosened its grip on New York City and many other parts of the country. His experience and abilities as a salesman were formally acknowledged when he was promoted to manager.

Meanwhile, Hugh and his high-school-age pals, Lennon and Zimmer, cocooned by adolescence, were carrying on as a bona fide trio of big-city sophisticates, given to irreverent commentaries, pranks, and hanging out in dapper porkpie caps near an ice cream shop frequented after school by some of the prettiest neighborhood girls. One day a man approached the boys with a complaint—he was Vinnie, the owner of a nearby fruit store.

"Why don't you bums get off the corner," Vinnie said, drying his hands with a towel. "All you do is hang around here and wait for my back to be turned and steal my apples and pears."

"Nah, we don't do that," the boys protested.

"Why don't you make something of yourselves?"

"Yeah?" Zimmer asked, more curious than challenging. "How?"

"Why don't you go down to the 101st Cavalry, sign up with the National Guard, and get paid a few dollars every day for training horses—if you can qualify."

The armory, which stabled the cavalry's horses, was just up the street. The boys wandered over and before long they were in the National Guard, as much for the prestige symbolized, or so they hoped, by their new high-laced boots, campaign hats, and monthly stipends, as for any awakening sense of nationalism or duty. Carey learned to love the horses and the companionship of fellow guardsmen. At first he and his pals were shown a mild-mannered horse and taught how to place a blanket on its back. By trial and error they learned how to mount and ride. The three became National Guard troopers of the lowest rank, pocketing a few extra dollars for their weekend work with the horses, and also attending summer outings in upstate New York, a break from the often sweltering city. Carey, who had a taste for expensive clothes, found out that Brooks Brothers sold uniforms, and soon his closet was filled with them; he could almost have been confused for a general some days, striding down Flatbush Avenue with polished boots and shiny buckles, while his brother, Denis, ended up with a less prominent role, cleaning the horse manure in the stables for the Guard.

The 101st Cavalry, New York National Guard, would become Carey's gate of entry into the military and the war to come.

By 1939, still raw and untested at age twenty, Carey enrolled in St. John's College in Brooklyn, and chose to major in history while tending to drift, like many young men, unsure of what lay ahead. He continued working part-time jobs, including as an office assistant at a funeral parlor, where he became familiar with the terms "embalming," "floaters" (corpses found floating in the river), and "potter's field" by listening to the conversations of pallbearers who bided their time between funerals talking about their morbid but necessary line of work. Carey's sense of his future was not much brighter. England and France were already at war with Germany and Italy. The conflict was a world away, yet it was still possible for an observant and exceptionally curious young man to detect the gathering indications of international strife. He and some classmates formed what they called the "Life Stinks Club," which was not an organized fraternity but a collective, cynical statement of sorts about what their prime years seemed to hold out for them and their generation: a bad economy, military conflict, and limited horizons.

College life left Carey with his late afternoons free, and his Aunt Mary, who worked at Abraham & Strauss, the major department store on Fulton Street, Brooklyn's primary business strip, told him that they were hiring for the winter holidays. Taken on as a temporary for thirty-five cents an hour, he labored in the store's basement, sorting stray shoes that had been strewn all over the sales floor. Responding to cries from the salesmen to rematch the pairs, he and his coworkers send them back up to be tried on and, with any luck, purchased.

Hugh was subsequently hired for grounds information work at the 1939 World's Fair in Queens by a man who formerly worked for A&S. In his new role, he wore the official World's Fair staff uniform at an information kiosk, directing visitors to the likes of General Motors' futuristic car city, the USSR Pavilion, and a huge globe and planetarium, among many other exhibits. One of his coworkers at the sprawling "world of tomorrow" on the former site of a Tammany Hall–controlled ash dump near the Flushing River was the chiseled, dark-haired Gregory Peck, not yet the American movie idol he was to become. Hugh felt he was doing pretty well for himself because not only was he making friends, but he had been able to cash in a disability insurance check following a horse kick he suffered while training horses at a cavalry weekend camp upstate; he'd purchased the accident policy for ten dollars, and collected a three hundred dollar indemnity. He had even survived a military arrest, along with Zimmer and Lennon, after crossing the border into Canada in their Guardsman uniforms in pursuit of a weekend of entertainment, in violation of the U.S. Neutrality Act. It led to a penalty assignment as a horse exerciser, which was when he was injured and sent home to recuperate.

In January, 1941, President Roosevelt began readying the nation for the possibility of war, despite the still-strong non-interventionist sentiment among the public. One of the early steps was federalizing the National Guard.

Carey went home and told his parents.

"What does that mean," his mother, becoming alarmed, asked.

"It means I'm going to be a soldier in the Army."

"You're not in the Army, you're in the National Guard," she said.

"Instead of going a couple of times a week in the summer to cavalry camp," he explained, "I'm going to be in uniform. My regiment is going to Fort Devens, Massachusetts, in a couple of weeks."

She paused. "No, I want you to just give them back the soldier suit and tell them you don't want to play anymore!"

It was not to be. On the night of January 21, 1941, in frigid winds, twenty-one-year-old Hugh Carey joined a long line of men and horses marching down Flatbush Avenue in Brooklyn to the Vandemeer railroad station, where they helped load the animals into dingy cars and then climbed into other cars and made their way on the slow-moving train to Fort Devens. There, Pvt. Carey soon shifted from riding horses to riding and servicing mechanized rolling stock as a member of a new regiment, though he knew relatively little about how a motor vehicle worked beyond what he had read in a textbook somewhere or heard about from his dad, a lover of automobiles. "I faked it," he recalled. Which was fine and dandy until a sympathetic military overseer was replaced with a new one, who approached him one day.

"I've been watching you—you don't know nothing about the engine," the new commander said.

"I'm learning," said Carey.

"That's not good enough: I'm demoting you, and you're going to ride a motorcycle."

"I don't know how to ride a motorcycle."

"You better learn," warned his commander.

"But I'll kill myself," said Carey.

"That," said his superior, turning to walk away, "is the general idea."

In time Carey grew to love riding the motorcycle. But one night in the winter of 1941, as he was helping to escort a rumbling column of forty military vans carrying horses, men, and equipment through Baltimore on the way to Fort Devens, trouble found him again, as it did when he was a boy. On cobblestone streets made slippery by ice and rain, Carey's bike hit a curb and he lost control. He went flying while the vehicle continued on without him and crashed through the window of a German bakery, sending broken window glass and baked delicacies flying everywhere. Bloodied and dazed, he was not, however, in need of hospitalization; he was driven along with the rest of the caravan to the U.S. Military Academy at West Point in New York, where he slept through the night. Early the next morning the caravan of now-rested soldiers, Carey among them, was back on its way.

Accustomed to being called "dog faces" by loudmouth civilians they encountered on roads and byways, they instead heard unfamiliar cries of support on that cold day in early December as they rolled through Hartford, Connecticut, with people shouting "Great going, boys!" and "We're behind you!" and handing them Devil Dogs and bottles of Coca Cola. Carey quickly learned the reason for the change in attitude: the Japanese military had just bombed Pearl Harbor. It was December 7, 1941.

Given a choice of military services in the days to come, Carey leaned toward the Air Force, but a medical examination showed problems with depth perception in his right eye. He selected the Army infantry and was assigned to the 104th Infantry Division, known as the Timberwolves. The assignment would eventually lead him to the Normandy coast, forty days after D-Day, and a 280-day tour of combat duty until Germany's defeat.

Well before D-Day, the Timberwolves were trained by Major General Terry Allen, a strutting, brave, third-generation military man, a veteran of World War I and most recently a general of the 1st Army Division in Sicily and North Africa during World War II, a command that ended after a highly publicized clash of strategy and personality with General Omar Bradley. Allen was then handed the command of the 104th Timberwolves by General George Marshall. Under Allen, the new fighting unit took its place in the expanding army and was formally activated at rainy Camp Adair, Oregon, which was where Carey, a city kid, began learning how to dig a fox hole, shoot a rifle and machine gun, read aerial photos, swim, employ maps and compasses, and endure harsh conditions on scant rations in simulated combat conditions in a mountain or desert.[5]

Viewed as leadership material, Carey was assigned to lead a platoon at Camp Adair. To impress his commanding officers, who constantly monitored him, he improvised when he could, a valued trait since battlefield conditions were rarely predictable. The army term that caught his fancy was one that defines a soldier who could fix anything, be it a broken weapon, saddle, or Jeep: "Artificer." Hugh Carey always wanted to be known—first, as a boy looking to impress his siblings, and now, as an infantryman seeking recognition by his commanders—for his ability to fashion something out of nothing, or anything that might craftily turn adversity into advantage.

Leading his platoon into the soggy Oregon mountains for an overnight camp, his opportunity came when he unwittingly led his men into a patch of poison oak. On the morning they returned to base, they all developed an itchy and infectious rash and were confined to their barracks and its rain-soaked grounds. Carey was glum but found a way, beyond giving out calamine lotion, to buoy his soldiers' morale: he purchased bags of sawdust for a nickel each, and spread the mixture over the outside athletic field, giving the men an area to play ball and enjoy other physical activities. He also developed a dry firing range in the barracks, pulling up the cots with makeshift pulleys to clear some space and using rifles that projected beams of light against cardboard boxes used as targets. By the time the poison oak rashes disappeared, every single one of his men—cooks, clerks, carpenters, sons of poverty or privilege—were judged as qualified marksmen.

Carey must have made a good impression on his superior officers because he and an army buddy, John R. Deane, were sent to Fort Benning, Georgia, to attend officer candidate school, the pair making the long trip in Deane's Chevrolet. After completing the school they succeeded in becoming "ninety-day wonders," or certified graduates as second lieutenants, and were sent back to Camp Adair to serve as commanders of a company and prepare it for battle. From there it was on to additional training maneuvers near Camp Hyder in the Arizona desert along the Southern Pacific Railroad between Yuma and Phoenix. In a thirteen-week training program designed by General Allen, Carey and his fellow GIs conducted battle drills by night—Allen's main emphasis was night-fighting. Carey became acquainted with packs of wild rats, hunger, and scorching days and freezing nights. He learned about communicating by once- or twice-clicking a rifle to announce the detection of enemy combatants in the immediate vicinity. Just as important was evincing a gung-ho attitude and keeping complaints to a minimum. "Nothing in hell can stop the Timberwolves," was one of General Allen's oft-repeated mottos throughout the war, and the soldiers were made to understand that he meant every word of it.

In the middle of 1944, Carey joined the trainloads of infantry men heading east from still another area where Carey trained, near Colorado Springs. Soon, he boarded the USAT motor vessel *Cristobal* in New York as a member of the Division's 415th Infantry Regiment. The *Cristobal* was one of many ships bearing the Timberwolves toward the western European front. Allied Forces had just liberated Paris, and Supreme Commander Dwight Eisenhower was being cheered on the Champs Elysees by ebullient French crowds. The liberation of France, a bloody and costly campaign that had begun June 6—D-Day—on the coast of Normandy, also marked the beginning of a new push through the Netherlands that proved far more difficult than General Eisenhower had anticipated. The arrival of the 104th's thousands on the Normandy coast (Carey himself arrived at the Port of Cherbourg in France, his vessel escorted by submarines) brought new recruits who replaced or complemented the exhausted troops shoving inland against Panzer tanks, buzz rockets, mines, snipers, and armies.

On the Normandy coast the infantrymen resumed training in the late summer heat of 1944, while awaiting their marching orders. The British and American forces had regained control of northwest France and enjoyed air superiority. While there was little threat of attack on these new additions, an occasional German warplane swept by and dropped a random shell on their encampments. One of these bombs landed near Carey and he suffered a concussion. Taken to a field hospital, a doctor wondered if there was something wrong with his appendix and transferred him to a surgical tent, where the physician who examined him confirmed the diagnosis: "This guy's got appendicitis!" His appendix was promptly removed. Drifting in and out of consciousness after his operation, Carey recalled, "I saw some badly wounded guys brought in—some of them lasted, some didn't last."

When he emerged from the deep sleep of anesthesia, he was eager to leave the medical tent but unable to find out where his regiment was. To his shock, he learned it had moved on without him, headed to Belgium by way of Paris. Alone, with only most general information, he decided to set out to find them, jumping on the first train to Paris he could get, though he had not yet fully recovered.

Overnight, Carey developed a raging fever and dysentery. Finally, on reaching his destination, the rail-thin American officer walked the streets of an anarchic city in which Frenchmen were rejoicing and some Germans were still to be found here and there amid thousand of Allied troops. Carey, exhausted, searched in vain for a room to let. Hardly able to walk, and stumbling down a broad avenue, he stopped at the Cathedral of Mary Magdalene, climbed the stone steps, and entered the warm, dry sanctuary, where he fell asleep. The next day, when he awoke, his fever had subsided and the dysentery was gone. To him it was a miraculous recovery, "The Miracle of Magdalene."

It was October, and Carey headed for the airport at Orleans, where he asked troops in the area if they had any information about the Timberwolves. A handsome British officer overheard him.

"You mean . . . why yes," the man told Carey. "I saw them in Brussels. They're up around Brussels."

The officer explained he was working as a courier between the British General Bernard Montgomery and the American top command, and invited Carey to join him on his small plane, which was, in fact, headed to Brussels. He warned the American that because there were no armaments on board, the trip would be risky. Still, Carey accepted the offer, and only later learned that the British soldier who helped him was the actor David Niven.

After the plane landed in Brussels, he hitched a ride to Antwerp and the next day found the road leading to his unit, where the men of his regiment greeted him with amazement, having pretty much given up hope of seeing him again. In the reconnection, the company commander approached and said, "OK, major, you're going back to work now." Carey corrected him—he was not a major.

"You are now—you've just been promoted," he was told.

With his battlefield promotion in hand, unexpected though it was, he and his Officers Candidate School buddy John Deane, also a major in the regiment, were back together once again, and ready for whatever happened next.

The Germans retreated from Antwerp, and the Timberwolves went after them, avoiding counterattacks by the Nazi soldiers, who were hiding in thick clumps of trees, high ridges, farmhouses, and bombed-out factories. Maintaining pressure on the retreating Germans through the Netherlands, Carey and his fellow soldiers were experiencing the initial, heady taste of combat. Relying on General Allen's night-fighting techniques under actual battlefield conditions, they were soon joined by other Allied Forces as they fought all the way to the Ruhr River en route to the historic German city of Cologne, which they then helped liberate, in a sharp blow to the prestige and confidence of the vaunted Nazi military machine.

"As you can imagine," said Carey, "the dikes of Holland and the map of Brussels were like squares on checkerboards, ideal for artillery placement by the Germans. Depending on where the action was, they'd move their artillery from one dike to another dike, so we were like ducks in the water, and at times we suffered heavy casualties as we shoved forward through the dike country and out of it by means of the construction of bridgeheads, until the German line of defense was broken."

Carey's unit first pushed through the town of Aachen, a German stronghold just west of the Siegfried line of defense and protected by a massive array of German troops. As a brutally cold winter set in, frostbite became a principal enemy, too. "We fought night by night," said Carey, "and kept up our night-fighting techniques, made extraordinary advances, and also suffered our share of casualties," By the war's end, more than fifteen hundred Timberwolves had been killed, including many whom Carey had counted as friends. "There was the unavoidable impression that if you didn't get hit today, you'd get hit tomorrow. You'd say today was not my day. Does this mean we were demoralized? No. We'd become hardened to combat."

The 104th Infantry Division became the first American outfit to enter Eschweiler, a German city of fifty thousand that had been on the receiving end of air and artillery bombardment for almost a month. Next was the campaign for Lucherberg, a town of seventy-five buildings with a tall steeple at the center. Ahead of it, a German Panzer division was preparing to push back against the Allied invaders and drive them back toward Aachen. German soldiers burrowed into the sides of enormous slag heaps that dotted the town's charred perimeter. Maj. Carey's assignment was to devise a tactical plan to get his troops over those mountains and take Lucherberg with the fewest possible casualties and then advance across a heavily exposed plain to the Rhine River. Carey's strategies at Lucherberg were often effective, though the unit lost one of his close friends, Lt. Jack Ulst, whose bravery he admired and long remembered. "I was on the phone with him. He told me that artillery was being directed to a position where he was. I said Jack, you're already wounded and you're going to be killed if you keep at it. He said fine, I'll take a lot of them with me. He was killed that night. A typical experience, repeated time and again."

Never far from the front, Carey recalled that "the Germans had a monstrous gun called an '88,' or 'Screaming Mimi.' If you heard it, it was wonderful because it meant it had passed overhead. If you didn't, it had landed—it tore you apart. And we were out-gunned on the ground by the German Army. If you heard the clank of a German tank, we had nothing to equal it. Once we were sleeping in haystacks and we looked around and the haystacks started to move. A German Panzer was in the stacks, rolled out, surveyed the area, and just sprayed bullets all over. Did I experience actual fire? Yes I did in that case, and in many other cases, but I never got wounded, never got hit."[6]

Finally, in fierce fighting, the 104th fought its way across the Ruhr River to capture Cologne, where Carey happened upon the well-appointed bunker of the former provincial governor of the city, one of the highest ranking civil employees in Germany, from which he came away with a book about the exploits of Hitler autographed by the Fuhrer himself.

"The most amazing thing was the bunker had an elevator, so my men and I were conducted several stories below the shattered city, and there was a cache of Weimar whiskey from all the places in Europe they'd occupied. And a grand piano," said Carey. He and his company wanted to linger awhile in the exotic opulence, so, to keep their superiors away, they wired dire warnings about their position and small-arms fire on the streets above them.

"I'm sitting in a luxurious chair, enjoying myself with my men, and all of a sudden out of the elevator comes General Terry Allen himself, as tough, profane, and pugnacious as ever, stepping out of the elevator to disrupt the party." "Small-arms fire?" Allen scoffed. "Get yourself out of that chair. This is my command post now." Allen wasn't amused to see his troops enjoying themselves in the resplendent lair. "Now you're on your way to Remagen," the general said, ushering Carey and the others out the door. "Good luck."[7]

Remagen opened a new chapter in Carey's military service. The town's bridgehead was one of the last remaining spans across the Rhine River that the Germans had not yet destroyed to prevent their foes from crossing into the homeland. The Germans left the bridge alone so it would be available, if necessary, to use for the pullback of tanks, guns, and troops in late March. But the Germans sought to destroy the crossing when the first American infantry men, led by Lt. Karl Timmerman, made a daring bid to cross it after attacking the town. Major Carey and his regiment, too, together with the 3rd Armored Division and the VII Corps, fought their way across the span, also known as the Ludendorff Bridge, leading them deeper into the German interior.[8]

The United States' capture of the bridge so infuriated Hitler that he ordered the execution of five German officers he singled out for blame, four of whom were shot and the fifth one captured by the Americans. Hitler also ordered an all-out attack on the Allied troops, Carey among them, as they crossed the bridge. The battle followed by three months the failure of a massive German counteroffensive in the heavily forested Ardennes Mountains of Belgium, France, and Luxembourg, which became known as the Battle of the Bulge. The defeat of the German armies in that campaign came at the cost of nineteen thousand American lives, one of the largest and deadliest battles in U.S. military history.

"The surprise crossing of the bridge saved thousands of American lives that would have been lost by an assault crossing of the river," said World War II army combat historian Ken Hechler. In addition, it enabled the Americans to encircle and trap three hundred thousand Germans east of the Rhine, causing the war to end earlier that it otherwise might have.[9]

For Carey, the war—its havoc, its misery, and the wounding and death of so many fellow soldiers and civilians—became an integral part of who he was. Arguably, they contributed to his sense of himself as a leader who could make tough calls and take responsibility. As a governor, he would see success as a soldier might experience it, measured by observable results and incremental advances. He applied the soldier's instinct for self preservation with the ability to think on one's feet and take risks.

"Anybody who ever said he was in battle and wasn't scared is either a big liar or a big fool," Carey later observed. "It's a traumatic experience, especially when you are in a foreign country: you have the alien character of the scenery, of the terrain; you don't speak the language; and you are a tremendous distance from your home and family. But what you have to compensate for that is the morale—I don't know of a better word—or the cohesive nature of the army unit that trained together, and its leadership—in my case Terry Allen, who prepared us as much for the shock of combat in a foreign theater as anyone could expect."

Carey's service won him the Bronze Star, Combat Infantry Badge, and the French Croix de Guerre, but his most vivid memory was not of receiving a military honor but of entering Nordhausen, a German slave-labor camp his regiment helped liberate in Germany. On April 12, 1945, Carey's unit was among the first to come upon the facility some sixty miles southwest of Berlin. The site Carey encountered was a smaller base camp within the larger Mittelbau-Dora concentration camp, where some sixty thousand prisoners had been worked to death manufacturing the German V1 and V2 ballistic missiles. Unlike the abattoirs at Auschwitz, Buchenwald, and Dachau, which were essentially reserved for murdering Jewish men, women, and children, Nordhausen was populated by prisoners forced to work in underground workshops, who were physically abused, starved, tortured, and, when no longer able to perform their assigned function, killed.[10]

At Nordhausen, five thousand of the six thousand captives the infantrymen found were dead, and the remaining, skeletal survivors were clinging to life. Years later a French survivor of Nordhausen, Jean Mialet, said of his imprisonment there: "This is what hell must be like."

"Rows upon rows of skin-colored skeletons met our eyes," remembered Sgt. Ragne Farris of the 104th's 329th Medical Battalion. "Men lay as they starved, discolored, and lying in indescribable filth."

The troops who had fought their way into the camp immediately began searching for living victims.

"We went up the stairs and under the casing were neatly piled about seventy-five bodies, a sight I could never erase from my memories," said Farris. "We went downstairs into a filth indescribable, accompanied by a dead-rot stench . . . It was like stepping into the Dark Ages to walk into one of these cellar cells and seek out the living . . . I saw one man feebly stagger to attention and salute us as tears slowly trickled down his cheeks. Too weak to walk, the man was genuinely moved to pay tribute to those who were helping him, showing him the first kind act in years."[11]

Carey's remembrances are equally stark, ranging from the moment he and his fellow soldiers emerged from a tunnel leading to the compound, to his observation of bodies "stacked like cordwood . . . There were Danes, there were Dutch, and there were Germans, Russians, certainly lots of French. They simply worked them until they were done."

"I remember very well the chaplain of our unit pulled up in a Jeep to conduct a mass for the dead—the stench was overwhelming, the sight was unbelievable," Carey recalled. "You saw lifeless bodies, worked to death, literally, and some of these people had been brought in because they were scientifically adept. They didn't herd up women and children and put them in the gas chamber, as in other parts of the ghastly Nazi empire. They took skilled people and worked them to death. In my own way I've never seen anything in the world to echo this horror at Nordhausen."[12]

The people of the Nazi-fortified town of Nordhausen denied knowledge of the camps. The American troops didn't accept that, and led these farmers and merchants through the maze of tunnels burrowed into the mountains and put them to work burying some of the corpses.

As a candidate for Congress and governor, Carey would encounter people who identified themselves as former inmates at Nordhausen—in one case, it was a Jewish shopkeeper on Thirteenth Avenue in the Brooklyn neighborhood of Borough Park; he raced outside when he recognized the gubernatorial candidate on his sidewalk in 1974. Running up to him, he grabbed Carey by his lapels, hugged him, and fell to his knees, weeping tears of gratitude. Carey, though, never highlighted these kinds of emotionally freighted experiences or his role at Nordhausen to win votes.[13] Though his media consultant, David Garth, wanted to tape the candidate's encounters with Holocaust survivors because of their potent political value, Carey's attitude was simply, "Leave them alone; they've suffered enough."[14]

Yet Carey's wartime encounter with the German labor camp undoubtedly shaped his political future in one key respect. "I came to the conclusion that guided me in the governorship, that no government should have the power over human life. I don't know when it began, but I became firmly opposed to capital punishment," he said.[15] And indeed, he appeared to conduct himself without his own political advantage uppermost when he announced in the spring of 1977 that he would veto a bill that would bring back New York's death penalty. His stance presented a formidable challenge to his own political prospects, with polls showing huge support in the state, and among most Americans, for capital punishment.

As Governor Carey said in one of his many public statements on one of the most volatile issues he grappled with as a public official: "By inflicting the death penalty on one who has killed innocent people, justice is not done."

His views reflected his own reading of the Catholic Church's teachings and Jesus Christ's turn-the-other-cheek example. State legislators' untiring promotion of bill after bill to make capital punishment the law of New York State led him at times to be less formal and more sarcastic toward the sponsors, and he once had only dismissive things to say about a prominent state senator who was pushing legislation to bring back the "hot seat," in the glib, popularly resonant shorthand for "electric chair" employed by headline writers at the *New York Post*.

"If he can get Resurrection into the death penalty," Carey said, more than thirty years after his military service ended, "I might be willing to give it a second look."[16]

# 2

# "Oh, Now What Have You Done?"

*Mr. Carey goes to Washington.*

Although Irish Catholics began arriving in America during the formation of the North American colonies—with the first Mass in the New World celebrated by a Jesuit in 1634 on St. Clement's Island in Chesapeake Bay—it was not until the mid-1800s that a huge influx began. This torrent of arrivals, beginning before the U.S. Civil War, was set in motion by Ireland's Great Hunger, the tragic epidemic of starvation and disease between 1845 and 1852 that killed or sent into exile some 20 to 25 percent of the population. By 1880, there were upward of six million Catholics of European stock in the United States, up from six hundred thousand in 1840.

The Irish settled heavily in America's cities. They were blessed with verbal gifts, the inheritance of an exploited people who were denied their written language under the rule of the English. Their skin was white, another decided advantage in post-bellum America, and they spoke the English language. Their history as an oppressed minority and their campaign, past and present, for Irish independence and Catholic emancipation paved the way for them to get involved in politics in their adopted land, to confront and compromise with the ruling elites on behalf of the mother country and themselves.

As William Shannon, a historian of the Irish American experience, has written, the Irish immigrants had acute political awareness, and rather quickly made their presence felt in local politics in cities, organizing their fellow countrymen's votes by block, by parish, and by neighborhood. They lifted into office those who promised and could deliver physical results—coal in winter, beer in summer, and patronage jobs on the public payroll. For the Irish, politics meant power, protection from exploitation, and enhanced social status, and was the opposite of the more genteel, upper-class notion of political involvement as an means to achieve efficient and honest "good government," better services, and lower taxes.

"The Irish concept of politics as another *profession*—practical, profitable, and pursued every day in the year—diverged sharply from the ordinary civic code that draped politics in the mantle of 'public service.' . . . Like every other profession, it was expected to reward its practitioners with money, prestige, and if possible, security. It was generally expected that a politician would make money out of his office, collaterally, if not directly, and that if he lost he would be 'taken care of' in a sinecure," wrote Shannon.[1]

Life was often harsh and violent for the newcomers. Competing for jobs at the bottom of society, many Irish laborers in nineteenth-century New York City were by no means sympathetic to Northern aims in the Civil War or to the former slaves liberated by the Emancipation Proclamation.[2] Tensions erupted into bloodshed in the city in 1863, when Abraham Lincoln issued a call-up of hundreds of thousands of additional soldiers to battle the breakaway Confederacy. Though the Irish already were disproportionately represented in the Union Army—signing up brought some remuneration, however meager—the terms of the Republican president's conscription allowed the rich to buy their way out of service for three hundred dollars. After enlistment stations targeting Irish men and boys sprouted in Manhattan, five days of mayhem ensued, which became known as the Draft Riots. Street gangs of Irish men and boys and other poor whites burned, lynched, and looted. By some historical accounts, as many as eleven blacks were hung during the rioting, which the local police—their ranks too thin because so many of them were off fighting in the war—proved no match for the mayhem. A Brooks Brothers store was smashed in a spasm of class and racial fury, while the Colored Orphan Asylum on Fifth Avenue, erected by white philanthropists, was set aflame, the attack intended to rid the city of black workers, who the Irish workers saw as competition. The city's elected leaders got out of town and telegraphed Washington for reinforcements. By the time federal troops arrived, in part to protect City Hall and other federal buildings from takeover by the rebellious mobs, swaths of Manhattan lay smoldering and in shambles.

Few Irish residents of the city were likely to be especially embarrassed or offended by the rise at that time of William Magear Tweed, the great fixer of Tammany Hall. A Scotch-Irish Protestant who depended heavily on Irish votes, he developed the notorious "Tweed Ring" that took bribes and rigged public franchises, contracts, and judgeships for half a dozen years following the end of the Civil War. When Tweed's spate of greed and grandstanding finally ended with his own imprisonment, local reformers, moralists, and antagonists of the Democratic Party and the Catholic Church cheered, but the lower stratum remembered him more for his charitable largesse. Hundreds of working men converged on his house the day of his funeral and walked in solemn procession past the coffin.[3]

By the 1900s, the consolidated, five-borough port city expanded along with American industrialization and demanded more men and women to dig the subway tunnels, erect the skyscrapers, build the bridges (the Brooklyn Bridge was finished when future governor Al Smith was a nine-year-old boy growing up nearby), and keep the factory assembly lines and sweatshops rolling. Immigrant boys and girls often fulfilled the latter functions, and no laws yet existed to protect them from exploitation. The unremitting need for cheap labor kept the borders open to all comers, despite voices of anti-immigrant sentiment, and with that, the doors of opportunity for millions desperate or ambitious enough to begin life anew on behalf of themselves, or more commonly, their children.

In the late nineteenth and early twentieth centuries, a strain of progressivism ran through the American Irish political character, though there were reactionaries aplenty. During the fierce class conflicts of the era, James Cardinal Gibbons, at the time only the second American to have been named a Cardinal of the Roman Catholic Church in the United States, became an outspoken supporter of labor unions and their heavily Irish rank and file. Even the influential columnist H. L. Mencken, who couldn't abide clergy members no matter their denomination, found Gibbons appealing and called him "a man of the highest sagacity." In 1891, *Rerum Novarum*, the "Rights and Duties of Capital and Labor," an encyclical issued by Pope Leo XIII, encouraged more Irish Catholics to participate in the movement for labor rights. Those who did, like the New Dealers to come and pacifists of the Catholic Worker movement, pressed in their own way for the rights and advancement of the poor and immigrants in America.[4]

Brooklyn's Irish lived in ethnically cloistered sections of the city, although Park Slope had many Italians (and Al Capone as a boy lived there years before Carey was born). Like Carey's parents, the Irish of the city tended to send their children to parochial schools, while non-Irish immigrants generally favored public schools. Largely sealed off from other ethnic groups, Irish lives were centered on, and strengthened by, the church and the obedience and order it compelled. For the "self-made man" attracted to a more secular life, there was politics, and politics in New York City of course meant Tammany Hall. Decades before federal agencies were created to help people cope with the exigencies of illness, age, hunger, and poverty, and before there was anything remotely resembling the current state and federal safety nets, Tammany offered government jobs, free meals, help with landlords, and suggestions on whom to talk to in which city department. Their price was only votes and loyalty, or for those who wanted to feed at the public trough, kickbacks and other payments. Tammany's political program did not go much beyond the getting and keeping of power. "Bonds, rent, tax assessments, utilities, docks, streets, sewers, public transit—everything was for sale," according to one historical account of the Tammany period.[5]

While Tammany had its share of unrepentant thieves, its leaders also included some reformers such as "Honest John" Kelly, a former congressman who succeeded Tweed, rid the government of the vestiges of his rule and instituted political reforms. Charles F. Murphy, a baseball player, saloon owner, and trucking company owner, while far from an advocate for labor rights, improved tenement housing and women's suffrage, held power during the first decades of the twentieth century, and even fended off newspaper publisher William Randolph Hearst's reach for political office, among many other challenges to his supremacy. But, importantly, he did not prevent the Tammany machine from aligning itself with progressive causes in his quest to remain at the top of the political organization.[6]

No progressive of the late Tammany years was more popular and influential than Al Smith, a once-poor immigrant boy from Manhattan's teeming Lower East Side and, as of 1918, the state's first elected Irish American governor (Martin Glynn, the first Irish Catholic to serve as governor of New York, was appointed to the position, succeeding the impeached and ousted Gov. William Sulzer in 1913). Smith began his fabled political career as a clerk in the office of the Commissioner of Jurors in 1895, a foot soldier for Tammany Hall. In 1903, he was elected to the New York State Assembly, and went on to serve as vice chairman of the commission appointed to investigate factory conditions after 146 young women, many in their teens, jumped from windows to their deaths to escape the 1911 Triangle Shirtwaist Factory fire. The factory's doors were locked to keep the five hundred or so 59-hour-a-week, low-paid laborers in and union organizers out. The fire escapes gave way under the weight of those clambering down them, and the city's fire engine ladders reached only to the sixth floor. The tragedy prompted national outrage and epitomized the extremes of the industrial era. Smith, who strongly identified with the victims, became known for his relentless, crusading response. He was for many New Yorkers an incorruptible tribune of the people. Along with a fellow legislator, Robert Wagner Sr., who went on to become a champion of labor rights in the U.S. Senate, they pushed through progressive correctives in both Albany and Washington.

Even at the height of Smith's influence as governor, there was not much he could do to undermine Tammany Hall in the city. It took public revulsion to accomplish the change. In 1929, Tammany's debonair mayor, the infectiously charming Irishman Jimmy Walker, erected a casino in Central Park as a glittering tribute to his showgirl paramour Betty Compton and a late-night playground for his flatterers and toadies. For this, he was roundly denounced by Patrick Cardinal Hayes and others. Finally, Beau James's administration drew the attention of Judge Samuel Seabury, a stern and indefatigable reformer. Newspaper exposes and Seabury's heavily publicized hearings on Tammany corruption confirmed its most craven dimensions, such as an extortion scheme whereby cops arrested innocents for crimes they had not committed and paid witnesses to testify falsely to their guilt in the local courts, forcing the defendants to pay bribes or go to jail.

In contrast, the passionate and largely self-taught Governor Smith, a symbol of the rising Irish American community, provided a series of progressive programs that would became a model for FDR and his New Deal. Yet when he ran for the presidency in 1928, only to be beaten by Herbert Hoover, he drew vicious, bigoted attacks by those around the country who refused to cast their vote for a Roman Catholic, especially one hailing from New York City. When his presidential campaign train rode through the Midwest and the South, many voters arrived wearing the white hoods and robes of the Ku Klux Klan, and burned crosses to express their hatred of the first Roman Catholic presidential candidate.

Smith's career and ideals captivated the nation's Irish, including Carey's parents, and their enthusiasm for a politician remained unmatched until the ascent of FDR, who served one term as governor after Smith's departure and then, as U.S. president, appointed many Irish Catholics to positions of influence in the federal government and the courts. Those appointments, and of course the panoply of New Deal programs to help the average man and woman and child, ensured that Irish Catholics would remain in the Democratic fold for decades to come. At Smith's death in 1944, Frances Perkins, who started her political life by working with Smith in Albany before Roosevelt tapped her to be the secretary of labor and the first woman ever named to a cabinet position, delivered the eulogy at St. Patrick's Cathedral. A preeminent social reformer in the Smith mold, she described him aptly as "the man responsible for the first drift in the United States toward the conception that political responsibility involved a duty to improve the life of the people."[7]

By the time Smith died, Tammany's power had reached its peak. Its fate had been sealed by the 1934 election of the Republican Fiorello LaGuardia, another tireless visionary in the Smith mold who promoted economic and political justice as opposed to seeking power and control for its own sake. Along with Smith, LaGuardia, the successor to Jimmy Walker, altered the way many New Yorkers, the Irish among them, viewed politics and government. The beloved FDR followed in their footsteps, and the transformation from the days of Tammany was largely complete.

Hugh Carey was drawn to politics after his release from the army. Leaving active service with the rank of major after the German defeat in

1945 (he would receive an honorary promotion to colonel years later), Carey accepted during the following year the title of state chairman of the fledgling Democratic Veterans Association of New York State, which was one of the organizations the party set up to involve and win the votes of World War II's returning soldiers.[8] Although the position was unpaid, the decorated military officer was given a desk in a small office at the popular Biltmore Hotel in Manhattan where the State Democratic Committee was located. From his proud hole-in-the-wall he observed the comings and goings of many notables in New York politics, including no less a power broker than Edward Flynn, the Democratic Party boss of the Bronx who had risen to become chairman of the national party in 1940, and James Farley, the former campaign manager for Smith's and Roosevelt's gubernatorial campaigns turned New Deal postmaster general and patronage dispenser. Carey was not opposed to dropping the names of political luminaries as he gravitated toward the political sphere and warmed to his new title. He was increasingly ambitious for attention and influence, and interested in learning the art and craft of politics.

To garner some small amount of recognition for his efforts, Carey organized a political luncheon at the Biltmore, and went looking for a member of the New York congressional delegation to volunteer to be the keynote speaker to an audience of hundreds of veterans and other young Democrats. All but one of the two dozen or so he contacted—Representative Eugene Keogh, whose district comprised parts of Brooklyn and Queens—turned him down. One was candid enough to tell him why: There were no important political contacts or contracts to be gained, and nobody important was going to be there.

"It was a huge disappointment," Carey, then still young and untested in this complex arena, recalled.[9]

Still, one of the state committeewomen working at the Biltmore suggested he approach somebody from the family of President Franklin Roosevelt, who had died in 1945. "What? Franklin Jr.," he asked. No, she replied—Eleanor. It was a good idea, and the former First Lady agreed to come and was a big drawing card. In the Biltmore ballroom, it was Carey who introduced Mrs. Roosevelt to the enthusiastic audience of ex-GI's. In turn she said some kind, polite words about him.

In his mind, if no one else's, he had *arrived,* though his mother did not attach all that much significance to his accomplishments in state politics. "Did you meet anyone today who you like better than yourself?" she sometimes asked him, marvelously pricking his swollen sense of his own importance as he returned home, heady from all his activities.

Just as important as his first taste of the political spotlight—far more so, actually—was the mixer he attended immediately after the luncheon at the

Biltmore gathering spot known as Under the Clock (for it lay underneath a landmark Roman numeral clock). Looking at the faces in the room amid the hubbub of clinking glasses and conversation, Carey thought he recognized a beautiful and dignified brunette across the room. At least he hoped so. He recalled that he leaned toward a long-time friend standing next to him, a Miss Parisi, and asked her who she was.

"Oh her? She's a friend of mine," she said. "Helen Owen."

"Oh, yeah," Carey told Parisi. "She's married, isn't she?"

"No," said Miss Parisi. "Even though her name is Helen Owen Twohy, she became a war widow and is not married now."[10]

Helen Owen, Carey's future wife and great love, confidante, and anchor, was an only child from Brooklyn, six years younger than Hugh, who attended St. Angela Hall, a private Catholic school for girls located on the same trolley line as St. Augustine's. When Hugh was in the National Guard, a fellow senior from the St. Angela sorority had asked him to participate in a benign hazing ritual at a well-appointed Brooklyn Heights hotel, and he agreed. When Carey arrived at the assigned hotel, Helen was already waiting in a room on the ninth floor along with her excited classmates. She was all of thirteen and was solemnly advised, with the other St. Angela girls, that it was customary to kiss an upperclassman in order to qualify for membership in the sorority. Helen soon enough entered the corridor, where Hugh stood waiting as he was told for the ensuing peck on the cheek.

During the war years, Helen went to Marymount College and met John Twohy, a young Columbia University student who enlisted in the Navy. In his first assignment in 1945 as an ensign on a battleship in the Pacific, a piece of metal broke away from the chamber of the gun he was firing, killing him instantly. Months later, Helen's and her first husband's only child, a girl, was born. Helen's mother died the same year, and she and the baby, Alexandria, moved in with her late husband's parents in their home in Brooklyn. She had not had any interaction with Carey since their first innocent kiss when she showed up with friends at the Biltmore, and in later years never told her husband whether she attended the luncheon to hear the words of Eleanor Roosevelt or chance a meeting with the handsome young man from her youth. Either way, Hugh felt extremely fortunate.

Carey's entry into the early post–World War II political scene in New York State on behalf of young Democrats got him involved in the 1946 campaign for governor, when his veterans association and others pushed for greater recognition by the party and won the right to participate in the caucuses at the Democratic convention held in Albany early that summer. The veterans rallied behind Albany's Mayor Erastus Corning, a decorated army veteran. However, the boss of Albany County, Dan O'Connell, showed little patience for these upstarts, though many had risked their lives to defeat Germany and

Japan. The powerful O'Connell regime was not quick to make concessions, either. But Corning was a protégé of O'Connell, and so, to the cheers of Carey and fellow vets, Corning received the machine's nod as well as the formal nomination as lieutenant governor on the same ticket as the Democratic gubernatorial nominee, James Mead, a U.S. senator from Buffalo.

The veterans felt triumphant. But the feeling soon faded. In November, 1946, the Democrats lost in a big way to the Republican incumbent, Thomas Dewey, who two years later lost a very close presidential election to Harry Truman. Carey, though, convinced himself that the state Democratic organization—composed of many politicians who believed that the paramount purpose of government was to secure jobs and contracts for loyalists—owed him a good job for his two years of unpaid work as the head of the veterans group.

A party functionary laid out Hugh's employment prospects not long after the disappointing election.

"We've got something for you—they want to reward you," Carey said a party functionary told him in response to his inquiries. "Report to the Brooklyn headquarters of the party and see a man there named Lynch."

"In Brooklyn" Carey asked, perplexed? "But I thought my job would be in . . ."

"Oh, they got a really good spot for you in Brooklyn," the functionary said.

Carey was directed to the Board of Education headquarters with a slip of paper, where Mr. Lynch received him as expected and gave him his reward: "You're going to be a deputy attendance officer."

"A what?" asked Carey, aghast. "You mean a truant officer?"

"That's the job."[11]

Carey didn't want it. And to the extent the roots of his later political career were in the Brooklyn political machine, those roots were shallow, indeed. While he might have looked the part of the back-slapping Democratic regular, he was not a creature of the tightly run political power structure in his home borough, as was, for example, the future New York City mayor, Abraham Beame, who started his successful political career ringing doorbells for the party. Meade Esposito, the bail bondsman turned district leader turned—in 1969—the unchallenged leader of the Brooklyn Democratic organization would, in fact, back Carey's opponent in the 1974 governor's race. According to Carey, Esposito even put the arm on him to get out of the race, spouting physical threats.

In the post-war year of 1946, however, the offer of a mere truant officer position probably made Carey realize that his mother and father had been right and he needed to continue working with his brothers at Peerless Oil, which of course meant taking orders from his oldest brother, Ed, two years his senior, who still liked to have fun at Hugh's expense and whose stern and booming voice, in impatience, "could shake the paint off the walls."[12] Carey said goodbye to politics and went to see Ed, presenting him immediately with ideas of what he could or should be doing for Peerless, whose books Ed still oversaw though he was immersed in trying to crank up his New England Petroleum Corporation, or NEPCO, with his business partner, Fred Gilbert, the owner of Patchogue Oil Terminal in Brooklyn. Instead of a grandiose position with Peerless, Carey received the keys to an old delivery truck and a menial assignment to collect unpaid bills from disgruntled home-heating oil customers who complained of poor service.

In the brief time Hugh had spent in his first foray into politics, his eldest brother Ed had been learning to bid on government oil distribution contracts and in the 1950s began doing business with Con Edison and other major electric utilities throughout the Northeast. He would go on to build a refinery in Puerto Rico to meet the energy needs of the island. Helping him raise the capital for the project was George Woods, then the head of First Boston, where the youngest Carey brother, George, a graduate of Georgetown University, worked, and who helped work on that financing deal before dying tragically in a plane crash at age twenty-eight. The Puerto Rico facility was built and run by Ed's Commonwealth Oil Refinery Corporation, or CORCO.

Ed Carey had an uncanny facility for numbers—a veritable calculator in his head—along with a deep reserve of charm to compensate for his my-way-or-the-highway work style. His efforts were centered on importing, wholesaling, and retailing crude oil, and grew so large that he worked out deals around the world with such oil-rich nations as Nigeria, Libya, Saudi Arabia, and Venezuela. Before Hugh went to Congress, improbably winning a race that Ed had at first discouraged him from entering (he felt he could not beat the incumbent, Francis Dorn, and would not make enough money to support his family even if he did), Ed was familiar with people in Washington, dining or teeing up on the golf links with members of the New York delegation who could, say, help him beat back a proposed excise tax on fuel imports. His oil companies, which he solely owned and operated, grew to a combined value of some $5 billion, prompting him to build a second major refinery in the Bahamas with coinvestor Chevron. But this venture in the early 1970s left him over-leveraged, and was his last corporate expansion after more than a quarter century of profits and growth that, among other things, allowed him to help his equally determined brother to run for congressional office and reach for greater political heights.

Hugh Carey and Helen Owen were married February 27, 1947, at St. Patrick's Cathedral. After moving into the Carey family home in Long Beach, Carey, though he lacked experience as a workman, winterized it, prompting his mother to complain later that he turned the place into a "hotdog stand."

In 1949, the couple moved on, purchasing a three-story, one-family home on East 22nd Street in Flatbush, not far from Brooklyn College. By then, Hugh had enrolled in St. John's University to complete his undergraduate requirements and obtain his law degree. Though he was already a father of a growing family, and a breadwinner, part of Hugh Carey's character stayed wedded to innocent mischief. He nearly got himself kicked out of St. John's after he and some of his fellow veterans formed an association and reproduced old exams and sold them for five dollars apiece—answers included—in order to raise money for their group events.[13] Carey was the group's self-appointed chairman, and one of the authors of the successful fund-raising technique.

It was when the vets started pulling reliable A's on their exams—with some of the questions from the old exams repeated on current tests—that a school administrator grew suspicious and found out what was going on. In a confrontation recalled by Carey, the college official suggested that he might be only too happy to bounce Carey and his partners from the university and replace them with students less indifferent to worthy academic achievement. He gave them a single alternative to suspension: raise thousands of dollars legitimately, equal to the amount they'd collected and spent so far, and donate it toward the installation of stained-glass windows in a St. John's campus building.

"By when," Carey asked the university official. The administrator gave Carey and the other young men a deadline and was overheard mumbling in disgust "Lunkheads!" as he turned and left them. They met his mandate by putting on a musical show starring some of their professors. The event drew enough ticket buyers to cover their debt, and Carey went on graduate and in 1951 was admitted to the state bar.

After his brief stint practicing law, he made a modest living working with his eldest brother, leading the oil companies' early expansion into chemical derivatives, thanks in part to his college chemistry classes and due, too, to the easy rapport, and business deals, he cultivated with sales people from Pfizer and other drug companies. Peerless trucks delivered spent hops from the Schaeffer Brewery, which Pfizer used in a new process to manufacture penicillin. By the end of the 1950s, Peerless's annual revenues had ballooned from $700,000 to $7 million annually. Even Ed must have been impressed by his younger brother's powers of persuasion, later describing him as someone who "could sell wet watches."[14]

Still, Hugh grew restless in Ed's shadow. Returning home one evening swept by the excitement about John F. Kennedy's presidential bid, Carey opened his mail and found just the motivation he needed to seek office, though at age thirty-nine he was a political unknown.

The letter was an ordinary piece of political mail from Congressman Francis E. Dorn boasting of a poll conducted by his office purporting that the Republican presidential candidate Richard Nixon would beat Kennedy by a three-to-one margin in the Twelfth Congressional District, where Carey lived.

Carey bristled at the mailing.[15] He revered Kennedy and felt that the candidate's Irish Catholic lineage and sheer charisma would outweigh the district's usual inclination to embrace a conservative law-and-order Republican like Nixon over a liberal Democrat like JFK. Carey's view, though, didn't strike local leaders as so obvious. There had never been an Irish Catholic president of the United States, and the fear that the Vatican would direct a Kennedy presidency ran so wide that JFK would address more than a hundred Protestant ministers in Houston, Texas, that summer in an attempt to assure them that the Roman Catholic Church would in no way influence his political and policy decisions if he was elected. Meanwhile, in the Twelfth Congressional District, Dorn was not only well-respected, he was well liked. He appealed to voters and their core conservatism, whether the issue was crime, communism, pornography, or even the sanctity of the Pledge of Allegiance, the schoolhouse pledge that, since 1954, under a much-debated act of Congress backed by Dorn, was required to include the phrase "one Nation under God."

Off went Carey, undaunted, to see Al Hesterberg, a Brooklyn Democratic leader. Carey offered to help whoever the party was thinking of putting up for Congress, and showed the Dorn mailing piece to Hesterberg.

Hesterberg just shrugged.

"Well, you may not like his junk mail," Hesterberg said, "but he's been elected four times already."

"Who's going to run against him," asked Carey.

"We haven't got anybody, and down at county headquarters, nobody wants to put any money into it. They're sure he can't be beat."

Hesterberg paused. "You ever think of running, yourself?"

"What would that mean?" asked Carey.

"I'll take you down to headquarters, introduce you to the leaders."

They went to see one of Brooklyn's leaders, Joe Sharkey, who brushed off any talk of a Carey for Congress campaign, though he wasn't inclined to stop Carey from making a fool out of himself, either, if that's what he ended up doing.

Sharkey, a seasoned pro, looked straight at Carey.

"Let's get one thing straight," Sharkey said. "You don't get a nickel out of here."[16]

Carey returned home and told Helen what he was thinking. His announcement didn't arouse his family's enthusiasms, especially since it was clear the county leaders weren't going to help.

But Carey knew his wealthy brother would be willing to stake him. And little by little, he and Helen moved ahead with his seemingly quixotic plan. Carey made a stylish splash by purchasing a 1955 yellow Cadillac convertible. He painted it red, white, and blue, with "Carey for Congress" emblazoned on the sides. His children, who now numbered thirteen, campaigned for him.

Al Lewis, a Democrat who was politically active in the Twelfth District, met Hugh as the race was beginning; he and other young Turks had taken over the Bay Twenty-fifth Street clubhouse and were interested in Carey, eventually providing him with their endorsement. Since no one in their wildest fantasies expected the liberal newcomer to beat the well-ensconced Dorn, Lewis encouraged Carey at the time to attach himself to the legacy of the New Deal and the excitement surrounding Kennedy. But Carey's greatest momentum, he felt, came from enlisting his wife and children heavily.[17]

Renting a fleet of convertibles, Carey placed one son or daughter in each car, and at times Helen, too. The family caravan drew attention in Bay Ridge, Fort Hamilton, Sheepshead Bay, and Bensonhurst and at Knights of Columbus halls and in Italian, Swedish, and Norwegian communities. Carey never failed to mention his family's faithful attendance at church or his sons' roles as altar boys at Our Lady of Refuge Church on Ocean and Foster Avenues—or that he had served as the president of the church's Holy Name Society. Meanwhile, in Orthodox Jewish enclaves such as Borough Park, he was greeted warmly, as a working man, a family man, and a World War II veteran.

The Carey children handed out campaign rain hats, lapel pins, and shopping bags. Costumed characters given names like Mr. Yea and Mr. Nay staged street-corner debates to promote Carey's positions on various issues. No one could forget the charming sight of the "Carey Girls," consisting of his daughters and twenty to thirty of their classmates, who went around the district belting out songs wearing home-spun outfits designed and sewn by Helen and other moms. The campaign printed a postcard sent to every registered voter—thousands and thousands—featuring an endearing family picture in front of Brooklyn's Grand Army Plaza monument, with the girls lined up like charms in their pretty red coats and dresses, and the boys dapper figures in dark blue blazers, white shirts, and ties. Carey made the postcard a staple of his campaigns, and considered it a key to his electoral success, as it seemed to melt the hearts of all but the most hardened foe, and particularly appealed to senior citizens, who voted in large numbers.[18] Personal touches like that raised Carey's visibility, to be sure, and transformed him over the summer from an unknown to an underdog worthy of Dorn's increasing attention and concern—so much so that a pro-Dorn sound truck circled the neighborhoods, blaring, "Vote for a man, not a kindergarten!"[19] Dorn, also a military veteran, finally agreed to a series of debates, and the two candidates went toe-to-toe at an opener sponsored by the Brooklyn Chamber of Commerce. "Dorn showed up and insulted me from top to bottom: Who was I, what do I know, how could I dare . . . ? He beat the living daylights out of me." Luckily for Carey, the audience consisted of businessmen who lived, and voted, on Long Island.

In a subsequent debate before students of St. Francis College, Carey stressed his support for John Kennedy and cited his military service. Dorn vocally trumpeted his devotion to the Catholic faith, to which Carey responded, "Fine, but we're not choosing a bishop—we're electing a congressman here." He went on to charge that Dorn had accomplished little in six years in Washington, and voiced his support for federal aid for schools, part of the Kennedy platform, as well as construction of affordable housing across a district and a city facing an acute shortage. Dorn countered that the *Brooklyn Tablet* was supporting him—to which Carey said, accurately, that the Brooklyn Diocese paper did not make political endorsements. The audience booed Dorn when Carey pointed out his error, and Carey figured that he had won the debate. But a New York daily newspaper carried a story the next day quoting Dorn as claiming that the students had impertinently booed the *Tablet*. It was of little consequence, though, because the race was drawing attention and becoming tighter. Dorn stopped debating Carey.

One late-summer night, Carey's son, Christopher, then twelve, was standing alongside his father, and, like his dad, felt "supremely confident" that Dorn could be beaten. They were campaigning close to JFK's entourage, next to the Marine Theater near Kings Highway, when out popped Kennedy himself. The political star placed a quick kiss on Christopher's younger sister Susie's cheek, while her parents beamed. Soon after, the Kennedy campaign gave the Carey effort a largely symbolic donation of five hundred dollars. With the cash, Carey bought hundreds of rosebuds and stood at subway stops during rush hour and distributed them to husbands on their way home. "We knew there are family quarrels. The roses gave husbands a safe passage into the house," Carey later mused. The note accompanying each flower was succinct: "A rose to remember. On the 6th of November, vote for the Kennedy candidate, Hugh L. Carey."[20]

Kennedy's popularity was so pronounced that when he visited Brooklyn's Eighty-sixth Street and Bay Parkway for a campaign rally, the press of the throngs was great and at times uncontrollable. People had no room to stand and some had difficulty breathing (including one of the coauthors of this book[21]), so enormous was the crowd and the excitement. Al Lewis recalled that a cop's motorcycle's windshield was smashed, some people lost their shoes, and the fresh-faced JFK, smoothing his hair, had a hard time getting in and out of his convertible.[22]

Unlike Carey, the Democrats of Brooklyn and other impregnable bastions of New York political power never understood the challenge that Kennedy-inspired Democratic liberalism posed to their entrenched influence in the decade just then beginning. They were too grounded in the tightly organized, top-down ways in which past campaigns were conducted, and too armed with their own sense of political invincibility to notice. "Carmen DeSapio"—the Tammany district leader of Greenwich Village who was defeated by the staunchly liberal Edward I. Koch in 1963, three years after the Dorn-Carey match—"never knew what happened," noted Lewis.[23] A year later, in 1964, Robert F. Kennedy, in the wake of his brother's assassination, ran successfully for the U.S. Senate in New York against the Republican incumbent Kenneth Keating, though Kennedy, who had been the nation's attorney general, had only moved to the state shortly before the race and was attacked by his conservative opponent as a "carpetbagger."

In 1960, however, the winds of change that would help liberal Democrats in New York State politics were just stirring, so Carey's ability to compete successfully was all that much more surprising. Dorn's original campaign mailing—the one prompting Hugh to run in the first place—turned out to be accurate in predicting that Nixon would carry the congressional district in the presidential race. But Carey still beat Dorn by 1,097 votes because the challenger's total ran tens of thousands of votes ahead of Kennedy's tally (and because Kennedy brought record numbers of Democrats to the polls). William V. Shannon, among other commentators, took notice, portraying Carey's developing political style as the "blarneying, street-wise, fast-moving executive style of the Irish politician not seen since the days of Al Smith and Jimmy Walker."[24]

Carey proved he had not been a flash-in-the-pan when he beat Dorn again in 1962, this time by a razor-thin 383 votes, and in part with the help of an irrepressible anti-tax warrior named Vito Battista, of Brooklyn, and his obscure "United Taxpayers Party," which gave Carey its ballot line. Carey wisely courted Battista's endorsement after the Liberal Party leadership at the county level denied the congressman its ballot line because of his vocal support of federal funding for parochial schools. Carey prevailed all the same, and in spite of the fact that the Republicans had run Dorn for Brooklyn borough president the year before to keep him in the public eye and New York State Governor Nelson Rockefeller had approved a remapping of the district's boundaries and a new name, the Fifteenth District, to help facilitate Dorn's return.

After defeating Dorn the first time, Carey, who was then living with his family in a nine-bedroom home on Prospect Park West that he had bought for forty thousand dollars, eventually relocated the family to northern Virginia. It was 1961 as Carey arrived to take his seat in Congress, the same month the former supreme commander of the Allied forces during World War II, Dwight D. Eisenhower, departed from the White House with a solemn warning to the country about the dangers of the modern American military-industrial complex. The stylish era of Camelot was dawning, a time of optimism and fascination with the youthful president and the many issues that would engage his short-circuited presidency and beyond: Southern resistance to civil rights for blacks, which forced Kennedy to dispatch federal troops to protect black children and nonviolent demonstrators from white mobs; the near-apocalyptic Cuban missile crisis; the pushing forward of the space race; and the beginnings of the Vietnam War.

Carey, who earned twelve thousand dollars a year as a congressman while drawing a similar salary from Peerless as a company attorney, soon discovered the ways of Washington and its political culture. At first blush, its grandeur and historical weight were impressive, but it also seemed alien to an inveterate New Yorker—somewhat too small and staid a town to one so accustomed to the frantic pulse and daily chaos of New York City. Washington, he would learn, was populated with some honest and visionary people and more opportunists and self-promoters, as he had always read and heard. As a congressman, he discerned how it functioned, and met and befriended or at least stayed on the good side of those with much greater influence. He mastered the skills of the collegial legislator and the art of the tradeoff, and sponsored legislation. He could, and did, fall back upon the Irish storytelling tradition, incorporating many apocryphal stories, and he cajoled, finessed, humored, and avoided—all priceless skills for the ambitious politician. While garrulous, he was given, too, to private ruminations, mulling his next move intensely, even pacing in silence, hands plunged into his hip pockets.

Carey's first assignment was to help a fellow Democrat in a disputed Indiana congressional election to wage a lengthy recount battle. His role in the success of that effort won the New York freshman some attention from House leaders, including Speaker John McCormick. But McCormick was only the first among scores of legislative horse traders with whom Carey would share drinks, jokes, and stories, people in both parties who would, in 1975, prove essential to his securing, as governor, a federal aid package to keep New York City afloat. Among Carey's most important congressional contacts was Republican Rep. Gerald Ford of Michigan, the Minority Leader of the House from 1965 to 1973, who in 1975 would hold the city's fate in his hands as "accidental" successor to the disgraced Richard Nixon. Carey made friends, too, with Ford pal Melvin Laird, the Wisconsin Republican congressman who became secretary of defense under Nixon and who helped propel Ford up the Republican ladder.

Carey's ties to these Republicans owed a debt to Congressman John Fogarty of Rhode Island. Fogarty, a Democrat, took an early shine to Carey, a fellow Irishman. A former bricklayer, Fogarty was chair of the House Appropriation Committee's influential Labor–Health, Education, and Welfare Subcommittee during Carey's congressional tenure, a powerful panel that, with Laird's help as the subcommittee's minority leader, created the Centers for Disease Control and other lasting federal bulwarks in the fight against major diseases and epidemics.[25]

Fogarty liked having Laird visit his prime, first-floor office for the evening cocktail hour, and soon enjoyed Carey's company, too. So Carey and Laird got to know one another, all the more after Fogarty became so annoyed with Carey for regularly showing up ten or fifteen minutes late for drinks and abruptly had him relocated from an upper floor to another office just down the hall from him. Carey remembers returning to his upper-floor office while the forced move was under way. As workers hauled away boxes of papers and furniture, his executive assistant, Martha Golden, turned to him, sensing, mistakenly, that he had somehow offended the House leadership. "Oh, now what have you done?" she asked.[26] But he was not being punished. Rather, the move was a reward of sorts, the result of his enviable rapport with Fogarty.[27]

As their collegiality grew, "Carey watched with wonder as Fogarty and Laird took on fellow subcommittee members, full committee members, the House, the Senate, and three successive presidents to ram through hefty annual increases in medical research appropriations," wrote Dale Van Atta in an admiring 2008 biography of Laird. Fogarty and Laird were extremely knowledgeable about the issues of their subcommittee, and selected medical professionals who could speak ardently and without jargon on medical subjects to appear before them at budget hearings. "Their most effective technique," Van Atta, a Washington investigative reporter in those years, wrote of Carey's occasional cocktail-hour partners, "was to press HEW [Health, Education, and Welfare] officials to admit that they could use more money than the President's Bureau of the Budget had told them they could request. It infuriated Eisenhower, Kennedy, and Johnson, in succession, but the pair was unrelenting. During the Eisenhower era, Laird would be called to the White House for tongue-lashings, but he wouldn't budge. During the Kennedy and Johnson administrations, Fogarty similarly was denigrated by his party's presidents, but he also refused to cut the HEW budget."[28] Among the legacies of the Laird-Fogarty collaboration, of which Carey stood in justifiable awe, was the National Institutes of Health in Bethesda, Maryland, an institution that was begun in 1887 with a single doctor in Staten Island, New York, and operated on a shoestring until, from 1953 to

1969, its budget was increased twenty-eightfold in the legislatively nimble hands of Fogarty and Laird, thus affording the construction of the National Library of Medicine, the National Institute of Child Health and Human Development, the National Eye Institute, and other esteemed linchpins of disease research, treatment, and prevention.[29]

The liberal Democrat from Brooklyn, New York also made an ally of a man often referred to as the most influential congressman in Washington, Wilbur Mills. The Arkansas Democrat was the chairman of the fifteen-member Ways and Means Committee, which exercised broad jurisdiction over the tax code, federal budget, social programs, and the makeup of congressional committees.

In the mid-1960s, with the national treasury flush and no end in sight for the nation's economic expansion, President Lyndon Johnson set out to make his mark and complete the work of the New Deal. "Freedom is not enough," Johnson declared after his resounding 1964 election victory over Barry Goldwater, promising not only to pass civil rights laws but also to expand jobs, education, and health programs for the underserved. Mills, a fiscally conservative tax attorney, seized the political moment and positioned Ways and Means to get behind Johnson's agenda—and maneuvered to enlarge it in certain ways before Republicans could diminish it or, perhaps even worse, claim the lion's share of credit for its realization. With Kennedy's assassination providing much of the initial impetus in Congress, Mills assisted in the passage of Medicare and Medicaid, along with many other components of Johnson's domestic quality-of-life program known as the "Great Society" agenda.[30]

By this time, Carey himself was secure enough to take on the White House, when Johnson was at the height of his power, in the negotiations leading to the passage of the Elementary and Secondary Education Act of 1965, an extraordinary education law that represented the first time the federal government provided significant funding for schools, both public and parochial. Carey played a major role in these negotiations, marking what he and others consider his most significant achievement in Washington. For a hundred years, since 1865, many in the federal government had sought to pass such legislation, but their efforts did not came to fruition until the mid-1960s, when Carey was centrally involved.

Carey had started out as Kennedy's man on the landmark education bill, the touchstone of Kennedy's campaign pledge to address racial and economic inequities of all kinds. Subsequently, the Johnson administration sought to limit federal support for religious schools to work-study and work-training, tugged in that direction by the public-school teachers' unions and others who cited the danger of breaching the Constitution's separation of church and state. Johnson's bill was to channel federal education funds through public school boards of education, but to Carey, this meant the parochial schools would be frozen out of meaningful amounts of aid.[31]

"Now I'm serving on the Education Committee over there," Carey told Johnson and his aides as the president was simultaneously pushing for Congressional passage of a huge infusion of jobs-rich social service centers to be run directly by the residents of riot-marred ghettos, "and I'm handling your poverty program. And on the political facts of life, I got elected in my district because I went in and made an issue that I was going to do something for the kids in all the schools up there . . . [The] trouble is now that in today's papers we have a statement that this bill is going to exclude those kids [from any aid] and they're not going to get a chance."[32]

Carey's voting record was more liberal than that of his home district, which the conservative Barry Goldwater had dominated in the 1964 presidential election. But no one needed to remind Carey that securing even limited funds for parochial schools would give him bragging rights during election campaigns. (His fight, for example, led to a lifelong friendship with Rabbi Moshe Sherer, internationally influential president of Agudath Israel of America, and a supporter of aid to yeshivas as well as Catholic parochial schools.)

At a White House meeting in early May, 1964, LBJ aide Larry O'Brien reported to the president about the protracted negotiations in Congress, worried that the Carey impasse could undermine some of the Great Society legislation, such as the Model Cities urban jobs and services program.

"Now Carey is into this religious thing, as I indicated to you the other day," said O'Brien, according to a transcript of the discussion.[33]

LBJ snapped, "Oh, the hell with him."

But Carey wouldn't budge.

Meeting with Speaker McCormack and White House assistant Bill Moyers a few weeks later, Johnson returned to the education bill and that ungrateful New York City Democrat's objections.

LBJ to Bill Moyers, his aide: "I want to talk to you about this problem. We thought we had the church thing worked out where the local school boards could handle it, but that's not satisfactory to Carey . . . Bill, what is the language that Carey is objecting to in the bill?"

Moyers: "Carey objects to the language in Section 204b, Mr. President, that provides for the money to be given to these communities through the local school boards. Carey wants the language to be changed so that the money can be given directly to private institutions where . . . where available and where possible. This would include churches to run remedial reading courses, remedial arithmetic courses, and other kinds of instructional courses."

Carey was versed in the history of Catholics in America, and knew that some states had banned Catholic parochial school attendance entirely into the early twentieth century. It was not until 1923, in fact, that the U.S. Supreme Court, taking up an Oregon case, *Pierce v. Society of Sisters of the Holy Names of Jesus and Mary*, permitted all parochial schools in America to function as long as government did not allocate funds to those schools, which were paid for entirely by the families of the pupils and the Catholic community. And it was at about this time that a boy by the name of Hugh L. Carey started attending parochial school in Brooklyn. Forty-five years later, Congressman Carey insisted that the precedent-setting Elementary and Secondary Education Act must contain language that would permit some aid and money for special needs children whether they attended public or a parochial school.

In the end, a compromise was achieved, allowing the White House, public-school advocates, and Carey each to claim a measure of success in the most important education bill that the federal government had ever approved. Under it, federal money couldn't be used for "general education purposes," but certain taxpayer-funded programs could be carried on by nonpublic as well as public institutions. The deal meant that remedial education programs in parochial schools could receive federal funds for specific purposes.

Despite the success of the bill and Johnson's enormous domestic agenda, the president's escalation of the Vietnam War—measured in lives, dollars, domestic upheaval, and turmoil within the Democratic Party—proved too much for him to bear. With many in his party starting to resist the war, Johnson shockingly withdrew from seeking a second full term in March, 1968. This was a year of anguish and turmoil in the nation. The assassination of Martin Luther King Jr. in April spurred marches and riots in cities across America, along with a conservative backlash. In June, Bobby Kennedy, the Democratic presidential nomination within reach, was killed. And Richard Nixon narrowly defeated Democratic vice president Hubert Humphrey to become president, a figure of law and order.

Nixon soon sought alternatives to Johnson's "War on Poverty," terming some of its programs a welter of confusion and waste. He appealed broadly and deeply to the American distaste for centralized government with his "New Federalism" agenda, which meant altering or pulling back on the huge, direct federal commitments to the roiling inner cities desperate for decent housing and dignified jobs. While Johnson won the allegiance of the older industrial centers in the Northeast, Nixon bid for support among the fast-growing and predominantly white suburbs and Sunbelt states.

In 1970, Wilbur Mills placed Carey on Ways and Means, telling Carey's friend Jerry Cummins a few years later that Carey was the smartest man he'd ever met, and, as he described him to future state commissioner John Dyson, far and away the most popular member of his committee. In that berth, Carey's antiwar views were in line with those of the mainstream of his party opposed to Nixon's intensification of the Vietnam debacle, and, having supported the war early on, he served as a bridge between hawks and doves within his party. Separately, Carey led a push for a significant aspect of the New Federalism: federal revenue sharing. Carey was pivotal in getting the long-debated revenue sharing funds through Congress in October, 1972, representing $30 billion over the ensuing five years, which helped cities and states, particularly larger ones like New York, pay for an array of services at their own discretion.[34] Carey's involvement put him on Governor Rockefeller's side, for Rocky summoned the congressman to his baronial Fifth Avenue apartment as the congressional debate intensified and there, seated in front of the fireplace with a group of the governor's cohorts, as well as Brooklyn Democratic Party honchos Stanley Steingut and Meade Esposito, Carey agreed to track down Mills, who was then in Arkansas, and ask him to sign a letter pledging his make-or-break support for the bill. Rockefeller was grateful because he needed something in writing to convince New York State legislative leaders, whose support he was seeking in negotiations over the growing state budget, that an infusion of revenue-sharing money was coming. Carey made some calls and Mills came through with a letter endorsing the concept. Rocky immediately dispatched his special assistant, former journalist James Cannon, to retrieve the letter from its author in Arkansas.[35]

Another national political figure of the day, Thomas "Tip" O'Neill of Massachusetts, was noted for reminding his colleagues in Congress that "all politics is local"—wisdom his father had passed down to him—and certainly the truism was true in the case of the revenue sharing showdown. Carey knew his own 1972 election would not be a cakewalk. His district's voting patterns were becoming ever more conservative. Many voters viewed themselves as members of Nixon's "Silent Majority" and were upset by student protests over the draft, the rise of the women's movement, and black militancy. Carey's voting record, and stand on the war, positioned him well to their left.

Liberalism was in decline by the early 1970's though how much so was anybody's guess. In New York City, William F. Buckley, founder of the *National Review,* had framed a conservative's response to urban discord and disorder in his 1965 run for new York City mayor, though at the time his staunchly pro-police and anti-welfare positions were far outside the main-stream, and he was nearly alone in warning of the dangers of the fiscal mismanagement of the city. He didn't expect to win, and joked that that the first thing he'd do if elected would be to seek a recount (followed by placing nets under the window ledges at the *New York Times* to keep its liberal edi-tors from committing suicide). Still, another Buckley, James, in 1968 picked up on some of the ideas his younger brother had planted, bidding to unseat

Senator Jacob Javits. James Buckley didn't win, but he did pull a surprising one million votes statewide and two years later ran again for Senate and defeated anti-war Republican incumbent Charles Goodell. Carey's district, with one of the highest concentrations of conservative voters in the heavily Democratic city, pulled the lever for Buckley in large numbers.

It was amid such resurgent Republican tides that Carey offered his helping hand on revenue-sharing in 1972 to the then-reigning grandson of Standard Oil founder and chairman John D. Rockefeller. The forty-ninth governor of New York responded by helping Carey win his congressional race that year. Indeed, Nelson Rockefeller and his emissaries convinced the Conservative Party in Brooklyn to endorse a candidate other than the Republican nominee in the race, who was a local entrepreneur, Frank Gangemi. The endorsement was more than a little awkward, as the Conservative county committee had voted only a week or so earlier to endorse Gangemi. But the party chairman, Bill Wells, forced the committeemen and women to vote again for a Conservative leader from Bay Ridge, Franklin C. Jones. Having acquitted himself well, Wells went on to run for State Assembly the same year with Republican backing.

Thus, the anti-Carey vote was split that November, helping to ensure the congressman's reelection in the same year Nixon won reelection over George McGovern by a landslide.[36]

Carey would not ask his district to send him back to Congress ever again. He had been casting about for some time for a way to return to the noisy New York political stage, where he wanted to star. In 1969, after Helen had been diagnosed and treated for breast cancer, Carey announced a run for mayor but soon withdrew and ran instead for the comparatively insignificant post of city council president. Carey switched gears then because Robert Wagner Jr., former three-term mayor of the city and the son of the former U.S. Senate worker-rights champion of the same name—"a political barnacle that stuck to every hull that ever floated, and a very lovable man," in Carey's description—decided himself to run for mayor that year. Wagner made a secret deal with Carey: if both were successful, Wagner would resign after one year as mayor, and the top job would be Carey's. (The city council presidency is next in line to the mayoralty under the City Charter.)

If the agreement made Carey a pawn, he was willing since he could leap to the top of the most prominent urban government in the land, in the city closest to his heart and that of his wife and family. "I'm *that* kind of puppet," he shrugged years later.[37] But the Wagner-Carey pact of 1969 was unrealistic. Wagner's once-strong alliances with labor unions and machine bosses were in play that spring and summer in a large field of Democratic candidates that even included the rebellious candidacy of Norman Mailer and running mate Jimmy Breslin ("Vote the Rascals *In*" went their slogan). The front-runners in the party primary were Herman Badillo, then the Bronx borough president; Mario Procaccino, the city comptroller; and Wagner, still a mover-and-shaker in Democratic circles. Procaccino, a conservative who channeled "outer borough" disenchantment with Lindsay's first term, won the primary with just 33 percent of the votes cast, but Carey considered him a loudmouth and a hack and all but said so publicly. The feeling was mutual, based on what Procaccino had to say in return.

In his own election, Carey refused to challenge a recount after the results of a canvass of primary ballots in his tight race with Francis X. Smith of Queens nudged his rival into the lead—and even after it was discovered that hundreds of votes for Smith had been placed in the wrong column. Harold Fisher, a politically active lawyer from Brooklyn who managed Carey's campaign, advised the congressman, "You don't want the job." And indeed, Carey didn't want to be Procaccino's running mate.[38] He publicly termed the looming general election line-up a "real Hobson's choice: an incompetent liberal Republican"—by which he meant Mayor Lindsay—"an inexperienced conservative Republican"—Staten Island State Sen. John Marchi—"and an unimaginative conservative Democrat"—Procaccino. Carey wasn't going to be mayor any time soon, given the results of the primary, and he determined he was better off staying in the House of Representatives.[39]

The effort wasn't a complete washout. Carey managed to win more votes than the venerable, well-known, and well connected Wagner, and as a result, a few of Wagner's key allies, most notably Alex Rose, leader of the pivotal and important Liberal Party, came to appreciate Carey's vote-getting potential. At the same time, Wagner, apologetic, felt he owed Carey a favor, and promised to be his ally in future races.

Carey abruptly and immediately declared his intention to run for mayor as an independent Democrat in the same election, but the announcement drew sharp criticism from the Lindsay-friendly *New York Times*. Lindsay, having lost the Republican primary to Marchi in a GOP backlash, had switched gears and was now running on the Liberal and Fusion lines. Opined the *Times*, "Mr. Carey's willingness to offer himself once more as a mayoral candidate since his narrow defeat for the presidency of the city council by Francis X. Smith, the incumbent, indicates singular political flexibility. He appears to be willing to follow, rather than to lead, and to do the bidding of others."[40] The paper's editorial page feared that Carey's entry in the mayoral race would siphon support from Mayor Lindsay as a fellow liberal politician and "give over the city to Procaccino and the right-wing."

For all the tumult in Carey's public life, none of it could compare with the personal tragedy he suffered that July, when two of his sons, Peter and Hugh Jr., were killed in a car accident on Shelter Island on the eastern end of Long Island, where the family had a summer home.

Carey was asleep on a sofa at his friend and campaign assistant Tom Regan's place in Brooklyn after a day of shaking hands and courting supporters when Helen called with the news. Groping in the darkness for the phone, Regan heard Carey's distraught wife saying, "We've had a tragic accident."[41]

Regan went to get Carey and handed him a telephone, saying: "It's Helen."

"Oh my god. Yes. All three?" Carey said, speaking into the receiver. "Oh my God. We're on our way now."

He told Regan that his two sons and a neighbor's daughter were all killed when their car went off the road and hit a tree.

The two men drove for nearly two hours in silence. At the Greenport, Long Island, ferry terminal, Carey demanded to see his dead sons as the ambulance carrying the bodies rolled off the emergency ferry at the mainland dock. Morning's first light appeared. Tom Regan, a New York City fireman, caught the driver's eye, and watched as he slowly shook his head: the bodies were mangled and unrecognizable, and not to be seen by their loved ones.

"You're not going to see them," Regan instructed Carey, holding him back. "They're not your children any more. They're God's children now."

"I knelt there and he knelt too, and we said a prayer," recalled Regan.

They took a ferry to Shelter Island, and at the house, the family was waiting for them on the porch in a state of shock and disbelief. Carey, said Regan, blamed himself. "I wasn't there," Regan recalled Carey saying. "I should have been there. It might not have happened."[42]

Wounded, and profoundly so, Carey left the mayoral arena for good, and returned to Washington.

Two years later, Carey was considered for the post of House Majority Whip. He was in the running on the strength of his close ties to Louisiana congressman Hale Boggs, a fellow Catholic Democrat and champion of the Johnson-era civil rights laws. Carey had worked to rally the dean of the New York delegation, Emanuel Celler of Brooklyn, among other lawmakers, to support Boggs's successful January, 1971, bid for House majority leader. A lasting friendship ensued.[43]

Initially, Albert and Boggs considered Illinois Rep. Dan Rostenkowski—the product of Chicago Mayor Richard Daley's Democratic machine and, like Carey, a member of Ways and Means—but decided against it because House Speaker Carl Albert didn't want to hand the Daley crowd any more power than they already wielded in Congress. Boggs convinced Albert that Carey would be a perfect choice for Majority Whip, with Tip O'Neill a close second in their estimation. Boggs informed Carey, and he was thrilled, but he responded he wanted to talk it over with Helen first. She had already complained about his prodigious time away from her and the kids, for the life of the congressman meant hearings, speeches, benefits, campaigns, and weekend excursions to the home district. Then the Whip drama heated up. According to Carey, a Washington newspaper reported that this No. 3 job was his, as he had indeed been tapped on the shoulder and offered it. But the writer of the article was a bit ahead of the story, since, again, according to Carey, Helen made clear that she wanted him home more and they made up their mind that he would decline the position. With the newspaper article making the rounds, Carey and his wife went out that night for dinner at Paul Young's Restaurant, a watering hole favored by many senior members of Congress, to toast their joint decision. They bumped into Rostenkowski there. A mountain of a man, Rosty was nothing if not taken aback when Carey told him he could have the post as far as he was concerned. The next morning, Carey went to see Hale Boggs and withdrew, rueful yet convinced he was doing the right thing.

He only felt stung when, at the caucus vote to select the Boggs-Albert second choice for Whip—Tip O'Neill—Carey overheard John Rooney, a far more senior Irish Catholic member of Congress from Brooklyn, telling a mutual colleague that he "put the blade into Carey" and his ascension to the coveted post. Rooney, with twenty-six years in the House, had apparently paid a visit to Albert along with another New York representative, Jim Delaney, in the preceding days, warning: "Don't pick Carey—he's a troublemaker and a publicity seeker who takes credit for everything we've done. If you appoint him, don't ever expect loyalty from us." But Rooney's machinations had made little or no difference. O'Neill was grateful for the promotion, and used the post as a steppingstone to becoming the Speaker of the House.[44]

In what Carey remembered as a terrible coda to the Whip fight, he had an indirect role in the tragic fate of Boggs, who was killed in an October, 1972, crash of a small plane ferrying him to deliver a stump speech for campaigning Alaskan congressman Matthew Begich. Carey said he had gotten Boggs to agree to make the trip at a date of his choosing in return for Begich's vote for Boggs as majority leader. Boggs was quick to make good on the pledge.

"One of the saddest tales of my life," Carey said of his friend's death. He never forgot it.

Back in the early 1960s, Joseph Danaghy, a Brooklyn acquaintance with whom Carey often took Saturday or Sunday strolls all around Brooklyn, predicted Carey would one day run for governor against Malcolm Wilson, who was then lieutenant governor under Rockefeller.

"You'd be the logical candidate to run against Malcolm Wilson," said Danaghy. "You're establishing yourself as a well-known Catholic leader. The day will come when you'll be opposing him. Better get ready."[45]

It was a remarkably prescient statement by someone whom Carey considered an astute observer of New York politics and a mentor. It stayed in his steel-trap memory through his 1972 reelection to Congress, which Helen pressed him to make his last. Helen wanted him more than ever to achieve a steadier pace, preferably back in New York. She most of all wanted the whole family anchored and living together reliably under one roof, and she wanted the children to have more time with their father. Carey could work with his brother in the oil business or perhaps practice law, she reasoned.

During a family trip to Dublin the following year, Carey announced over dinner that he had made up his mind about his future: "I'll leave the House of Representatives," he said, "and run for governor of New York."

At first, no one in the family said anything that evening. Then Helen spoke.

"OK—and when are you going to do that," she asked.

"Soon," Carey answered.

Helen was surprised. There was another long pause as she considered the implications.

"OK, good," she said. "When you lose, we'll all be together again."[46]

# 3

# Party Crasher

*Congressman Carey makes a maverick bid for governor.*

In the 1974 gubernatorial primary in New York, businessman Howard Samuels was the clear favorite. His front-runner status lasted almost until the day Democrats around the state went to the polls. But Congressman Carey, from even before the race got started, maintained that Samuels was beatable. He set out to prove he was right.

Samuels, who hailed from Canandaigua, near Rochester, resembled Carey in that he had been an army officer in the European theater during World War II and was married, with many children (eight, in his case). A graduate of the Massachusetts Institute of Technology, he served as Under Secretary of Commerce in Lyndon Johnson's administration, and then headed the Small Business Administration. Fascinated by elective political office, he ran in 1966 for lieutenant governor on the Democratic gubernatorial ticket led by former Queens County district attorney and city council president Frank O'Connor, though O'Connor fell to incumbent Gov. Nelson Rockefeller and Lt. Gov. Malcolm Wilson. Samuels ran four years later for the Democratic nomination for governor, only to lose to the former U.S. Supreme Court Justice Arthur Goldberg, who, in turn, was beaten by Rockefeller. The silver-haired Samuels manufactured his own inventions, notably the plastic clothes line, which had been the subject of his doctoral thesis at MIT, and later the plastic Baggie; he eventually sold his Kordite Company (founded with his brother) to Mobil Oil for $5 million. He landed his first city government post in 1970, when Mayor John Lindsay named him president of the city's Off-Track Betting Corporation. Samuels became known widely as a "New Liberal" and was popular among Reform Democrats in Manhattan who had voted for Lindsay in both of his mayoral runs.[1]

Carey saw more political vulnerability than strength and prowess in the candidacy of Samuels, since Samuels never won an election or held elective office. Two of Carey's most influential allies in New York—Alex Rose and Robert Wagner—had commissioned a few polls during 1973 that detected softness in Samuels's popularity: Samuels never received more than 40 percent of the vote in his past two races for governor, and many had a less than positive opinion of him overall.[2] Rose had decided the Liberal Party would run their own candidates in the primary to siphon votes from Samuels. Former mayor Wagner, who at one point had considered running for governor himself, said he would also try to help Carey, agreeing to become his campaign chairman.

When on December 18, 1974, Rockefeller resigned to mull his future on the national stage, the governor's fifteen-year, larger-than-life presence in the political affairs of the state—"He owned one house and leased the other," Carey memorably remarked, referring to the Republican-led Senate and the Democratic-led Assembly—was over, and Carey grew still more excited about the Democrats' prospects, for Lt. Gov. Malcolm Wilson of Yonkers in Westchester County, handpicked by Rocky to finish the last year of his term and carry the Republican banner in the governor's race, was far less well known, formidable, or rich a political figure than his famous patron.

More importantly, Carey's wife, Helen, having overcome a return of cancer in 1973, was feeling much better and, pointed toward a full recovery, was now committed to helping her husband achieve his goal anyway she could. Win or lose, Helen knew that Carey would be more available following the campaign. His life of shuttling between Washington and New York—and Congressional hearings—would be behind them. They would be able to leave McLean, Virginia, and return to their Brooklyn roots in the event he lost the gubernatorial race. If he won, they could reside together in the Executive Mansion on Albany's Eagle Street.[3]

As Carey began preparing for the gubernatorial nomination in earnest, the first campaign manager he chose was Jerry Wilson, a former television-news reporter. Carey's nascent team consisted of just a handful of other staff people, such as friends Tom Regan, Hank McManus (who would marry one of his daughters), and Jerry Cummins, who soon succeeded Wilson. A very early office was in the rear of a building at 355 Lexington Avenue in Manhattan; it had just two phones and was one flight down from the far more impressively outfitted campaign headquarters of Samuels and his roughly forty staff people. Regan would race upstairs to pick up the statements that the Samuels team put out and trot them back down to Carey so he could read them and, if necessary, dictate a public retort.[4] As it grew, the Carey campaign relocated to larger quarters at 515 Fifth Avenue, where Jerry Bruno, a "renegade genius" in Carey's description, set up a phone bank, using the sale of Carey's Virginia home as collateral for a bank loan.

Samuels was the first to formally announce his candidacy for governor, in March, 1974. He, not Carey, had plenty of reasons for feeling confident of his chances, since leading Democrats, union presidents, and the heads of many county Democratic organizations saw him as the front-runner if not inevitable victor, and polls showed he was known by 91 percent of the voters in the state, compared to a mere 5 percent who knew Carey. In 1969, Samuels had become the first prominent Democrat in the state to endorse Lindsay's uphill run for reelection. Lindsay, in rewarding Samuels with the helm of the Off-Track Betting Corporation, effectively gave the industrialist a potential army of volunteers to man his field campaign—the people he hired to work in smoke-filled off-track betting parlors. "Howie the Horse," as the press nicknamed him, computerized the agency's transactions, enhancing his image as a business-minded political reformer.

Preparing to launch his campaign formally in midtown Manhattan, Samuels hit a pothole, however, in a telling episode. Members of Samuels's campaign staff found out that the *Village Voice* was working on a potentially damaging story about the late father of Samuels's second wife, Antoinette, a Frenchwoman, known to her friends as Loulette, who had married the businessman about a year earlier. The article was to assert that Camille Chautemps, who died in 1963 and whose portrait hung over the fireplace in the couple's Manhattan apartment in the elegant Hotel Beresford, had served as a minister of justice in the anti-Semitic Vichy government in France before fleeing with his family to the United States. When Samuels's wife was informed of the impending piece, she called it unfair and insulting. She wanted her husband to respond forcefully.[5]

Ken Auletta, Samuels's state campaign manager, who had first met Samuels as a public policy graduate student and gone on to become his speech writer and then his executive director at the OTB, immediately started to worry. He advised the candidate that the impending *Voice* dispatch from the archives of World War II must not be permitted to distract from the thrust of the kickoff, not only because it was substantively irrelevant—Samuels had never met his wife's father, and she was barely out of diapers when he worked for the Vichy government—but because it threatened to complicate enthusiasm for Samuels among his fellow Jews, who made up the largest bloc of Democratic voters in the city.

The *Voice* piece came out just in time for the campaign event, and Samuels's speechwriter, Doug Ireland, had a copy, bringing it with him, according to Auletta, on the ride to the inaugural press conference with Samuels, Loulette, and her three-year-old daughter. When she spied the front-page story, Mrs. Samuels became visibly upset and Samuels draped his arm around her. The press conference had to be delayed until she composed herself. And Auletta? "I'm thinking, Where's the nearest gun so I can shoot myself."[6]

The event finally began, about an hour late, and Samuels's wife stood loyally and bravely at her husband's side as he sketched his hopeful vision for the recovery of recession-mired New York State. When the time came for press questions, the article's author, Phil Tracy, lobbed the first, and it didn't deal with why Samuels was running for the state's highest political office or even his chances of success, but rather his wife's father. Auletta, watching intently, did his best to keep his game face on. But Samuels proved heedless of his campaign manager's earlier pleas to stay on message, and launched into a passionate defense of his wife's father. Loulette's tears welled up as cameras flashed and clicked.

Carey, a year older than Samuels at fifty-five, had flirted yet again with running for mayor in early 1973, but backed away when party leaders coalesced around Abe Beame, the genteel and well-spoken college-trained accountant out of the regular Democratic organization in Brooklyn, who would go on to win the election. Having made that choice, the would-be governor now cast about for a way to improve his credibility among local Democrats. He felt that David Garth, a well-respected media consultant to candidates, would give his gubernatorial candidacy a jolt of legitimacy if Garth could be convinced to sign on. Samuels would have loved to have Garth too; according to Garth, Samuels made a pitch on the primary's eve to bring him on.

Carey's key opportunity arose on a day he and Helen happened to board the same commuter plane as Garth, bound for New York City's LaGuardia Airport from Washington, D.C.[7] A one-time TV sports producer who grew up in suburban Woodmere, in Nassau County on Long Island, Garth had made a splash with his pioneering and prodigious use of television commercials in Lindsay's 1969 campaign. Garth's ads for Lindsay sought to buoy the square-jawed, athletic, and handsome six-foot-four-inch reformer after most of the unions and county political organizations had already turned against him. In Lindsay's first term, the city had been rocked by racial unrest, crippling transit and garbage strikes, campus sit-ins, and growing signs of civic destitution and disrepair. Garth sidestepped the questions about Lindsay's effectiveness and instead emphasized his battle scars; the mayor was perhaps most admired for having walked through a tense Harlem in the wake of the Rev. Martin Luther King Jr.'s assassination in 1968 to appeal successfully for calm even while other ghetto areas in the country rioted and were set afire. "It's the second toughest job in America," went the slogan Garth devised, and the message made a difference, especially after Republican voters cast him aside in the 1969 primary.

Other ads produced by Garth had Lindsay admitting his mistakes, including having been slow to dispatch snowplows to a blizzard-covered—and patently furious—Borough of Queens. The message was that Lindsay had faced adversity and learned from his successes and failures. As Garth knew, few things resonated as much with New York voters as hearing a politician own up to his mistakes.

By the morning of the plane ride to New York, Garth had not thought much about Carey as a potential statewide candidate, knew little about his congressional record, and wondered, like many others at the time, whether he was just testing the waters once again. To Garth's eyes, Carey was a pudgy Washington pol with a broad Irish face, and one whom voters might well see as another hack put forward by the self-dealing political machine of his home borough. Carey's fitful runs for city council president and mayor were hardly grounds for confidence in his political judgment.[8]

Even so, Garth admired Helen, her long-enduring marriage to Hugh, and their large, close-knit family—and Helen found Garth likeable, though he could be gruff and blunt. Immediately, Garth greeted her, warmly. He was aware that she had been struggling on and off with cancer for the past four years. And during their chat, she told him, with a smile, that she hoped her final epitaph would read "Loving Wife of the Governor of New York State." He took it to heart, though he realized she did not mean it literally. Probably more out of respect for "this very lovely person," as he remembered her, than due to any strong faith in Carey's potential as a gubernatorial candidate, Garth agreed before the plane had even landed to run Carey's media operation for him. He would become the prime mover in the day-to-day decisions and overall direction of the campaign

Carey, in addition to signing up Wagner to help him drum up support, drew assistance from his one-time law partner, Jim Tully, and his friend Harold Fisher, a politically influential Brooklyn attorney, and started making the rounds at political functions, union halls, and civic clubs. But profound troubles again hit the family: Helen discovered she needed further treatment, as her breast cancer had returned. From that point, Carey was regularly with her at her bedside at Lenox Hill Hospital, four or five times a day and then well into the night. Helpless as the dreadful disease took its toll, he one day asked Regan to pull over the car Regan was driving and stop in front of an antiques store on the East Side of Manhattan. There, Carey purchased a tiny glass bird, brought it to Lenox Hill, and placed it in her hands.[9]

It was to be a last token of his deep love and affection. On March 8, one or two days later, having contracted pneumonia, Helen died.

Three weeks later—March 27—Carey returned to his suspended campaign and made good on his promise to his beloved wife, formally launching his candidacy, inserting himself into a Democratic field of contenders that came to include, in addition to Samuels, Ogden "Brownie" Reid, a Westchester County congressman from the *Herald Tribune* family; Sam Stratton, a chiseled congressman and former mayor of Schenectady, New York; and

Donald Manes, the borough president of Queens, one of the largest Democratic strongholds in the country.

As Helen had hoped and foretold, the work of the campaign helped bind and carry the Carey children through the disorienting days and months of loss and grief, with the Carey sons and daughters, veterans of his congressional races, going to work to raise enthusiasm for and interest in their father. By the end of the campaign, Alexandria, 29; Christopher, 26; Susan, 25; Michael, 20; Donald, 19; Marianne, 17; Nancy, 16; Helen, 15; Brian, 14; Paul, 11; Kevin, 10; and Thomas, 7, would travel by bus to almost every corner of the state.

Jerry Cummins, who first met Carey as a Kennedy volunteer in 1960, attended a boisterous dinner in April, 1974, at a Manhattan steakhouse at which Carey and a group of political associates tossed around ideas on how to beat Samuels. With others, Cummins, who owned a printing business, made the argument to Carey—and Carey concurred—that in going ahead with the race, he could not possibly win the majority of votes to be cast by state delegates to the Democratic nominating convention slated for mid-June in Niagara Falls. Rather, everyone agreed, Carey would have to aim for just 25 percent—the proportion of delegate votes necessary to secure a spot on the primary ballot.[10]

If all went according to plan, then, Samuels—not Carey—would win most of the delegates to the convention and thus emerge as the party's No. 1 choice, leaving Carey as the underdog or insurgent taking on the party establishment's anointed candidate. Samuels would thus be forced to work with, and perhaps genuflect to, Meade Esposito of Brooklyn, Matthew Troy of Queens, and other party bosses, and might draw fire for compromising his profile as a political reformer. While placing Samuels in an awkward position, Carey's status as a challenger could resonate with the majority of Democrats in a year when public concern about bossism, corruption, and entrenched politics-as-usual was acute.

The congressman liked the idea of running as a maverick Democrat, not beholden to the county leaders or their demands for jobs and laws and contracts from the victor. He realized, anyway, that winning the party's backing at the convention was not in the cards for him: the majority of county and local political leaders were already climbing on the Samuels bandwagon, and many municipal and state unions were likely to follow. He was set to go it alone, but not completely alone. He still needed the votes of at least 25 percent of the three hundred convention delegates to secure a spot on the primary ballot.

With the plan of attack laid out, Garth lent Carey a spare apartment he owned, in a stately building where he himself resided in a larger spread overlooking Central Park. Each morning, Carey, able to thrive on little sleep, got up early to jog around the park's reservoir. At Garth's suggestion, or, more accurately, demand—for he was something of a puppeteer when it came to his candidates—the congressman went on a diet and lost twenty-five pounds. With the help of his daughters, Carey touched up his grays; he was now raven-haired. He needed no convincing to work, and surprised Garth, happily so, with his spontaneity, wit, and grasp of the issues. Just as importantly, he was willing to take direction and absorb the World According to Garth.

Garth sent Carey to a top-of-the-line men's clothier, outfitting him in some expensive suits and shirts. Though the campaign had a treasurer, the expenses were typically reviewed line-by-line by Ed Carey, who from time to time would erupt at the sight of frivolous spending, like fancy duds, but which Garth would defend as essential in the new age of politics rendered personal and immediate by the television lens.[11]

Carey's capacity to think on his feet and disarm listeners with a cascade of facts and humor were on display when he began his campaign formally at the Commodore Hotel in Manhattan, surrounded by all his many children, of course, and wearing his PT 109 tie clasp in deference to his modern political inspiration, John Kennedy. When asked by a reporter at the event if he was "the boss's candidate," Carey said that no Democratic county leader in Brooklyn or anywhere in the state had endorsed him. A natural crowd-pleaser, he drew big laughs when he added that he divided the county leaders into two categories: " 'Enlightened Leaders' who see fit to endorse me and 'Bosses' who have not."[12]

All the same, though their clout was on the wane, county leaders still controlled or heavily influenced the convention delegates. If Carey fell short of his 25 percent target, the only other way for him to get on the Democratic primary ballot would be to obtain the signatures and addresses of thousands of registered Democrats around the state. But the Samuels team would almost certainly fight to have the petitions tossed out on technical grounds by judges, who were likely to be beholden to the party leaders for their positions as jurists. It was a process no candidate wanted to endure.

One person in the Carey orbit knew most of the sixty-two county leaders at the time—Carol Opton, a freelance political consultant to the Carey campaign. She had previously worked in the mid-1960s as a staff director at the New York State Democratic Party. Opton had also worked on Bobby Kennedy's 1964 Senate campaign and his presidential race, and was, like so many others, devastated by his murder. She gravitated toward helping Carey, not because she knew all that much about him—she didn't—but because Samuels in her eyes had been on the wrong side of the great Kennedy-Johnson rift of the 1960s.

Opton placed an early round of calls to the state committee members in March, and discovered that the "Undecided" category was larger than anyone knew, representing a vacuum that Carey could exploit as people around the state got to know him. In April and May of 1974, she found herself increasingly in the hot seat, with Garth checking in with her many times a day and growling with impatience as she told him that the number of delegates likely to fall into Carey's column remained as uncertain as ever. "Then what do ya need from me, sweetheart," Garth would finally ask Opton, pronouncing it "sweet*hat*." "What can we do here? How about we get some ads on the air upstate!"[13]

Garth and his crew decided to create a dozen or so commercial spots, and cranked them out. Jeff Greenfield, a former speech writer for Robert Kennedy, helped excavate Carey's congressional record from boxes and boxes of letters, clippings, speeches, and legislation shipped from Washington. He and Garth, along with a handful of others, sat around Garth's office "spit-balling" themes for Carey television ads—these were the days before focus groups and extensive polling.[14] With Carey's help, the Garth team came up with a compelling slogan that appeared as a tagline at the end of each new thirty-second spot. However long-winded, the phrase was punctuated by one-syllable words, and aimed at the man and woman on the street. It spoke of a hard-working individual who placed substance above style, who had *produced* as a congressman: "This year, before they tell you what they're going to do, make them show you what they've *done*."

Garth and Opton carefully coordinated the preconvention ad buy with Carey's campaign schedule so that the TV ads would piggyback on the local news reports about his upstate activities. Opton also organized a weekly mailing to each state committee member, portraying a growing Carey momentum with reports on his most significant speeches, community and college-campus activities, and the endorsements he picked up around the state. It was a well-planned push whose impact on the delegates was missed by Samuels, who didn't give it much thought because he never anticipated facing an opponent in the primary. The media, too, clustered for the most part in Manhattan, did not notice the upstate media campaign or appreciate its potential significance.

Carey was a natural for the small screen and reflected his experience well. His tone was deep and burnished, the timbre resonating with the quality and authority of a talk show host. He showed up for the shoots wearing a navy blue suit or a tan overcoat, the latter attire striking a serendipitous chord with upstate residents because it made him look like a local. His hair trimmed, his sideburns long, and his face deeply lined, he spoke plainly of the need for lower taxes, more jobs, affordable housing, and better schools. And there were testimonials from political notables as well as everyday people—whites, blacks, and Latinos, men and women, old and young. Carey was making a play for the old New Deal coalition, and the ads focused on the hopes and frustrations of the average working man and family. In one ad, a Brooklyn

Navy Yard worker thanked the congressman for having saved his job and that of his fellow workers. A middle-aged man in another spot described how he bought and renovated a foreclosed house in Queens with the help of tax credits and other assistance made possible by a bill Carey shepherded into law. The principal of the National Technical Institute for the Deaf in Rochester, New York, was shown giving Carey credit for federal funds that permitted the pioneering school to flourish; an admiring student poignantly pronounced Carey's first and last names with heart and determination, if not correctly. Robert Abrams, a youthful reformer from the Bronx and a favorite among Jewish voters, was enlisted. The highly respected Peter Rodino, chairman of the Democratic Judiciary Committee investigating Watergate, offered unassailable words of praise.[15]

In the wake of these potent ads, and as the convention neared, the pressure from Democratic Party leaders on Carey to get out of the way grew.

Carey was invited to attend a private lunch meeting in the Little Italy section of lower Manhattan with the political bosses Meade Esposito and Matthew Troy, who were both working to get Samuels elected. The venue suggested by Esposito was Tiro a Segno, the New York Rifle Club, the oldest private Italian American club in the city. Founded in the 1880s, its members had included Fiorello LaGuardia and Enrico Caruso. In addition to being a restaurant with at least a hundred seats, it offered its patrons the rare attraction of a basement shooting gallery.

Carey wasn't sure whether to show up. It was a decided risk, for if a press-photographer plant popped up and took a picture of the candidate and Brooklyn's Esposito breaking bread, it might sink Carey's independent campaign. Still, when Carey checked with some of his associates, they reminded him that Esposito was upset by divisions within his party ranks that had been sparked by the Bloom brothers of Brooklyn—Bernard, a Democratic district leader and later Surrogate Court judge, and Jeremiah, a state senator. They advised him to go ahead and see what he wanted. Carey assented, and took Jerry Cummins along.[16]

It wasn't long after the candidate and his aide had arrived that Esposito, puffing on his ever-present stogie, told Carey, "Alright Hughie, you've had your fun now." The usually talkative and quotable Matthew Troy, a member of the city council and the chairman of the finance committee, and of whom City Hall reporters said possessed "the fastest jaw in East Queens,"[17] listened without a word. "You haven't got any money, Howie's got the money, Howie's *gonna* win," Esposito declared. The "cock-of-the walk" in political circles, as Carey depicted him, wanted Carey to bow out of the race before the convention started.[18]

"Howie's a nice guy," Esposito continued, according to Carey. "He wants to be good to you. Listen to this: you'll get nothing this year if you keep running against Howie, but how about we do this for you," and he promised Carey that the "whole organization" would back him if he dropped out and ran instead against New York's senior senator, Republican Jacob Javits, who was then 70. "You'll be the winner because he's an old man now," Esposito said. "And when you beat Javits, you'll be a national name. Next year there'll be a ticket. The man who beats Javits could become vice president, because Howie will be behind you."

In Carey's lively accounts of the episode, Esposito and Troy waited for Carey to respond to their offer.

"You didn't say to me what happens if I don't accept your offer," Carey began.

Esposito (according to Carey): "Well, your fucking head will roll in the gutter."

At which point Carey removed the cloth napkin from his shirt and rose, brushing breadcrumbs from his pants in an unhurried way, yet shaken by the threat.

"Gentlemen," Carey said, with Jerry Cummins getting up to leave too. "I had no idea, no recognition, that you were so powerful."

"Well, we wanted to do the right thing," Troy quickly offered.

"Just think of it," Carey went on. "One minute my 'fucking head' is rolling in the gutter, the next minute I'm vice president of the United States. You guys are magicians. But I'm going to go out there and beat the hell out of you."

Carey and Cummins headed toward the door when, as it happened, the Roman Catholic Bishop of Brooklyn, Francis J. Mugavero, arrived with a friend for dinner, offering Carey a warm, welcoming hello: "Hughie, how are ya? Hey Meade, it's wonderful to see you here trying to help Hughie. Hughie's our friend, you know. We're going to help him!"

"Your Excellency," said Carey, "I can't stay for dinner, I have to go somewhere. But if you choose to sit down with my friends, then please tell them I'm going to win."

"Oh it's great," said the bishop, "everybody's for ya."[19]

When the three-day 1974 Democratic convention opened, Opton kept tabs on each convention delegate on index cards, which she kept in a small, black metal box. Each cards contained the delegate's telephone numbers, the total of votes he or she represented, and notes on her and Carey's conversations or encounters with them. She apportioned the cards into three piles—those for Carey, those for Samuels, and the "Undecideds." The "Undecideds" pile slowly declined as the Carey pile grew.

Some Democratic Party leaders did not want to be seen as heavy-handed backroom bosses pulling the strings for one candidate at the expense of another, or meddling with the delegate voting process, especially during this summer of the brewing Watergate scandal. One in particular, Patrick Cunningham, fiery, broad-shouldered, with half-moon reading glasses, came through for his fellow Irish-American, releasing 50 percent of the delegates he controlled in Bronx County to Carey, while committing the remaining 50 percent to Samuels. The Bloom brothers of Brooklyn peeled away from Meade Esposito as expected. Help for Carey also came from Suffolk County's Democratic leader Dominic J. Baranello, the former Erie County leader Peter Crotty, and Albany Mayor Erastus Corning. Opton and other Carey people worked to ensure that the political leaders who were indicating that they were willing to offer some of their delegates to Carey stayed true to their professed intentions.

The vote was still uncertain when Carey delivered a well-received, ten-minute speech, drafted by Greenfield, in which he declared that once the hoopla of the convention faded and all the posters came down, the state's struggling residents would still be facing a host of urgent concerns about the economy and the running of the state and the real question on their mind would be not who would win the election but what would be done to make life more tolerable. "I'll tell you one thing," recalled Cummins, "Bella Abzug"—the Greenwich Village congresswoman known for her floppy hats, combative temperament, and uncompromising antiwar and feminist views, of whom Carey was not always a fan—"jumped out of her chair and applauded."[20] Manhattan Councilman Bobby Wagner, son of the former mayor and grandson of the former senator, broke from the pro-Samuels consensus among Manhattan Reform Democrats, and delivered the nominating speech for the long-shot Carey and seconded his nomination. When the delegates had all cast their votes, Carey had accumulated 31 percent. It was an indisputable victory for him: he was on the ballot.

For his part, Samuels claimed 68.27 percent and was now the party's nominee, but with an unexpected primary battle now ahead of him.

As the Carey people celebrated, Samuels was less ebullient. Talking with reporters in front of his seventy-foot-long trailer parked outside the convention hall, where free frankfurters had been dispensed all day, he said, "It's been a long, difficult struggle. More could have been done if we wanted to twist arms, but that would be against the political principles I stand for." He walked off to deliver his acceptance speech in the bustling hall with his "chic" wife, as a *Daily News* reporter described her, at his side. Samuels pledged "both compassion and tough management" if elected, and said the campaign would be conducted in the "shadow of the totally political Nelson Rockefeller and the morally corrupted Richard Nixon."[21]

Auletta, too, harbored regrets, as he explained years after. "Here I was, a kid under thirty years old" and not so long out of the Maxwell School at Syracuse University, where he had received his received a master's degree in public administration. During the convention, he said, the Samuels campaign had failed to use its leverage as the frontrunner to ensure that these hardened dealmakers, the county bosses with their blocs of delegates, kept their minions in line behind the prospective nominee. One county leader in particular, he said, got away—Cunningham. "When they said let's put Carey on the ballot just to look like we're not bosses, I didn't strong-arm them or tell them, hey, you want to fight us on this, we'll fight you—we're not going to make it easy for Hugh Carey."[22]

Before the banners and bunting were all gone and the stage dismantled, the delegates designated Syracuse Mayor Lee Alexander over two antiwar and civil rights leaders, the former Nassau County congressman Allard Lowenstein and former U.S. attorney general Ramsey Clark, to run for the U.S. Senate seat held by Jacob Javits. The Rockland County district attorney Robert Meehan was chosen to vie for state attorney general against Louis Lefkowitz, 69, the Republican incumbent who had begun his political career as an assemblyman when Calvin Coolidge was president. Arthur Levitt, 74, another long-time figure in state and city politics, was chosen to seek his sixth term as the state comptroller, while Mario Cuomo, 42, a public-spirited attorney from Queens come to prominence as a conciliator in a furor over a Lindsay administration plan to build public housing in middle class Forest Hills, was selected to run on the Samuels ticket for lieutenant governor.

Carey and his small group bolted from the convention hall to the municipal airport while the political deliberations and jockeying were still afoot, although Carey probably would have liked to stay for what remained of the procedural debates, for he relished this kind of internecine battling. But Cummins wanted him to get out of Buffalo and away from reporters for two or three days in service to his new image as a maverick. On balance, he was in a good place, a confirmed outsider in an election year when party-anointed candidates were suspect in the eyes of most voters. Emerging from the convention, he was largely free of binding commitments to Democratic leaders, and thousands of feet above the fray.

At the time, a new state campaign finance law had become effective June 1, two weeks before the convention, limiting campaign contributions by a candidate and members of their families to $105,000 per person. The Samuels people were happy the state legislature had approved this cap, as Ed Carey was then Hugh's only heavy contributor; the Samuels people believed their opponent's campaign would be low on cash once the congressman's big brother reached the campaign donation limit. But Ed, who was reported to have a personal net worth of $1 billion, advanced hundreds of thousands of dollars to the campaign, all the same. The Carey team, meanwhile, put together a plan to raise enough outside money to replenish his funds so he would be technically within the limit by the September primary (the date when every candidate was required to disclose his campaign contributions since June 1).[23]

It was an artful tiptoe around the spirit of the law, perhaps, but it was legal. And if the Carey campaign worried that Ed's money might become a troublesome issue, it didn't let it be known. Typically, campaign finance is too arcane to engage voter interest. But Cummins said he wasn't altogether sure until a campaign stop with Carey at a community center in Brooklyn. That morning, he listened as a senior citizen talked with another in conspiratorial tones about Carey's brother in the oil business, and the woman who was taking it all in shrugged and said, "What's a brother for?"

"After I heard that," said Cummins, "I didn't worry about it."[24]

Carey's success at the convention did not attract much media interest in him or his campaign. Gubernatorial campaigns rarely arouse intense public attention until their final weeks, and 1974's was no different. The *New York Post* and the *Daily News* instead published prominent stories in July and August about an intraparty contretemps between the prideful Mayor Beame, 68, (whose campaign slogan had been: "If you don't know the buck, you don't know the job—and Abe knows the buck") and his sometime rival City Comptroller Harrison J. Goldin, 38 (who had been proffered to voters as a "Young Dynamo" who will "Make Waves"). At issue were audits from Goldin's office alleging that Beame previously ran the comptroller's office in a sloppy manner and even lost track of millions of dollars in city bank deposits. Beame strongly denied the attack on his credibility and convened an investigation, which in short order accounted for the whereabouts of the funds and bond securities, found at the back of desk drawers, tucked away in the wrong set of envelopes, or obscured by piles of scuffed ledgers.[25]

Carey had picked up endorsements from Edith Lehman, the widow of the late Governor Herbert Lehman, and W. Averell Harriman, the last Democratic governor of the state, when a young reporter from the *Times*, Linda Greenhouse, was dispatched from the paper's headquarters to the upstate "hinterlands," far from the bright lights, and squalor, of Times Square. Her assignment was to cover Carey on the upstate campaign trail. She recalled her editor asking her to catch up with "some guy who says he wants to be governor," or words to that effect, and off she went.[26]

She first encountered Carey that July at the offices of a Syracuse newspaper, where the candidate had gone to meet the editor in chief. She often found herself the only reporter around as Carey traveled in search of an audience. "Which one is Carey" was a comment she would hear from those who stopped by to listen to the candidate and whoever he happened to be standing next to. At one point she found herself sitting knee-to-knee with Carey aboard a tiny two-seat aircraft as it carried them over rustic hamlets and rusting cities. In Schenectady, Carey waited outside the gates of a factory to shake hands with workers, she recalled, but none of the employees showed up; most, it turned out, were on vacation. As Carey turned to leave, he said, "We can't lose—we outnumbered them." Greenhouse nodded and chuckled to herself as she jotted down the quip in her pocket notepad.[27]

The midsummer assignment provided Greenhouse with her introduction to Carey, as it did for a few other reporters who would go on to cover him closely, like Frederick U. Dicker of the *Albany Times Union* and later the *New York Post*. In her first weeks with the congressman, Greenhouse couldn't help but notice his good-natured and self-effacing humor, especially when he apologized to her for having drawn the solitary assignment of chronicling his upstate politicking. He was clearly well-informed, determined, and a good storyteller. Perhaps, she thought, there was more to this Brooklyn pol than she or her editors knew.

The national media, meanwhile, was appropriately riveted by the possibility of the impeachment or resignation of the President of the United States, and eventually even the local oriented New York City tabloids began to cover it play-by-play ("Nixon Not Quitting," the *Post* headlined on August 6, followed up by "Report: Nixon Ready to Go" on August 7, and finally, on August 8, "Nixon To Resign Tonight").[28] Not only would Nixon be ousted from the Oval Office with little more than a month to go before the 1974 gubernatorial primary, but New York's own Nelson Rockefeller would be nominated to be President Gerald Ford's vice president. And when Ford began weighing the extremely volatile question of pardoning his predecessor, the governor's race in New York was pushed even farther back in the papers. Besides, summer was a season generally reserved for more enticing distractions—baseball, beach-going, and barbeques—and a year when a French high-wire artist defied death and common sense by walking a tightrope between the lids of the Twin Towers. *The Power Broker: Robert Moses and the Fall of New York,* a blistering biography by Robert Caro, came out, and Charles Lindbergh, the first person ever to fly a plane alone non-stop across the Atlantic, died.

Samuels and Carey nonetheless worked hard to get attention and contrast their views in televised debates around the state. Their differences were often subtle and difficult to detect. Liberal in their views, both voiced support for such things as amnesty for Vietnam War draft evaders, campaign finance reform, and holding the line against any deregulation of rents in the city's tight rental housing market. In addition, both candidates said they would not, if elected, force parents to accept busing over long distances to integrate their children's schools, nor seek to reimpose capital punishment or build so-called scatter-site public housing, as Lindsay had tried and failed to do in Forest Hills. Carey wanted more methadone clinics for heroin users. Samuels, whose twenty-two-year-old son from his first marriage had struggled with drugs, wanted the state to concentrate on promoting drug-free therapies as well. Though *Roe v. Wade* had been decided by the Supreme Court only the year before, it had not yet assumed the flashpoint significance it would in later years nationally. Samuels backed the landmark court decision guaranteeing a woman's right to choose whether to curtail a pregnancy. Carey said that while the ruling was sharply at odds with his personal views about the sanctity of life, he would not support any push for a constitutional amendment to overturn the decision of the nation's highest court.

On state fiscal issues, Carey talked about returning power and money to local governments around the state. He cited the federal revenue sharing bill he had sponsored. "I'm for doing things at the lowest possible level of government where judgments can be made," he said, adding, "Let's have the neighborhood work, give the means, if you will, to have the borough presidents fix potholes." Samuels put the emphasis on government efficiency and reform—"tough management" and "management and productivity standards" that, he argued, should be directed from the top, in Albany. "My first priority," he said, "is that I have to stop the escalating costs of state and local governments, which have gone up 12–16 percent a year. I have to provide the leadership. It costs fifteen thousand dollars to keep a person in a nursing home, and only three thousand in home care."

The two rivals traded charges over the source of their financial backing, with Samuels blasting Ed Carey's heavy bankrolling of his younger brother's campaign, and, citing Ed's oil deals with Con Edison and Long Island Lighting Company, he claimed ratepayers were essentially underwriting Carey's campaign. At another point, he criticized Ed Carey's Puerto Rico refinery and residency there as a tax dodge. Carey reacted by saying his brother had created "thousands of jobs" for the people of Puerto Rico. He charged that since Samuels had sold his plastics company to a division of Mobil, he too could be considered to have "ties" to Big Oil. The Carey campaign further highlighted Samuels' self-financing: he loaned his campaign $134,000 before May 31, exceeding the state's legal limit, and guaranteed another loan of $50,000. What was worse, they said, Samuels hadn't paid income taxes that April to the city, though he had made $40,000 as the OTB president. The Carey campaign labeled it "an outrageous application of the tax loopholes." But Samuels contended it was simply a matter of his charitable giving and medical costs exceeding his taxable income.

On and on they went with their charges and countercharges, rounds of TV and radio advertisements, press conferences, accusations, and promises.[29]

The campaign took on an air of unreality near the end, because the consensus that Samuels was headed to victory held. *The Times* gave Samuels a less-than-wholehearted endorsement—"It's like chicken soup—it's lukewarm," Carey described it, "but it doesn't hurt." The Samuels team cited internal polls indicating he would win by 10–20 percent. Voters headed to the polls to decide the contest; some newspapers described the race as too close to call.

But victory in the end was decidedly Carey's—not a close call but a stunning upset. He received 580,733 votes to Samuels' 433,901, winning 55 percent to 45 percent, and captured all five boroughs of the city, its suburban counties, and virtually all of the counties upstate.

Gone, as a result, were the long days when Carey enjoyed something tantamount to privacy as he trekked around the state in search of support and attention. Not only the local press but the national newspapers and magazines were now caught by his unexpected triumph. Samuels termed Carey's campaign "brilliant," and the deluge of coverage of his ascendant efforts eclipsed even that of the incumbent governor, Malcolm Wilson. Now it was Carey who was widely favored to win.

Part of the reason for Carey's success was related to Wilson's decision in May to push through a bill shifting the date of the primary from June to September. The shift was intended to give the public more time to become better acquainted with Wilson and his candidacy, and the Democrats additional time to engage in their usually fratricidal ways. But the move only helped Carey, affording him extra months to campaign at an ideal time—when the Republicans' Watergate scandal was unfolding and voter's suspicions of party-anointed candidates like Wilson as well as Samuels were deepening.

Wilson had other challenges. Far from emotional or dynamic on the stump, Wilson instead boasted he was fluent in Latin and never drank alcohol. Not surprisingly, such pronouncements failed at times to excite the public's imagination. He sometimes came across as an upstate Abe Beame—able, connected, loyal, and knowledgeable about how things worked and how to get things done, but not particularly dynamic.

"When you ask him what time it is," the journalist Richard Reeves wrote of Wilson during the 1974 campaign, "he not only tells you how to build a watch, but also recites the history of chronology." Addressing a friendly campaign crowd at Lake Placid, according to Reeves, Wilson began, "It's been a very interesting day for me. Under the felicitous concatenation of circumstances, I've had a day where I've seen the microcosm of all New York State—what makes the state tick."[30]

Still, Wilson won admirers by presenting himself as a proud conservative who would hold tight to the state's purse strings. He was first elected to state office in 1939 as an assemblyman. He served as naval officer during World War II and was a graduate of Fordham Law School. When, starting in mid-December, 1973, Rockefeller chose him to take his place as governor, he inherited the first signs of very serious budgetary problems. He was one of Albany's most experienced political players, having served as lieutenant governor for nearly twenty years.

The beginnings of the city's fiscal crisis were also percolating quietly. As early as the sixth week of 1974, well before the gubernatorial race, representatives of the big commercial banks headquartered in New York City had privately raised questions about the city government's growing volume and frequency of short-term borrowing under Beame and Goldin, who, as Beame's successor as city comptroller, negotiated borrowing rates and bond transactions. A few of the bankers warned at the time that the market for city securities was becoming over-saturated, and investors' appetite for purchasing the city's debt paper was waning. Their assertions to the newly installed comptroller and mayor were polite yet persistent.

This was no minor matter. The city relied on long-term, thirty-year loans from the municipal bond market for the huge expenditures needed to build and fix schools, hospitals, bridges, and highways (even the section of the West Side Highway in Manhattan that collapsed shortly after Beame's election, becoming a symbol of the city's deferred maintenance), and relied, too, on higher-priced, short-term notes, which typically came due within six to eighteen months. The latter loans helped fill temporary gaps in operating cash flow over the course of a fiscal year.

During good economic times, the banks earned fat fees underwriting city notes and bonds and marketing them to other banks, insurance companies, public employee pension systems, and well-off individuals. They were tax shelters: interest from these investments was triple-tax-free for New York–based purchasers. Gains typically exceeded those to be reaped in the stock market. Until 1974, there was never any outward worry about the city's ability to meets its debt obligations. But the banks greeted the January, 1974, arrival of Beame at City Hall with intimations that they might ask the city to pay a higher interest rate on bonds and notes. That seemed to be their only way to assure that the securities marketed on New York's behalf would sell, and that no banks would be left holding unsold, devalued city securities from upcoming offerings.

From the start, Beame dismissed their qualms, though there was no way to deny their significance, since even a fractional rise in interest would mean an increase of millions of dollars in city debt-service costs at a time when revenues from local taxes and federal aid were falling and the poverty rate, and the city welfare rolls, were ascending to all-time heights. The new mayor was wrestling with a city operating budget that, he complained, Lindsay had left riddled with greater-than-anticipated expenditures and overestimates of revenues. The new mayor privately reproached the bankers for their doubts, calling on them to work harder to market the bonds of the great center of finance, culture and ambition which he was elected to steward and advance on the strength of his budgetary experience and expertise.[31]

Still another fiscal debacle was developing outside of public view during the 1974 gubernatorial race—increasing fiscal problems were jeopardizing the mission of the New York State Urban Development Corporation, a Rockefeller creation, and threatening to cause it to default on its loans. But a new infusion of financing provided over the summer by a group of underwriters led by Chase Manhattan Bank, headed by David Rockefeller, the former governor's brother, ensured that the agency would have enough cash at least until the end of the year. It did not in any case become an election-year issue for the incumbent.

Blithely unaware of these undercurrents in Albany and at City Hall, Democratic nominee Hugh Carey started racking up endorsements from union leaders and elected officials seeking to join forces with the clear choice of Democratic voters. Carey, in due course, moved to tar Governor Malcolm Wilson with the troubles besetting his scandal-scarred party in Washington, from which Wilson tried to distance himself (and no, the governor said when reporters pressed him, he would not be asking Nixon to campaign for him).

More worrisome for the Wilson campaign was that while he expected the state AFL-CIO to endorse him, as it had Rockefeller in 1970, the politically potent union went with Carey, partly at the urging of Albert Shanker of New York City's United Federation of Teachers, or UFT. In addition, the umbrella New York State United Teachers (NYSUT), with two hundred thousand members statewide, came out for Carey after word got around that Wilson, at a private meeting with the union president and Assemblyman Joseph Margiotta, a powerful Nassau County Republican, referred to teachers who went on strike as "outlaws." True or not, that was just about all Thomas Hobart, the president of NYSUT, needed to hear.[32] A number of other labor organizations, including the Seafarers International Union, headquartered in Carey's congressional district and led by a long-time Carey supporter, the rough and ready Paul Hall, helped the Carey fund-raising effort remain competitive with Malcolm Wilson.[33] (The seafarers union donated $43,000.)

Stephen May, the Republican nominee for state comptroller, told reporters that Wilson's record was "a winning story, but I'm not sure he has the winning personality." Polls were showing Wilson trailing Carey. Complicating matters for Wilson, his supporter Senator Javits was running for reelection on both the Republican line and the Liberal line, the latter also giving its ballot line to Carey—and so, too, was Republican state Attorney General Louis Lefkowitz. Meanwhile, although the Conservative Party endorsed Wilson for governor, it was conducting a national push to try to unseat Javits.

Still, Wilson swung hard at Carey, highlighting Carey's inexperience with Albany while airing a commercial depicting the funeral of a murdered policeman in an effort to characterize the anti-death-penalty Carey as soft on crime. But polls showed that most voters were desirous of a change, and cared less about crime than about inflation, unemployment, and taxes. Carey pledged he would not increase the state income tax. Handing Carey a political gift of sorts, Wilson dismissed the vow as irresponsible.

In a head-to-head debate, Wilson sought to blame Carey for "the move toward inflation and the huge deficits." He termed the trend "Careyism." But Carey, one of 435 players in the House of Representatives, responded, "I'll accept all of the responsibility for the Johnson-Kennedy inflation if you'll accept the responsibility for the Nixon inflation"—meaning, effectively, the current inflation.

"It is good," said Wilson, "that you accept your full responsibility for all of the inflation which came about during the first eight years that you have been down in Washington."

Carey: "What was the average inflation rate, Governor?"

Wilson: "The average rate depends upon the cumulative deficits which were built up during that eight-year period."

Carey: "The average rate, Governor, for your information, varied between 3 and 4 percent. The growth rate, Governor, was over 6 percent."

Wilson: "I'm talking about deficits. When the Congress votes for deficits, which is to say, in simple terms, the Federal Government spends more money that it takes in revenues, that is what causes inflation."

Carey: "Governor, Nixonomics . . ."[34]

In the wake of the debate, Wilson fell still further behind in the polls.

The *Times* published an editorial on November 4 entitled "Near-Bankrupt City," indicating that the current city budget deficit could be as much as $1 billion, a fearsome hole, and maintaining that "the city is sliding into bankruptcy with dismaying speed."[35] But the editorial prompted a joint letter to the editor from Beame and Goldin. They questioned the choice of the word "bankrupt" on the grounds that the term stirred "unwarranted fears for the safety of their investments among the city's bondholders."[36]

On Election Day, November 5, Carey swamped Wilson, 58 percent to 42 percent. In the nearly statewide sweep, Carey rode a wave of voter dissatisfaction with Watergate, uniting a broad coalition of traditional Democrats—liberals, the poor, and blue-collar workers. His victory was so overwhelming that he even stirred quick speculation in the Washington pundit loop that he could emerge as a Democratic challenger to President Ford come 1976.

His victory was indeed striking. Four years earlier, the Rockefeller-Wilson team had swept heavily Jewish areas of the city, such as Forest Hills, in the 1970 race against Arthur Goldberg. But this time, Forest Hills, still considered a bellwether for Democrats, voted strongly for Carey, and he also won in the more conservative neighborhoods of the city such as Ridgewood and Bay Ridge. Carey's margin of victory was a lopsided 7 to 3 in the city and an equally impressive 3 to 2 statewide. Wilson even lost to Carey in Long Island's Republican-led Nassau County, which had last been carried by a Democratic gubernatorial hopeful in 1910.

Of 4 million votes cast, Carey got 2.4 million, Wilson 1.6 million. Carey's running mate, Mary Ann Krupsak, a state senator of Polish descent in upstate Amsterdam who Carey liked to refer to as "the star of the ticket," became the lieutenant governor–elect and the first woman ever elected to a major New York State office. Arthur Levitt, meanwhile, powered to his sixth term at the age of 74, collecting more votes than any candidate for statewide office in the history of New York State. Bronx Borough President Robert Abrams fell short in his bid to defeat Attorney General Lefkowitz, while Sen. Javits was reelected over Ramsey Clark.

At the Roosevelt Hotel in Manhattan, Governor Wilson nursed a toothache as he conceded his defeat and congratulated his opponent.

"This has not been a good day for the Republican Party," he declared, capping his thirty-six years in public life. Two hundred misty-eyed supporters cheered. "But let no one say the Republican Party is dead."

Over at the Commodore, where Carey had kicked off his campaign eight months earlier, a band played "Happy Days are Here Again," and Carey, who emerged to wild clapping, gave his victory speech, also evoking the solidly Democratic era of Franklin Roosevelt. He mentioned Al Smith as well, and began several lines with John Kennedy's famous phrasing, "Let the word go forth," arousing even more frenzied applause.

"Let the word go forth that the divided and disaffected Democrats have come home tonight," he said.

Accompanying him, of course, were his children, the six youngest of whom were going to move with him to the Executive Mansion in Albany in a fulfillment of their parents' wishes.

Their only disappointment was that Carey had prevented them from electioneering in Broome County—home base of state Senate Republican majority leader Warren Anderson—as he had required them to return to school on time in September and concentrate on their studies.[37]

When the election results were tallied in the state's sixty-two counties, Broome was the only one that Carey didn't carry.

4

# On Borrowed Time

*The fiscal crisis emerges.*

The sweeping gubernatorial victory was sweet but not long savored.
Like many a candidate, Carey had given more thought to running his campaign than to how he would run the state if elected. Malcolm Wilson had been right about one thing: his Democratic rival knew relatively little about the characters and habits of the state capital. Still, by the time he delivered his first State of the State speech on January 9, 1975, the new man in Albany figured out he was inheriting circumstances far more difficult than either Wilson or Wilson's towering predecessor and patron, Nelson Rockefeller, had indicated. On top of the widely discussed problems in education, health care, poverty, and urban life, New York State had 200,000 fewer jobs than at the post-war employment peak in 1969. Despite this, the state government's expenditures from the general fund had risen and risen, an average 18 percent annually from 1969 to 1972, fueled in part by generous federal revenue sharing and matching grants.[1]

By the time Carey became governor-elect, the once-buoyant optimism and heavy borrowing of prior years were being tested by broader conditions and constraints. Rockefeller embodied an era of soaring state ambitions, but in the wake of his leadership, New York State faced ever-leaner times for which it was less than well-prepared. Rockefeller seemed to acknowledge as much, at one point telling the former Democratic congressman and federal revenue-sharing-law sponsor, "I drank the champagne—you got the hangover."[2] Awakening to the wide-ranging effects of the mid-1970s recession, Carey started thinking early about what others would come to describe as the "politics of less," and moved to embrace state-budget economies in place of the well ingrained habit of growth. The state had weathered recessions before, including under Rockefeller, but this one marked "the most severe recession in postwar history," according to the President's Council of Economic Advisers.[3] It began in November, 1973, and would continue for the nation as a whole through September, 1975, a period of massive job losses coupled with stratospheric inflation and tightened credit. The Governor-elect readied an alien concoction of budget cuts and tax increases that members of his own party found surprising and some most distasteful, coming as they did from a liberal Democrat from the party's Brooklyn base who had not made slowdowns and cutbacks a theme of his campaign.

As he developed his approach to the state's budget difficulties, Carey also began the work of filling the key positions in his administration. His transition team opened offices in an undistinguished prewar office building on lower Broadway in Manhattan, a short walk from the World Trade Center and its tens of millions of square feet of then mostly vacant office space made possible by Rockefeller and his banker brother, David. The transition team, directed by Matthew Nimetz, a corporate attorney, was made up of academicians, retired judges, and business executives. It quickly took up the work of sifting through thousands of resumes, interviewing applicants, and ultimately assembling what amounted to a high-caliber group of staff and commissioners. It did so without interference from county Democratic bosses, who, with the exception of Patrick Cunningham of the Bronx—whom Carey pushed, starting within a week of the 1974 election, for chairman of the state Democratic organization—had all bet on the wrong horse in the governor's race and thankfully had no claim to the spoils.[4] David Garth sent over a handful of recommendations for top jobs. Former mayor Wagner and the Liberal party chief Alex Rose, the duo to whom Carey readily returned for political advice and talent referrals, sent more, and so, of course, did Cunningham. Still, the governor-elect, having won a relatively independent run, enjoyed unusually wide latitude to make his own decisions. "Carey wanted a strong, independent, administrative, nonpolitical transition group," says John Dyson, who, then thirty-four, put in his name and was interviewed by an assistant dean from the Woodrow Wilson School of Public Affairs at Princeton University, and received the post of state commissioner of agriculture and markets in part because Carey, a city boy, knew no one else who had majored in agricultural economics (Dyson did so at Cornell University as an undergraduate) or run a farm (which belonged to his family and was situated in New York's Hudson Valley). "Because Carey wasn't the party favorite, the Meade Espositos of the world did not have a hook on him very much to try to get their people into the administration," said Dyson.[5] And with help of his staff, the months-long selection process, continuing into 1975 under Carol Opton, was based on Carey's instinct to hire the best person for each job—and was arguably the most critical component in the administration's accomplishments to come.

Dyson, the son of a Park Avenue investment banker, had served in an army intelligence division in Vietnam. Upon returning to New York and marrying, he volunteered to help the then nearly bankrupt state Democratic organization headed by Joe Crangle of Buffalo to drum up contributions in a solidly Republican era. Through Carey's congressional office, the young Dyson also met Wilbur Mills, chairman of the House Ways and Means Committee, and Mills asked Dyson to help raise money for twenty-two members of Congress in danger of losing their seats in the 1972 elections because of the anticipated drubbing of Democratic presidential candidate George McGovern at the hands of President Nixon. Seven of those Congressional candidates were from New York, and one was Carey.[6]

Carey as a rule looked for those with whom he could establish a rapport and who had government experience, a sense of independence, intelligence, and creativity. Even though he rewarded a small number of close friends, supporters, and campaign staffers with jobs in Albany—Jerry Cummins, his campaign manager, would be named commissioner of the New York State Thruway Authority, a traditional patronage post; Carey's childhood buddy Jake Lennon, who had experience in the insurance business, became a deputy commissioner of insurance; and Dr. Kevin Cahill, a highly regarded expert on tropical diseases who had been Helen Carey's physician and a close family friend, was named special assistant for health affairs—those were all exceptions to the rule. Carey in his own way succeeded in cobbling together a "brain trust" in the mold of John F. Kennedy's cabinet of confidantes, experts, and advisers. The Carey "cabinet" came to include a group of highly talented men and some women, to whom he granted leeway to initiate and negotiate decisions.

Democrats had been out of favor for so long that Carey faced a choice in stocking his administration. He could fill its senior ranks with entrenched, usually older Democratic operatives, or he could select younger Democrats with little or no New York State government experience. Carey chose men and women who were, in the main, younger than he was, sometimes by up to two decades and in their thirties and early forties. Many were in awe of the confidence and trust he placed with them, and would prove willing and able to work unusually long hours, as well as weekends. Many, too, were idealistic, believing they could solve problems that others dismissed as unconquerable. To them, he was a prickly, moody father figure, feared and respected, and above all appreciated. His administration, as he shaped it according to his moral dictates, emerged at odds with the history of patronage-steeped state government. At the time, few noticed that so many key people he hired had had little or nothing to do with his campaign for governor.

Further gearing to take charge of the affairs of the state, Carey held several meetings with the Democratic state comptroller, Arthur Levitt. It was somewhat unusual for a governor-elect to sit down with another statewide elected official at this stage, especially one who would be looking over his shoulder as the state's top person in charge of audits. But these two professional politicians had known each other for at least a decade, and, what was more, Levitt, a long-popular public official, appreciated the younger Carey's prior service on the House Ways and Means Committee and his grasp of business and finance, which was relatively rare for an elected official.[7] Levitt, who had an office in the same building, brought Carey to meetings of his private-sector advisers, among them municipal bond specialists Gedale Horowitz of Salomon Brothers and Frank Smeal of Morgan Guaranty. State government expenditures, Carey learned quickly enough, were expected to outstrip revenues by about $700 million by March 31, 1975, the end of the state's fiscal year. Some of Levitt's private sector advisers noted that further tax increases risked additional erosion of the state's economic base. State and local personal income taxes had grown from 14 percent above the national average in the 1960s to 25 percent in the early 1970s.[8]

In the movie *The Taking of Pelham 1 2 3,* which hit cinemas in 1974, sinister criminals and a disgruntled former motorman hijack a subway car under the streets of Manhattan and send it on a terrifying downtown ride. In real life, it was the recession that was taking the state and its largest city hostage, hog-tying it with high unemployment as well as inflation, a rare and painful double whammy. Around the state, many businesses had left or were packing up for the Sunbelt states and the suburbs of the New York region and beyond. In midtown Manhattan, office vacancies, including at the World Trade Center, were extensive and rising. Tax collections were declining, challenging the city's ability to scour up revenue. The civic fabric—parks, hospitals, subway stations, schools, public safety—was frayed.

Mayor Abraham Beame, who had a penchant for seeing a silver lining in almost every dark cloud, was hopeful that the election of a governor from their shared home-borough of Brooklyn might result in fresh installments of funds to patch up the gaps in the city's budget, which, he complained, were larger than his predecessor had reported—a total $600 million by his initial estimates. Given the stalled economy, Beame warned the shortfall could hit $1 billion during the city's next fiscal year, which started July 1, 1975. Following Carey's election, Beame told reporters that Carey had indicated to him his willingness to work with the city to plug its budget gap. But when reporters at City Hall got their first chance to ask Carey directly about the subject, Carey only patted Beame on the shoulder. "Well," he declared, "we both know the way to Washington."[9]

Beame soon lined up Democrats in the State Assembly on behalf of another Brooklyn Democrat, Assemblyman Stanley Steingut. A former Democratic leader in Brooklyn, Steingut had been elected Assembly Speaker by his fellow legislators during the first week of January, 1975, a role that Steingut's father, Irwin, had also played for one term in 1935. When Carey, during the governor's race, had tried to win Steingut's backing, there were a lot of personal and political resentments between them. Steingut's first bid to become Assembly Speaker had been thwarted in 1965 by Carey's current ally, Robert Wagner Jr., who, having been reelected to his third mayoral term in 1961 by denouncing the same party bosses who had supported him twice before, decided to line up his Democratic allies in the state legislature behind Rockefeller's choice for Assembly Speaker, the Democratic Minority Leader Anthony Travia of Brooklyn. Wagner's decision helped Rockefeller's candidate Travia prevail, breaking a deadlock that paralyzed Albany for six weeks. Later during that session, then-mayor Wagner made sure that virtually all of the Democrats who had voted for Rockefeller's choice also backed his proposal for a state income tax increase, as well as approval for the city to raise its sales tax.[10] When, in the summer of 1974, Carey visited Steingut's office to ask for support for his race for governor, Steingut indicated his preference for Carey's rival, Howard Samuels, and flipped Carey the finger.[11]

Even so, Beame, whose political image was built upon his facility with numbers as a former city budget director and city comptroller, knew how important the state legislature would be for the city budget, because federal aid was slowing. The White House was now in the hands of Gerald Ford, who was seen as little likely to go out of his way to help the disproportionately Democratic city—a city, moreover, which was still portrayed by many Republicans as a swamp of corruption and profligacy. Beame certainly understood that LBJ's Great Society approach to directly funding cities and their inner city programs was fading, along with the overflowing national black ink that underwrote so much of it. At the same time, important Democratic constituencies were demanding a sustained level of aid even though federal matching dollars for antipoverty work was going by the wayside. And the public employee unions, which for years had put on both muscle and girth,[12] and to which Beame owed his election to no small degree, were not in any mood to surrender hard-won contractual gains of the prior fifteen years.

More pressing than the troubling trends confronting the city was the financial condition of New York's largest public authority, the Urban Development Corporation, which, on close inspection by the newly forming Carey team, could only be described as worse than expected and acute. Carey was dismayed.

During the gubernatorial campaign, he had raised only general questions about the state's increasing dependence on its public authorities, for the issue was not new and the state's habit of reliance on public authorities was well ingrained. New York State pioneered the use of public authorities nationally; in the early nineteenth century, under Governor DeWitt Clinton, the first large-scale state and local financing ever undertaken in the country was used to build New York's Erie Canal, an engineering feat that helped propel the rise of Wall Street as the financial center of the United States. In the twentieth century, Robert Moses appreciated the vast potential of public authorities and almost single-handedly used them to direct the modernization of the New York area. The tax exempt bonds issued by the Moses-controlled Triborough Bridge and Tunnel Authority were probably the safest and highest-yielding of any municipal or corporate bonds ever. As such, the TBTA and Moses became a favorite of David Rockefeller and his Chase Manhattan Bank, the trustee of the authority's bonds and, followed by Chemical Bank, the largest beneficiary of the lucrative service fees connected with marketing them.[13] While such generous terms for investors placed upward pressure on tolls, the TBTA bonds covered the cost of building bridges, parkways, concert halls, and public recreational areas. In 1974, *The Power Broker*, Robert Caro's biography of Moses, depicted the near-unilateral clout of an ironclad political constituency that rose up to support Moses—leading bankers and construction-trade union leaders and their allies in the political world.[14] The state legislature, too, could be counted on to go along, as the growing reliance on authorities relieved them of the need to raise taxes to support these projects. Yet their financing mechanisms posed a risk to the treasury: if an authority failed to pay off its bonds, the state treasury was legally required to come to its rescue. But a default even quickly remedied threatened the state's reputation in the credit market and, at the very least, was likely to drive up its borrowing costs.

Delegates to a state constitutional convention in 1938 argued that public authorities were carrying out too many functions traditionally performed by state agencies and exposing the state to too many liabilities for their debt. The state adopted a constitutional amendment mandating that authorities could henceforth be created solely by a special act of the legislature. There were about forty public authorities in the state at the time.[15] But by 1956, another twenty-four authorities had been approved to build bridges, ports, water treatment systems, and parking facilities, the latter a result of the era's burgeoning suburbanization. The new generation of authorities shared a common trait: they generated revenues from specific services that they provided, such as electricity. The fees paid by their customers guaranteed repayment of the bonds. These traditional authorities were called "revenue authorities" and attracted government officials from around the world to visit and learn about them. Starting in the 1960s, the state legislature began sanctioning new financing authorities that sold bonds to finance construction of projects that the authority did not itself operate, but leased to the state, which then paid them back with taxes or fees for the use of the facilities. The Urban Development Corporation, created during this period to build affordable housing in low-income areas of the state, was one such entity.[16]

But the UDC's bonds were its most exotic feature. Unlike traditional revenue bonds of most state authorities, the UDC's financing instruments were called "moral obligation" bonds, as they were built on a promise—not a requirement—that the state legislature would dip into tax revenues to make bondholders whole in the event of a default. Absent was any legal obligation to replenish the reserves of a troubled authority for the purpose of paying off bondholders, and any requirement to obtain voter approval for large bond issuances, as existed for more traditional bonds.

Governor Rockefeller, speeding to address urgent social problems plaguing cities, embraced the concept, and the moral obligation bond soon was used by many other public authorities, both in New York and other states. Its inventor was John N. Mitchell, who at the time, 1960, was a New York bond attorney. Years after, he became the U.S. attorney general convicted and imprisoned for his role in the Watergate scandal.

Carey believed the state's borrowing through the authorities was unbridled and out of hand. "In New York State," he told reporters during his transition period, "we haven't found only back-door financing, we've got side-door financing. And because of New York's borrowing over the years—through the state government, its authorities and agencies, and UDC and MTA [the Metropolitan Transportation Authority]—we got money going out the doors, the windows, the port holes."[17] Malcolm Wilson, according to Carey, spent only an hour briefing him on what to expect in his new role, and said nothing about the perils threatening the UDC with imminent default. "Either he didn't know or was asked to keep silent by Rockefeller," said Carey.[18] Meanwhile, former campaign staffers Stephen Berger and Carol Opton, among other transition aides, traveled to Albany to find empty file drawers, papers strewn and shredded, and overflowing receptacles—little of what might be called an organized plan to help smooth the changing of the guard. Opton said it looked as if the job appointments office on the second floor of the Capitol building, down the hall from the governor's office, had been abandoned in anticipation of an invasion by a foreign power.[19] Luckily, long-time state professionals like Howard ("Red") Miller, since 1956 an official in the state budget division on the ground floor, and John J. Corrigan, another veteran budget official, offered a helping hand to the twenty-nine-year-old Opton, the new deputy appointments officer.[20] Robert J. Morgado, soon to be the governor's first director of operations, also helped; his experience had included service within the budget division and as the director of tax and fiscal studies for the Assembly Ways and Means Committee, and he would go on to become the deputy secretary to Carey, and then secretary to the governor, filling the critical chief-of-staff role from 1977 through the midsummer of 1982.

Carey's own look around the Executive Mansion, the picturesque two-story Queen Anne–style house erected in 1856 and used as the official residence for governors since the 1870s, provided another clue as to how much things were going to change. As he prepared to move into the official governor's residence, one of the building's staff members explained that the state attorney general, Louis Lefkowitz, and the state comptroller, Arthur Levitt, had been and were still occupying their own bedrooms at the head of the stairs, a convenience that had been extended to them by Rockefeller, since the governor lived with his wife, Happy, in Manhattan and Pocantico Hills. As delicately as possible, for Carey knew he would be working closely with both men, he sent word to them that they would have to part with their apparently rent-free accommodations to make way for his children. "I had to tell them the ball was over," Carey recollected.[21]

The new boss was arriving, and things would be different.

His first annual State of the State message to the legislature on January 7, 1975, set the tone.

"In the very simplest of terms," Carey said not long after beginning the televised address, speaking to lawmakers assembled in the lofty Assembly chamber, "this government and we as a people have been living far beyond our means. There has been scarcely an activity, a category of public spending, in which we did not lead the nation. What we did was limited only by our imagination and our desire: our buildings were the tallest and most sumptuous, our civil service the most highly trained and paid, our public assistance programs the most expensive. Indeed, so lavish was the style of our government that we came to depend on it for life itself, forgetting that government was only the result of our industry and not its source. As the state's private economy stagnated, government became the principal growth industry in New York. Fewer New Yorkers are gainfully employed today than in 1958. But those who work now bear an enormously increased burden for the support of their fellows, and for the expenses of government. To pay for all of this, our taxes also became the highest in the nation . . . and every interest and group and advocate came to think of the state budget, and of state subsidy of local budgets, as a cornucopia, a never-ending horn of plenty that could pay for more and more each year.

"Now the times of plenty, the days of wine and roses, are over," Carey declared, in what became one of the most famous, and trenchant, lines of his tenure. He then went on: "We were in the lead car of the roller coaster going up, and we are in the lead car coming down. So we must first recognize the immediate burdens we inherit. We do this not in a spirit of recrimination, nor in criticism of any man or party. There is responsibility enough to go around for all. But if we would master our fate, we must first acknowledge our condition."[22]

Democratic and Republican legislators were in no mood to do so. Carey's prompt call for immediate economies and tax hikes irritated Democrats in particular. Carey was among the first in the party nationally to emphasize that there were limits to what state governments could do to improve people's lives. Though they were soon echoed by Democrats, Republicans, and independents running for political office all over the country, at the time Carey pronounced them his words sounded unfamiliar and dissonant, especially to liberals in his party, who identified them with conservatives, bankers, and a chamber-of-commerce mentality.

But, drafted with the help of Adam Walinsky, formerly Bobby Kennedy's speechwriter,[23] Carey's speech made an imprint on nearly everyone: the new governor would be tougher and less predictable that expected. The sense that surprises were in the offing was underscored by the impression left a week earlier by Carey's children at his inaugural address. *New York Times* reporter Francis X. Clines recalled that the young ones, "so cute," had gone "skylarking" to their seats with other members of the Carey clan; their youth signaled the end of one party's control of Albany and the start of a new chapter. It was, remembered Clines, as if someone threw open the windows of the capital and allowed air to circulate through the musty chamber for the first time in a long while.[24]

Carey delivered his first budget address two weeks after his State of the State, proposing an instantly unpopular ten-cent increase in the gas tax, a job freeze for state employees, a cut in the cost of governmental administration over the next year and reduced aid to localities to reduce by $450 million the gap in the state budget. More in celebration than complaint, the *Economist* wrote that Governor Carey was "sounding more like a conservative Republican than the liberal Democrat he is."

But the UDC drew Carey's first focus, for the agency was undergoing an astonishing slide toward insolvency, with no easy way out. Unknown to Carey or anyone else, this was only the beginning of a period in state history that would mark the wildest, most dynamic, and most dangerous crisis a governor had ever confronted.

David Burke, secretary to the governor, a lanky, pragmatic, twenty-eight-year-old Bostonian whom Carey recruited from the Dreyfus Corporation after he had served as Ted Kennedy's top Senate aide, laid it on the line for Carey very early, saying "You've got a problem here. There's no legislation, no appropriation, no money—there's going to be a default here."[25]

At the time of Burke's red-flag warning to the governor, the Urban Development Corporation was little more than six years old and had already had a dramatic history closely identified with "one hell of a salesman," as Carey described Rockefeller. Rocky had been the driving force behind its creation, just as he had created the State University of New York from a smattering of small colleges, the construction of a dramatic, postmodernist civic mall in Albany to "lift us above the scurrying ant heap of those absorbed only in survival," as he put it, and the planning, begun in the mid-1960s, that led to Manhattan's Twin Towers. It was when the Rev. Martin Luther King Jr. was assassinated in April, 1968, that the "Master Builder" of New York dusted off a bill to create a new authority to build affordable housing in distressed or partially abandoned urban areas. He rammed it through the Republican-dominated state senate, but the assembly, led by Democrats, voted it down because it contained a provision to allow the new agency to supersede local zoning.

Confronted with the assembly's recalcitrance, Rockefeller rushed back from King's funeral to rescue the bill, as outrage over the civil rights leader's murder touched off rioting in many large and small American cities. In the predawn hours the next day, the governor had the State Police round up New York State legislators to ensure that he had enough assembly votes for the bill, and the measure was passed by the same margin by which it had been voted down in the chamber the day before. Capping the triumph, Rockefeller chose someone of note to head his new agency—Edward Logue, a former development administrator who had carried out major renewal programs for New Haven and Boston and who had also worked for a year or so as housing coordinator under Mayor Lindsay. Logue, perhaps the leading housing and neighborhood renewal figure in the country, said later that his mission for Rockefeller was "a directive to go out and build, build, build."[26]

The UDC was the largest state government agency of its kind in the nation. It began by building affordable housing in poor, minority communities that had long suffered from red-lining by banks, discrimination by real estate brokers, wide-scale bulldozing by state and local governments under the banner of "urban renewal," and neglect by landlords. The national commercial banks headquartered in New York City eagerly marketed and bought the UDC moral obligation bonds, supported by the agency's anticipated rents and federal housing subsidies.

But the credit market's support for the UDC didn't last. Though U.S. Housing and Urban Development secretary George Romney and Logue enjoyed what the *Times* described as a notably cooperative relationship during Nixon's first term—allowing Logue to go into construction in advance of assigned contracts from HUD, and assuring the availability of the subsidies needed to market the housing—Romney announced a nationwide moratorium on new commitments to housing subsidies in the latter part of the term, reflecting the administration's disillusionment with these programs.[27] After Nixon was reelected in 1972, Romney left the agency. Then, in December, 1973, Rockefeller resigned from the governorship. The UDC's champion was gone from Albany.

By the end of 1974, the UDC had more than $1 billion in outstanding moral obligation bonds, many half-finished projects, no money from either rents or HUD to complete them, and no one who could be counted on to force the state legislature to cover the gap. A deadline to make payments on the latest series of maturing bonds loomed in late February, 1975. Alarmed, the New York banks were no longer interested in helping the agency secure additional financing.

In general, when a bank (or group of banks) was chosen by a government agency to be its underwriter, the financial institution purchased the bonds issued by the public agency in the expectation of reselling, at profit, those bonds it chose not to hold. Banks also earned "service fees" for such tasks as authenticating and delivering the bonds, acting as "paying agents" for the interest payments, or collecting and destroying the old bond coupons when the issue matured on a given date and was paid off by the agency at the negotiated rate of interest. Under federal securities laws dating to the 1930s, the bankers and bond dealers known as underwriters were required to advise prospective investors of any adverse circumstances or risks associated with any particular series of bonds or notes. Independent ratings agencies, such as Moody's and Standard and Poor's, were supposed to do the same. But in the case of the UDC, underwriters who had promoted moral obligation bonds as high-quality instruments from the beginning—as ultrasecure investments providing high, tax-free yields, like the Triborough Bridge and Tunnel Authority debt paper of old—feared they would be unable to recoup their investment in the agency's ongoing projects and walked away.

Carey brought a measure of level-headedness to this, his first fiscal crisis, as he would again and again when confronted by other unwelcome inheritances from the Rockefeller era, such as the legal case against the grossly inhumane Willowbrook institution, the bitter suspicions left by the governor's handling of the 1971 Attica prison uprising (for which only inmates, not guards, were indicted in the deaths of forty-three inmates and guards), and a widening scandal in the state-regulated nursing home industry (Carey and Attorney General Louis Lefkowitz would appoint an independent prosecutor to comprehensively investigate industry fraud and abuse, resulting in high-profile cases and a state-based Medicaid fraud-control approach funded nationally by Congress in 1977). Some of Carey's aides urged him to step gingerly through these political minefields and others, but Carey, a lightning-quick study, came to the governorship with the implicit understanding that blaming the prior governor wouldn't serve him well for very long. It was one thing to remind the press that many problems he faced were not of his making, like the UDC mess, as Carey did, but it was quite another for him to deflect ownership of those ongoing concerns. One way or another, he realized, he eventually would have to answer for his own actions or inaction. Blaming Rockefeller and Wilson, or ignoring the problems they helped create or failed to address, was not going to resonate beyond the conflict headlines the attacks would inspire. The only thing that would matter to voters, and pivotal Republicans in the state senate, would be whether and how he would make his own mark.

"There was a definite body of opinion among well-meaning advisers that the public should be impressed that everything from the imminent collapse of the UDC to the scandals at Willowbrook were part of the same pattern of neglect and abuse of power," Carey said in an interview with political scientists from the State University of New York near the end of his public career. "That theoretically would enhance the image of the new administration by pointing up the glaring deficiencies of the previous years. I rejected that approach for these reasons: First, the nation, and certainly New York, had had a full diet of Watergate—of corruption in high places and the shortcomings of government from the federal on down. I felt the blame and shame technique, the 'wailing wall and crying towel,' would generate more skepticism and cynicism among the people of New York. Second, I felt that it would be better to use our talents and energy to fix conditions instead of fixing blame. I strongly felt that, in due course, people would draw their own comparison, and we would be judged fairly on the record we would develop ourselves, rather than the negatives we could point to in the past."[28]

So it was that Carey had used his first State of the State address not only to frame for the legislature his prudent approach to the public purse, but also to reveal to legislators the fiscal woes besetting the state Urban Development Corporation. To save this giant from default, Carey told the legislators, he planned to submit emergency legislation even before proposing a proposed state budget for 1975–76 to the legislature. The authority, said Carey, was short $106 million, due February 25, on a series of bond anticipation notes.

"The UDC," he declared, "is facing an imminent exhaustion of funds. All of its ongoing projects will grind to a halt within four or five days unless we take immediate action."[29]

Shortly before giving the speech, Carey met with the newly installed Democratic Assembly Speaker Stanley Steingut and the longer-serving Republican Senate Majority Leader Warren Anderson, as well as the minority leaders in each chamber, to explain UDC's precarious position. Steingut, Anderson, and the others were surprised not only to be invited to meet with the newly minted governor prior to his State of the State address, but to hear, too, that the largest public authority in New York State was in imminent danger of imploding. As Anderson and other prior and current state legislative leaders would later tell an investigative Moreland Commission set up by Carey to uncover the factors that led to the UDC crisis, they had no idea, until Carey told them, that the grave problems at the agency, with their implications for the entire state credit rating, even existed.[30]

Carey, along with Anderson, asked for, and received, a $30 million loan from several of the UDC's long-time underwriters. The financing was modest in comparison with the authority's immediate need for cash, and needed to be repaid no later than February 28. It at least bought the state legislature some extra time in which to consider Carey's request for a larger emergency appropriation. Carey requested $178 million by February 25, 1975, to cover both the UDC's short-term debts to bondholders falling due on that day and the agency's operating costs through March 31. He also requested $50 million to replenish the agency's reserve fund.[31]

If the legislative aid was approved, Carey and his top aides reasoned, a long-term solution to the UDC's longer-term problems could then be cobbled together.

Carey also replaced Logue with Richard Ravitch, a Manhattan construction company executive. Ravitch came highly recommended by the governor's senior counsel, Judah Gribetz, who was familiar with key people in the local building industry from his former positions as the buildings commissioner under former New York City mayor Robert F. Wagner and deputy mayor for governmental relations under Mayor Beame.

The chubby-cheeked Ravitch was surprised that Carey offered him the job of UDC chairman, as "I'd never met him before in my life."[32] He'd only talked with him on the phone during the gubernatorial race, when Carey called seeking his help. But Ravitch had demurred, explaining that as chairman of the board of his children's school, and with his mother struggling with cancer and his business partner serving as the president of a general contractors association, he was too busy. "I may end up voting for you, I don't know, Congressman," said Ravitch, "but I make it a practice not to contribute to two candidates in the same race," and he went on to explain that he had already made a modest contribution to Howard Samuels—his tennis partner in a weekly doubles game.

Still, after mulling Carey's offer with his wife, Diane, an education historian at Columbia University, Ravitch accepted it.

One Saturday in the beginning of February, shortly after Ravitch assumed the helm of the storm-tossed UDC,[33] he and Carey sat down for a meal at Rose's, a cozy but far from posh restaurant in downtown Manhattan favored by the governor. They were getting ready for a meeting the next morning with the top bankers of the city, who Ravitch had asked to come to Carey's Manhattan office. Ravitch told Carey that he intended to bring a bankruptcy petition to the meeting, and had had the rather-ominous document drafted by a well-regarded bankruptcy-law attorney with an eye toward impressing the bankers with the grave seriousness of the UDC crisis and to underscore that their own coveted assets—the UDC bonds in the banks' portfolios—were very much part of the high stakes. "Governor," said Richard Ravitch, "from the information I've received, the UDC crisis has some very significant risks associated with it—the stakes are high not just for this agency but the entire state." He paused. "Maybe, governor, you should get the opinions of someone with more gray hairs than me."

But Carey wouldn't hear of it. "I'm glad I've picked you, and I have confidence in your judgment," he responded, making an indelible impression on his charge, who had recently turned forty.[34]

At the Sunday morning summary meeting, where Carey met many of the bankers for the first time, Carey described the UDC debacle in a straight-forward way and solicited the finance gatekeepers' suggestions and, he hoped, offers of additional loans and financing. But it was not to be. Walter Wriston, the square-jawed, tough-minded president of First National City Bank—later Citibank—and an unofficial spokesman for the eleven Clearing House Association big commercial lenders based in the city, set the tone. Like other fiscally conservative, Republican business leaders, he viewed the Democratic city and state governments as ineptly run, local taxes too high, and the labor unions too cozy with politicians and too influential. When Carey asked the nation's leading underwriters if any had advice for him on how to get through a period of difficulty, Wriston glared at Carey. "Yes I do, Governor," he said tersely. "Pay your debts."[35]

Carey and Ravitch did not have much luck, either, when they approached, hat-in-hand, the leaders of the state senate and assembly, who seemed intent to test the new governor's resolve in a time-honored Albany tradition. Despite Anderson's earlier help in persuading some banks to provide a short-term loan to the UDC, he and assembly leaders now ignored Carey's request for a UDC bailout package. State Comptroller Arthur Levitt, meanwhile, indicated he was not comfortable with investing workers' pension funds in state agencies' moral obligation bonds, which he regarded as an inappropriate use of state employees' retirement money.

Ravitch returned to the bankers, offering a proposal aimed at raising $700 million in financing regardless of whether the legislature responded to the Carey administration's bid for stopgap aid. Ravitch believed that because the lending institutions had made hefty profits handling UDC's securities during years of easy credit, it was incumbent on them to throw a lifeline to the now-overextended agency, provided, to be sure, that in so doing they would not violate their legal, fiduciary responsibilities to depositors and investors. The agency had twenty thousand partially completed affordable-housing units, the largest bloc of which was slated for Roosevelt Island in New York City, projects which represented potential homes for some eighty thousand residents and thousands of jobs for the tradesmen, construction workers, and suppliers involved in their creation. The banks, however, had different priorities. They wanted evidence that the legislature would meet its previously untested "moral obligation" to replenish UDC's debt service reserve fund on behalf of the bondholders. They turned down a plan developed by Ravitch, who worked closely with Peter Goldmark and Judah Gribetz and their staffs, to create a new state authority that would capture the rental revenues and federal subsidies from all UDC projects, and, freed from the agency's current liabilities, would create a sound basis for a new offering from the credit market. Its authors called it the "New Finance Agency." The underwriters called it too risky.

So it was that on February 25, 1975, the UDC, having failed to pay its debts due on bonds and loans due that very day, became the first large government agency in the country to default since the 1930s.

It was a huge blow to the new governor and the financial and managerial credibility of the entire state.[36] Reverberating far and wide, the UDC default caused the municipal bond market to back away from bond issues by other housing agencies, including Michigan's, or to demand higher interest rates, as in New Jersey. The New Jersey Housing Finance Agency soon reported that $54 million in short-term bonds were commanding rates of 7.4 to 7.9 percent, nearly two percentage points higher than expected. New York State's Medical Care Facilities Finance Agency would be forced to pay interest of 9.6253 percent on a $62 million bond issue in April, and 10.04 percent to sell $72 million of Dormitory Authority bonds in May.[37]

The Carey administration raced out with a new bill to create the "Project Finance Agency," designed to operate along the same lines as the New Finance Agency. Burned by an actual default instead of merely the feverish and perhaps politically inspired warnings of one yet to come, the New York State Legislature this time rammed the bill through, authorizing the PFA to issue bonds and receive state appropriations to take over UDC's riskiest mortgages.

Carey then met anew with Anderson and Steingut and the minority leaders of both houses and requested that they appropriate emergency funds to the Project Finance Agency for completing UDC's construction projects, and again the reality-checked legislative leaders went along. In doing so, the legislative leaders affirmed the state's "moral obligation" to bail out investors holding these bonds, treating them with the same deference that the state constitution afforded to traditional municipal bonds of the state. They cleared the way for a $105 million appropriation to pay UDC's debt, while banks, in the wake of the legislative flourishes, approved a $140 million revolving line of credit.[38]

The default was remedied, lawsuits by creditors were averted, and wider collateral damage such as a bankruptcy filing was prevented, although when bond dealers had first suspended trading in the UDC bonds, there was a heavy sell-off of the moral obligations of other state agencies and authorities, and Moody's lowered its rating of the moral obligation agencies and withdrew the once highly regarded state Housing Finance Agency's credit rating altogether, forcing it to become entirely dependent on state funding. Ravitch, surveying the damage, began the task of rebuilding investor confidence in the UDC, and sharply scaled back the agency's ambitions to start new projects. His weeks-long "game of chicken," as Ravitch described the high-intensity negotiations with the bankers and legislators, demonstrated to all the clout of the underwriters and the vulnerability of the state's elected leaders, whether Republicans or Democrats, to the gatekeepers of the municipal credit market. Carey said years later, "If we had let the thing collapse, it would have really been devastating. This was a hell of a house of cards."[39]

Carey, the fifty-first governor in a state of seventeen million people, had gone to Albany with expectations, perhaps, of a well-deserved honeymoon period after his overwhelming victory. He had hoped to begin to set right the state's troubles, taper its high expenditures, and rebuild its business sector. Instead, he had raced, like a firefighter headed to a five-alarm blaze, to the center of a fiscal emergency threatening to engulf his broad goals and aspirations. The problems he encountered initially were more fundamental than anyone anticipated. "The level of irresponsibility of the state government was beyond all apprehension that I had," Carey told Francis X. Clines of the *Times* in late April, when asked about his eventful first one hundred days. But the worst—far worse—was yet to come.

Stephen Berger was as familiar as anyone in the new Carey administration with the precarious condition of New York City's budget, because he had served as director of the Scott Commission set up in 1971 by Rockefeller to examine "the management, structure, organization, and fiscal and governance practices of the city of New York and its agencies," and which, in 1973, telegraphed the city's approaching fiscal crisis (which no one believed at the time, especially in light of the Republican rivalry between Governor Rockefeller and Mayor Lindsay, both of whom claimed the title of unofficial national spokesman on urban issues). Shortly after Carey defeated Howard Samuels in the primary, Berger shared with Carey his view that the city was headed down a dangerous path. Though the city's tax base was eroding, the costs of salaries, labor contracts, and social services were growing, so at some point soon, Berger believed, something was liable to give way.

Berger had first met Carey in July, 1969, when Berger was the campaign manager for Herman Badillo of the Bronx, the first Puerto Rican to serve in Congress, and who was then making his first unsuccessful run for the Democratic nomination for mayor (he would come closest to capturing City Hall in 1973, when he lost a runoff primary to Beame). As fate would have it, the day Berget met Carey was also the day Carey's sons Peter and Hugh Jr. would be killed in a car crash on Shelter Island, creating, for Berger, a sympathy for the future governor and a bond with him. But when he showed up to see Carey during the general election phase of the 1974 gubernatorial campaign, Carey must have experienced him as "Mr. Wet Blanket."

"Arthur says there's plenty of money," Carey told Berger, referring to Levitt, the state comptroller.

"Arthur is wrong," Berger replied, and he summarized the Scott Commission's findings. The room got quiet. Soon the suspender-clad thirty-eight-year-old budget hard-liner, who was new to the campaign, having been invited to join by David Garth, got up and left. "I'm sure that was the first time anyone suggested to him that we were heading toward a fiscal mess," said Berger, who became the state's social services commissioner, though he'd hoped to be the governor's chief planning officer for policy.[40]

In the spring of 1975, Peter Goldmark Jr. brought concrete warnings about New York City's fiscal condition to the governor, handing him a memo he'd prepared.

Since becoming budget director, Goldmark had been hearing a lot about the private worries—brewing unabated since early 1974—of the major banks as well as staffers in the city comptroller's office. He had gotten his hands on a working paper by a group of bank representatives seeking to learn more about the city budget and its cash flow challenges. To bring the governor up to speed, and perhaps influence his actions, Goldmark's memo laid out a train wreck in the making.

At thirty-four, the keen, metaphor-loving Harvard graduate, the son of an electronics pioneer credited with inventing the stereo LP, could have been mistaken for one of Hollywood's Rat Pack—lean, with quick movements, flashing eyes, dark hair swept back, and long sideburns. He started out in JFK's Federal Office of Economic Opportunity. When his boss there, Frederick Hayes, left to head Mayor Lindsay's budget bureau, Goldmark followed. Three years later, in 1969, he rose to became Lindsay's chief of staff. Then, in 1971, Massachusetts Governor Francis Sargent chose him as the Commonwealth's first secretary of human services. It was not long after Sargent was defeated for reelection that Carey attended a retreat for new Democratic governors held in Massachusetts and met Sargent's successor, the much-talked-about Michael Dukakis, who chatted with Carey and at one point called Goldmark restless and ambitious, as he appeared headed for a comparable government post on the West Coast. "That's our man!" Carey told David Burke, who was with him. He soon became one of Carey's most important hires.[41]

The March 24, 1975, memo by Goldmark began, "All of us have received reports on New York City's financial situation over the past few weeks." It tread gingerly at first: "This memo was not written to make recommendations for action now; it simply tries to organize and present some of what is going on now, and to indicate broadly where it may lead."[42] At the top of Goldmark's worries was New York City's outstanding short-term debt—notes that typically matured within one year or less of their issuance and had to be repaid from the city's annual $11.5 billion expense, or operating, budget. The short-term tab was estimated at $5 billion to $6 billion—clearly a whopping sum—and "many people believe there is little or no real security or receivables behind these obligations."

In addition, wrote the budget director, the city's current budget appeared to be underfunded by as much as $1 billion, a larger-than-revealed gap that could grow still larger by the beginning of the city's next fiscal year on July 1, 1975, and greater still during that year.

Goldmark, of course, realized the state, with its own, albeit far more manageable, budget gap, was not in an ideal position to help the city, nor was the legislature in a mood to participate; Carey's proposed statewide gas tax, for example, was going nowhere. Thus, argued Goldmark, the governor should use the city's cash shortages to force the city to restructure its short-term debt and its expenditure base, in keeping with the New York financial community's desires. Later on, he suggested, the national government would be likely to demand the state require such changes before seriously considering giving the city any stopgap assistance. He described the kind of possible "flashpoints" the city could face in the coming months—"no bids on a city offering; default on a repayment; postponement of a payroll, or some such similar event." The one entity that could respond rapidly, he added, was the Federal Reserve, but it had no contingency plans for doing so, and was merely watching the situation. "What may be needed here," wrote Goldmark, "is a three-to-five-year plan to restructure the city's debt and budget, worked out among the following parties: New York City, New York State, the U.S. government, the New York banks, and the labor unions. At this moment, most of the focus is on the short-term borrowing crisis. In the months ahead, attention will broaden, I believe, to include the more difficult question of how to restructure the City's debt and budget. This will be pivotal for us."

Carey didn't like what he was reading, remembered Goldmark.

"Carey exploded and said, 'Don't you know the first rule of politics of New York State: the governor does not interfere in the mayor's governance of his own city.' He threw me out of his office." It was evident Carey at that moment "was a man hearing something he was afraid might be true, and he didn't want to hear it," Goldmark said.[43]

The governor's reluctance was understandable. For any governor to meddle in the financial affairs of the city and its mayor only courted a showdown the interloper was bound to lose. Playing Big Foot to the popular Democrat would, too, cost Carey the support of state legislative leaders in Beame's camp, and endanger his entire legislative program. Voters in the city would resent Carey. Voters outside the city would complain about his giving undue attention to the Big Apple, a point of sensitivity even in the best of times for a governor who hailed from the city. Ethnic fault lines were never far from the surface in New York politics, and since Carey was Irish and Beame was Jewish, the potential for ethnic tensions was huge. The idea of a confrontation with New York City's elected leadership over its budget must have seemed, to Carey, akin to cutting his own political throat.

Even so, Berger, and with greater specificity, Goldmark, had done their job as they saw it—flagging a new fundamental danger that made even the UDC mess seem small: the city's huge—and fast-growing—reliance on short-term debt and its murky but clearly vast budget shortfalls. These were the problems that had already raised blood pressures in the executive offices of the Clearing House banks. Sooner or later Carey would have to face them, as would many others, including President Ford.

The problems were long in the making. Indeed, well before New York City's biggest banks began losing confidence in the city government's ability to meet its debts in 1974 and early 1975, several historical trends had tested their mutually beneficial partnership.

During World War II, New York City's manufacturing sector was robust, and the city was a magnet for hundreds of thousands of job seekers from Puerto Rico and the Southern states, where agriculture had become mechanized and rural employment was in decline. Blacks were propelled north, too, by the fear and reality of racial discrimination and violence.

During this great migration, the U.S. government maintained its usual ideological resistance to stepping in to stem population dislocations caused by economic and social trends, while doing little to assist the cities to which masses of people moved in search of opportunity and security. New York, like other older metropolises of the Northeast and Midwestern states, accommodated the waves of poor people in its schools, housing projects, hospitals, and large and small factories, where manual and skilled labor was in high demand.[44]

But it wasn't long after these great postwar migrations that the city's landscape of rail depots, teeming harbors, and smokestacks began to change, with even the deep-water port of Manhattan's West Side relocating to modern containerized docking built with New York and New Jersey state assistance at Newark. Many heavy industries relocated to the suburbs, and others states beckoned private industry with cheap land, nonunion labor, and low taxes.

Development of the nation's interstate highway system began in the 1950s, making it much easier for people and businesses to detach from the older, union-concentrated Northeast and Midwest manufacturing belt cities. Federal assistance encouraged the creation of new industrial corridors in the Sunbelt. Federal spending for domestic growth favored emerging industries such as aerospace technology and plastics, subsidizing the growth of regions where they were drawn, even as the densely populated New York metropolitan region continued to be among the most powerful engines of revenue generation for the federal budget, and the city sent significantly more tax money to Washington than it got back in aid.

As troublesome as deindustrialization was for the city's prospects, the growth of the suburbs in the post–World War II decades and especially the 1960s and 1970s proved even more worrisome. The green lands of Nassau, Suffolk, and Westchester counties drew the city's white middle class with their uncongested towns, good schools, lower taxes, jobs boom, and racial homogeneity; on the other hand, blacks, Puerto Ricans, and the poor were discouraged if not directly barred from migrating to the suburbs by a variety of mechanisms, from the zoning laws that barred low-income housing to the lack of public transportation. The work of real estate brokers and banks often reinforced the invisible wall in violation of federal fair-housing laws of the mid-1960s.

While the city's employment rate grew by 2 percent a year in the 1950s and 7 percent annually in the 1960s, the city lost a crippling five hundred thousand jobs from 1969, the postwar employment peak, to 1976. The city's historic strengths—its efficient transit system, heavy concentration of working people, and industrial jobs aplenty—were undermined by the country's inexorable shift from a predominantly manufacturing economy to a more consumer-driven, service-oriented one. As the city's economy weakened, TV news told an unrelenting narrative of a dystopia beset by homicides, racial strife, and poverty. The average age of city residents crept upward, a symptom of a steady exodus of younger families; the proportion of households with incomes below the national median rose sharply, from 36 to 49 percent. The city's welfare rolls swelled. By the 1974–75 recession, almost

1 million adults and children received cash assistance. The city's annual $1 billion yearly outlay for welfare was the highest in the nation.

Successive mayors—Wagner, Lindsay, Beame—struggled to keep the city going strong, to feed rather than curb its appetite for growth and improvement. Their political efforts and budget expedients came at a price: as a percentage of personal income, the individual municipal tax burden rose from 7.6 percent in 1963 to 10.2 percent in 1974, giving New York City the highest taxes per capita in the country.

By early 1975, when Goldmark wrote his prescient memo, the city was well on its way to becoming a national joke. Probably only a comic master like Woody Allen could depict its crumbling piers as romantic and beautiful in black-and-white. While Allen drew inspiration from a city's mad tenacity, others played to the crowd. Muggings, quipped late-night TV host Johnny Carson, were New York's most promising cottage industry.

Tourists still arrived, girding against pickpockets and ogling prostitutes who dotted midtown Manhattan streets, decked out in sky-high heels and, in winter, fur coats. Subways were fast becoming graffiti canvasses in motion. Drug trafficking was anything but furtive, while junkies quaked in the shadows of hollowed-out tenements on the Lower East Side.

The red-light district of West Forty-second Street became "murder central," with the Port Authority bus terminal a cavern of destitution and squalor that the destitute, the mentally disturbed, and the drugged and inebriated called "home." The majestic New York Public Library drew the homeless to its entrance steps, as did bedraggled Bryant Park just behind it. The city wore an edgy, desperate demeanor that competed with its long-enduring symbols of wealth, power and ambition—the limousines cruising Fifth and Park avenues, the New York Stock Exchange, the Broadway theater district, and some of the most famous restaurants in the world.

In many other big cities, such as Chicago, the local cost of hospitals, schools and other public services was shared with the surrounding suburbs, since city and suburbs occupied the same county. New York City, though, was its own jurisdiction. Its nearly 8 million residents covered the cost of the city's schools, medical services, police and fire department, and world-class (largely tax exempt) libraries, universities, stadiums and museums, with the help of broadly apportioned state and federal aid. Commuters who earned their living in the city but lived elsewhere paid a city income tax totaling one-quarter of 1 percent to the city, a minute proportion of what Mayor Lindsay had asked Governor Rockefeller and the increasingly suburban-oriented State Legislature to approve in 1966 to help balance the city budget.

New York City was also responsible for one quarter of the state's annual cost of reimbursing local hospitals and physicians for treating the poor. In many other parts of the country, states footed the entire Medicaid bill for their localities. Same with welfare: New York City paid the highest proportion of this social expenditure of any city in the country—one quarter of the total tab for poor families—while California's localities were responsible for 14 percent of the total, North Carolina's 8 percent, and, in 28 other states, the federal government picked up the entire tab.[45]

Responding to budget pressures in the decades before World War II, the city could have slashed public services, as some reformers urged it to do. But retrenchment would have been out of character: New York City had never had a shortage of pressing social needs, with aging, substandard, and unsafe housing conditions, rampant health deficiencies, and outdated and crumbling schools, roads, and parks.[46] Indeed, from the earliest days of Tammany Hall, there had always been too many mouths to feed, too many conditions needing remedial attention. A report to Mayor Jimmy Walker in 1927 found "a third of the city's population—over two million people—[residing] . . . in unsatisfactory conditions, many under distressful conditions, some under disgraceful conditions."[47] Overcrowded tenements were home then to the city's poor, and the heat of summer turned them into "an inferno of torture to little children, the sick, and the weak"—firetraps with shared bathrooms and common water sources that were, according to depictions by the crusading journalist Jacob Riis as far back as the 1880s, "a menace to health, safety and morals."[48]

The impulse to grow was reinforced by Mayor LaGuardia's progressive leadership, which supported many projects to modernize the city and improve life for the working class in the wake of the Great Depression, and by dramatic increases in federal spending during the war. The rise of municipal unions starting in the Wagner years furthered the city's tendency to rise at *whatever* the cost to meet social needs. Brought into existence were not only modern labor standards and the rights of municipal workers to unionize and collectively bargain on their own behalf—the city's first collective-bargaining agreement emerged in 1958—but also the continuation of a free and open City University system, which grew from 91,000 students in 1960 to 271,000 in 1975, as well as the largest municipal hospital system in the country, with 17 major facilities serving the underprivileged. The city government committed itself to providing safe and affordable housing, new and rebuilt schools and parks, and a viable transit system with a 35-cent subway and bus fare, accessible to the working and middle class.

Even so, Robert Wagner Jr., who as mayor had enjoyed largely favorable times that permitted him to focus a great deal of city resources and attention on rebuilding the city's housing stock, faced for the first time, in 1964, a significant amount of difficulty balancing the city's annual expense budget. This had not happened since the Depression and its wake.

Wagner sought permission from the state legislature to use $26 million in city capital funds to help plug a gap between projected expenditures and revenues. He drew some criticism in the press, since issuing bonds under the city's long-range capital construction budget to cover current operating expenses flew in the face of accounting orthodoxy, which held that operating and capital expenses should remain separate. If the city expense budget was akin to a person's checking account and available only for ongoing expenses, then the capital budget was equivalent to a homeowner's mortgage, a debt to be paid back at a fixed rate of interest over, say, 30 years. Some in Rockefeller's budget division complained the funding sources must not be co-mingled.

But the controversy soon was forgotten and in 1965 the city gained still more flexibility to deal with its deficits: state legislation sponsored by the city authorized the Wagner administration to begin issuing short-term notes in anticipation of revenue to be collected in the *next* fiscal year. As a result, the city for the first time was allowed to use the following year's hoped-for revenues to balance the current year's books. This time there were fewer objections.

Wagner, in his final mayoral budget in mid-1965, turned anew to borrowing under the capital budget to help balance a now record-sized city operating budget—"borrow now, repay later," he termed it. Echoing the liberal ethos of addressing social needs, Rockefeller's almost limitless horizons, and the Democratic quality-of-life agenda then taking shape under LBJ, the mayor declared "I intend that we shall press ahead with the war on crime, the war on poverty, the war on narcotics addiction, the war on slums, the war on disease, and the war on civil ugliness." Wagner wasn't going to yield on any of these important objectives because of passing budget pressures, nor turn away from borrowing to get the job done." "A good loan," he declared at one point, "is better than a poor tax."[49]

Beame, who was the city comptroller then, criticized Wagner's handling of the city budget, including what he described as the tendency to overstate anticipated revenues and underestimate anticipated expenses. In 1965, Beame went further, contending that Wagner's tactic of using the capital budget to pay current operating expenses was reckless, akin to a family man who lacks the will to earn a living and prefers first to drain his bank account to pay his regular living expenses, then avoids working by borrowing. Finally, Beame warned, there comes "a day of reckoning."

Later in 1965, Republican mayoral candidate John Lindsay, who had served as a member of the New York Congressional delegation along with Carey, warned during his election campaign that the growing city practice of borrowing under the capital budget to pay for a wide variety of current expenditures was imprudent. However, once elected mayor, Lindsay moved

$564 million in expenses for the ongoing costs of government into the capital budget, easing pressure on the crowded city budget, and enabling still more spending.

Beame succeeded Lindsay in January, 1974, and he, too, turned to the city's capital budget rather than seeking to cut spending or raise taxes. That spring, $750 million was buried in the capital budget for operating expenses. The city's true budget gap, therefore, was larger than the $600 million operating shortfall announced, and decried, by Mayor Beame a bit later. As pressures to make ends meet grew, Beame unveiled "the tightest austerity program undertaken by the city since the Depression," projecting draconian layoffs of 12,000, while pushing for more state and federal aid. It was a classic mayoral play for greater levels of state and federal assistance. In the end, the firings didn't happen, and the city went back to budget expedients and business as usual.

# 5

# Visible Means of Support

*The Carey administration issues "Big MAC" bonds backed
with city revenues to tide New York City over.
The credit market finds the emergency bonds unappetizing.
The fate of the isolated city hangs in the balance.*

On an early spring afternoon in 1975, as New York City's problems with
its lenders mounted, Hugh Carey traveled to Felix Rohatyn's vacation
house, perched on dunes at the edge of the Atlantic Ocean, in Long Island's
East Hampton. Accompanying the governor was Peter Maas, the author of
*Serpico,* a best-selling book about a whistle-blower cop who nearly brought
down the New York Police Department in the Lindsay years. Maas was
friendly with Rohatyn, a player in the world of securities and corporate
reorganizations, and Carey was planning to ask for Rohatyn's help placating
and winning the cooperation of the financial community.[1]

With his puckish grin and flecks of gray hair, Rohatyn, forty-six, was
no stranger to the ways of prominent politicians, though he had never met
Carey before. Two years before, he had been innocently caught up in a classic
Washington brouhaha involving allegations that, in exchange for a pledge
of four hundred thousand dollars to help pay for the Republican convention, the Justice Department had dropped its lawsuit against International
Telephone and Telegraph. The suit had charged that ITT's acquisition of
a string of businesses, including the Hartford Fire Insurance Company—in
what was then the largest corporate merger in U.S. history—ran afoul of the
nation's antitrust laws. ITT contributed a hundred thousand dollars through
a subsidiary to the Richard Nixon–led GOP eight days before the settlement
of the government's case against the conglomerate.[2]

Washington buzzed at the first hint of possible scandal. With the
1972 presidential election approaching, one of Capitol Hill's most colorful

lobbyists, the salty, chain-smoking Dita Beard, who worked the halls of Congress for ITT, was allegedly involved with a memo, which she denied writing, that supposedly linked the settlement of the antitrust case to ITT's underwriting of convention costs.[3] At a Senate Judiciary Committee hearing, Attorney General John Mitchell denied any knowledge of ITT's promise of a contribution to the GOP. Rohatyn, who was then helping ITT's president and chief executive Harold S. Geneen, appeared before the committee along with Mitchell's successor-designate Richard Kleindienst. The two men acknowledged having met with each other before the settlement, but said their exchange was limited to a discussion of the implications that the collapse of the merger might have on the stock market. Kleindienst also said he had not known about any ITT pledge of funds to the GOP until he read about in a newspaper column, and didn't have anything to do with the settlement. He, Rohatyn, and the head of the antitrust division all denied any wrongdoing, and none was found. Yet Rohatyn decided he had had enough of the Washington scene by the end of the affair.[4]

When, three years later, Carey showed up with Maas in the Hamptons, Rohatyn, divorced with two sons, was still a senior partner at the international investment firm Lazard Freres. Detractors tagged him "Felix the Fixer,"[5] but Carey was impressed by Rohatyn's excellent reputation in the financial world. He took Rohatyn aside and popped the question he'd come to ask: Would he be willing to turn his full attention away from his successful career and serve instead in the less lofty world of state government?

In return, Carey told Rohatyn, he'd receive all the credit he would be due for helping to save the city, and would become known by his fellow citizens, not to mention his own sons, as "Felix the Savior" rather than "Felix the Fixer."

"It's up to you," Carey said. "Fixer or Savior."[6]

Around the time Carey made his sales pitch, Rohatyn got a call from a bond broker he didn't know, offering to sell him New York City notes paying an unusually high 9.5 percent interest. Rohatyn, suspicious, declined, saying, "If you're paying 9.5 percent for a triple-tax-free notes of the city, they can't be a very good risk."[7] He also heard from the Democratic National Chairman, Bob Strauss, who told him he'd recommended him to Carey.

"Well, it would have been nice if you had asked me before you went and did it," Rohatyn responded; he "had never heard of a bankruptcy of a *city*, but certainly for a city like New York. I thought it would be a devastating thing, even global."[8]

In Rohatyn's remembrance, the most pivotal encounter with Carey occurred later in the "kind of shabby" governor's midtown Manhattan office. The governor and David Burke began that meeting by presenting Rohatyn with some grim facts and figures. Carey pressed: Would he or wouldn't he help save the city from possible bankruptcy?[9] Burke had already worked on the Viennese-born finance man, reminding Rohatyn of his public declarations that he owed his life to the United States, as his family had escaped to America from the Nazi occupiers in France, and wanted to repay the debt to his adopted country.[10] Now was that day, Burke urged.

Rohatyn laid down conditions to Carey.

"I don't know enough and I can't do it alone," he said. "But if you would put together a responsible group of business types, both Republicans and Democrats, I'd be happy to be one of them."

Over the next ten minutes or so, Carey and Burke made a list.[11]

The New York City underwriting community had begun to wrestle with and reconsider its historic habit of indulging the city's appetite for borrowing and profiting handsomely from the relationship. In 1974, Beame's first year as mayor, banks weighed their wish to continue earning great underwriting fees against their growing concern that the city might be unable to meet its debts to bondholders. For the first time, the bankers raised questions about the city's management—an issue that had never come up before. Meanwhile, they walked a fine line: On the one hand, they realized that they could be exposed to liability under federal securities laws if they knew of any risks associated with the city's securities and failed to disclose them to prospective investors. On the other hand, they didn't want to panic the market, because doing so would cause the value of the city securities in their portfolios to plummet, damaging the wealth and stability of their institutions.

Their nervousness made it difficult if not impossible for Carey to avoid getting more directly involved in the city's money woes for too much longer, for by the time he headed out to see Rohatyn on the dunes, it was becoming evident that the city could easily default on short-term debt payments any time now, with its monthly payments to bondholders totaling hundreds of millions of dollars. At the same time, some editorial writers and budget watchdog groups began faulting Carey for keeping his distance from the city's problems, as he continued to make trips upstate and resolutely focused on many other things. But his attempt to be governor of the entire state and not just one part of it was growing more challenging by the day.

For he was also aware that if the city defaulted and filed for bankruptcy, there would be hell to pay—possible walkouts by police, firefighters, sanitation workers, and teachers, and perhaps even outbreaks of looting, arson, and violence. In an atmosphere of civic breakdown, a federal judge would be empowered to take the entire city government and its day-to-day affairs under receivership, superseding all elected officials, labor agreements, and existing rules and regulations. The judge would seek to create immediate mechanisms for continuing public services and running the city's many departments down to the most minute levels—deploying police, regulating schools, ordering supplies, dispatching child protective workers, all the while beginning the possibly decade-long process of sorting through the claims of perhaps tens of thousands of creditors—bondholders and their lawyers, city employees, welfare clients, and suppliers. In the wake of such dislocations, some argued, fear and loathing would roil the municipal bond market. The borrowing costs of cities and states might spike, causing service cutbacks and job losses if not additional governmental defaults. If large or small banks tottered or closed, the troubled national economy, if not the entire international banking system, would be disrupted.

So Carey and his financial advisers worried at the time. But the implications of a city bankruptcy were less than agreed upon or clear to the public at large as his staff debated how deeply he should involve himself and the state in the mounting series of New York City payment problems that were, after all, not of his making, and perhaps beyond his powers to contain or control.

In the spring of 1975, around the time Rohatyn was recruited, some aides to the governor, including Peter Goldmark, warned that if the Big Apple failed to pay its obligations, the state government would follow, so interwoven and interdependent were their finances. Staying out of it, therefore, could be suicidal for the state.

Other aides noted that in their upstate travels, they regularly met people who made no secret of their distaste for the big city—a drain on the rest of the state, in their eyes—and who felt just as adamantly that Carey should force its leaders to finally feel the consequences of years of financial profligacy. John Dyson, the state's agriculture commissioner, noted dutifully that Carey might alienate Republicans like Senate leader Warren Anderson if he intervened too forcefully on the city's behalf, especially since communities across the state were also experiencing hard times. At one such staff discussion at the Executive Mansion, the issue reached a boiling point. Having listened to the back-and-forth for nearly an hour, Carey finally stood and jammed his hands deep into his pants pockets—the telltale sign that his fuse might blow.

He would not, he said, even consider standing idly by as the city sank. He rendered the case for assistance in the most personal terms. "I have a big family. If one of my children came to me and said he's broke, I'm not going to put him out on the street; I'm going to do what's best. I'm not going to leave him out in the cold. We're stopping this right now," he said.[12]

New York City, the governor added, was legally a child of the state—it existed only because the state granted it jurisdiction.

He sat down at his desk. No one spoke. The staff shot glances around the room. And then for good measure Carey added that if any or all of his aides strongly disagreed, he would be more than happy to accept their letters of resignation immediately.

Always influencing his judgment, Carey recalled years later, was his late father's view that bankruptcy was an irreversible stigma and what he had most sought to avoid for the once-soaring Eagle Petroleum during the years of the Depression. After Carey articulated his position to his staff, he never really looked back, or veered. Soon, in fact, he unilaterally advanced the city $400 million in state aid, directly involving the state in the city's quest for survival and thereby putting the state's own credit in potential harm's way. This was money raised from the sale of state short-term notes and technically requiring voter approval for its use. The cash narrowly allowed the city to avoid default on notes that had to be repaid at the end of April, 1975. And Carey would advance the city a total of $400 million more in the months ahead.

"His force of will," said Paul Gioia, who was an assistant counsel to the governor, "was the most important feature in keeping the city out of bankruptcy. When someone at the top makes a solid commitment like that, people working for him respond, 'We've got to figure out how to get it done'—and that's what happened."[13]

The word Carey would elect to describe a New York City bankruptcy was "unthinkable."[14]

Unthinkable, yes. But whether the collapse of the city was avoidable was another question completely, as was the continuously delicate matter of how far the "parent" could safely stick its neck out, and get involved, to protect its troubled "child."

One of the first newsmen to dig into the city's financial problems was the third- or fourth-ranked reporter at the *Times*'s City Hall bureau, Steven R. Weisman. He was in his twenties and had recently reported on Jacob Javits's 1974 Senate race against former U.S. attorney general Ramsey Clark. He had also covered housing issues, learning the rudiments of how public debt works, and wrote a freelance piece for the iconoclastic *Washington Monthly* on the UDC failure, "because I felt that was huge."[15] By the spring of 1975, he was better prepared than most political and government reporters to appreciate confidential memos being written by a couple of "whiz kids" in the city comptroller's office, Jon Weiner and Steven Clifford. These confidential assessments were grim, depicting the city's deepening problems as perhaps inescapable, given the resistance of the Beame administration to fundamental change. The memos, some of which Weisman and his *Times* colleague John Darnton were shown, were reaching the desks of bank executives, fueling their worries. In one missive, Clifford speculated that as much as $2.7 billion of the receivables supporting the city's growing pile of debt would have to be disregarded if the city were to start using recognized accounting standards.[16]

The timing of these internal critiques couldn't have been any worse from the Beame administration's standpoint.[17] The city was turning to the credit market as never before for its operating funds. The Big Apple borrowed a record $2.5 billion in just a two-month period concluding in November, 1974, bringing its outstanding short-term debt levels to about $4.5 billion, a $1.5 billion increase over late summer's levels. The latest figure represented a fourfold increase over the city's outstanding short-term indebtedness in late 1970.[18]

And still the city borrowed even more in the short-term market to pay workers, suppliers, welfare clients, and mounting interest on its growing debt. About $600 million in short-term notes were sold that December.[19] The financial community stopped discussing and started demanding higher interest rates to ensure they could quickly turn over the New York City securities they agreed to underwrite. Merrill Lynch reported losing $50 million on the marketing of a $475 million city note after failing to discharge all of its assigned shares.

Short-term borrowing was not a new or unorthodox practice. The city turned to such temporary means of financing to cover its expenses until anticipated revenues from local taxes and state and federal aid arrived according to staggered schedules. Tax Anticipation Notes (TANs) and Revenue Anticipation Notes (RANs) were the main short-term financing instruments available. The city also issued short-term Bond Anticipation Notes (BANs) to help pay for affordable housing, with an eye toward refinancing the debt with long-term bonds when national interest rates became more attractive. Unfortunately, the opportunity for conversion was rare in the mid-1970s, for the recession just went on and on. The city's need for TANs, RANs and BANs grew. "A disturbing aspect of short-term operating loans, "one intergovernmental study warned in 1973, "is that cities slide into an abuse of these loans without planning to do so."

In the closing months of 1974, New York City held a stunning 29 percent of all outstanding short-term notes in the country, and more than any other city.[20] Its short-term debt grew from 8.5 percent of its total indebtedness in 1966 to 36.9 percent by 1975, or from $747 million in 1969 to about $4.5 billion. By comparison, Boston accumulated just $65 million in annual notes outstanding, and Chicago, $300 million. Even more worrisome for New York City, by 1975 banks could take their business elsewhere. Recent changes in federal banking and tax laws were affording institutional investors a wider range of investment options, including foreign tax credits, equipment leasing, and increased holdings of the mushrooming national debt.[21]

Many banks began to reduce their own holdings of New York City's debt paper, selling off large numbers of city securities in their portfolios between October, 1974, and April, 1975, and thus contributing to the "over-saturation" of the market, about which they complained to Mayor Beame and City Comptroller Harrison J. Goldin, and which was their rationale for forcing the cash-pressed city to offer prospective investors in city bonds higher interest rates. The instances of major banks dumping their city bonds and notes, documented in a voluminous report on the city's fiscal crisis that the U.S. Securities and Exchange Commission presented in August, 1977, were not known to city officials negotiating with the banks at the time, or to the large institutions and the individuals still willing to park their money with the cash-strapped metropolis.

Beame, in December, 1974, sent a delegation of local officials to Washington to make the case for increased federal assistance for the city, while Goldin remained home to tell unhappy bankers and bond counsel on his debt management liaison committee, men from such institutions as Salomon Brothers, Morgan Guaranty Trust, Chase Manhattan, and First National City, that he was canceling a city bond sale that had been planned for January of 1975—only Carey's first month in office. He sought their ideas about how to regularize the city's somewhat unpredictable borrowing schedule. The conversation appeased some of the financiers, but others complained that it was only a "gimmick" that would not override "severe market conditions."[22]

The next morning, members of the same committee breakfasted with Beame at Gracie Mansion, the official mayoral residence.

"No one questions the city's ability to pay its debt," Wallace Sellers from Merrill Lynch's bond division told the mayor that morning. "It is a question of the ability of the market to absorb issuances of such magnitude."

Sellers also pushed into new territory, linking the city's climbing interest rates to its financial management practices. "Borrowing to finance deficits is no longer a viable procedure," he declared.[23]

The usually dignified Beame responded angrily and defensively, brushing off the bankers' admonitions and adding that he was "outraged" by a 9.5 percent interest rate the city was forced to accept in its most recent note sale, four days earlier. "In the real world," he said, "all government budgets must go up annually and, as a consequence, borrowing will also go up." As for the allegation of deficit financing—an illegal practice for the city—Beame said he was "taking some very tough steps to economize," and seeking financial aid from Albany and Washington. "We want to work with the financial community . . . the banks can and should help the city and should not just sit by and tell the city to reform."[24]

Deputy Mayor Jim Cavanagh, who formerly held a senior job in the city budget bureau at the time Beame was the city comptroller, summed up how the mayor viewed the banks: "The banks and us are a community of interest. If we go down, they go down."[25] In other words, if the city didn't want to accommodate Wallace Sellers and his pinstriped pals, it didn't have to, and if the banks didn't think city paper was marketable anymore, they needed to buy the city's securities for themselves and hold them until the economy improved, as inevitably it must. They—the banks and the city—were in this boat together.

After the Gracie Mansion showdown, Beame nevertheless sought to calm the underwriters by forming the "Financial Community Liaison Group." Appointed to the new advisory panel were such titans as David Rockefeller of Chase, Elmore Patterson of Morgan, and Walter Wriston of First National City Bank, among a total six large and smaller national lenders headquartered in the city. Setting out in January, 1975, on a long-range plan to retool the city's financial management, they sought to compile data on city fiscal operations and provide extensive revenue documentation to support the city's continuing offers to the municipal bond market. On February 11—just two weeks before the market would be shaken by UDC's default on $100 million in BANs—the city was successful in selling $141 million in bonds.

But the victory didn't matter a great deal.

Jay Epley, a thirty-eight-year-old junior partner at the law firm White & Case and the son of a former president and chairman of Texaco, was among the first bond counsels to insist that Goldin certify financial data for *current* tax receipts at note issue closings, not those of the previous months, as had been customary in hundreds of previous situations like this.[26] Epley's demand represented an unprecedented push for specificity that other bond counsels had seen as best to avoid because, once such financial details were in the underwriters' hands, they needed to be disclosed to investors under federal law, and might well send them fleeing. It was a radical request, one pondered for a long time—because some lawyers believed the banks they represented had a statutory obligation to probe the city for risks—but one that was not directly and openly voiced until now.

"We simply asked the questions that we thought were necessary," Epley said later.[27]

Meanwhile, Jac Friedgut, a vice president at Walter Wriston's First National City Bank, traveled to Washington, D.C., and met with the city's congressional delegation, matter-of-factly presenting the jaw-dropping news that his leading bank would no longer purchase or market city notes, and he added that if the city defaulted, there was widespread concern in the financial community that local elected officials might ignore bondholders' right of "first lien," or first claim on remaining city revenues—a constitutionally enshrined privilege which undergirded the entire municipal credit market and arguably the national economy. Edward I. Koch, a liberal congressman from Greenwich Village who had launched a brief, unsuccessful race for mayor of New York City in 1973, said he didn't know the city government was on the edge of losing its access to the borrowing market. "It was a shock," he said.[28]

The city forged ahead with a planned $537 million note offering scheduled for March, but the comptroller insisted he was unable to provide the banks with current city data on the receivables supporting the offering to the market. With Wriston warning that there might not be a market for this, not a single bank placed a bid in the small tin box at the city comptroller's office to become the underwriter. In this instance, there was another complicating factor: the redemption of these notes were to be guaranteed with the proceeds from the sale of "moral obligation" bonds of the city's Stabilization Reserve Corporation, an entity whose existence was being contested in a lawsuit filed by Leon Wein, a Brooklyn Law School professor. The thirty-four-year-old academic claimed the SRC was unconstitutional because it allowed the city to exceed its constitutional debt limits. Thus, the banks, which at the time had 20 percent of their equity tied up in the debt, now had yet another reason to steer clear of further involvement with the city's borrowing arrangements.

With no underwriters stepping up, Goldin canceled the March sale. No amount of political theater—city council president Paul O'Dwyer called for an investigation of the banks, while Beame earnestly reached into his personal savings by investing in fifty thousand dollars worth of city notes, "to indicate my confidence"—made any difference.[29] The credit markets couldn't, or wouldn't, fulfill the city's capital needs, with the bankers having come to the perhaps unshakeable conclusion that the city government lacked both cash and credibility, and probably couldn't pay off its maturing bonds except, of course, by borrowing over its head even more.

When the city nevertheless managed to issue $375 million in RANs to a fifteen-member syndicate headed by First National City Bank, the group agreed to sell them under only the most drastic terms: these notes had to be repaid in 102 days at the nearly unaffordable interest rate of 8 percent.[30] And White & Case, a law firm relatively new to the role of bond counsel, wrote and disseminated a truly bombshell letter advising financial institutions to refrain from selling any more city securities "in the absence of what may be agreed upon as full and meaningful written disclosure" of adverse information concerning the city's finances, or they'd be subjecting themselves to "substantial exposure" to potential lawsuits by the purchasers of city securities.[31]

David Rockefeller, Elmore Patterson, and William Spencer (First National City Bank president, and No. 2 under Wriston) requested and were granted a private meeting with Beame on March 17, at Gracie Manson, telling him the lending window was closed now and for the foreseeable future, and politely suggesting he look to the state government, the Federal Reserve Board, or the U.S. Treasury for assistance.

Beame took in the dire news without comment.[32] But their message was inescapable: these capitalists were on strike against New York.

Days later, though, the mayor appealed for public support. At a televised press conference on March 23, with a mixture of defiance and submission, he said the city had every intention of paying its interest and redemption costs on time, meeting its payrolls, and maintaining "our basic fiscal strengths . . . By no stretch of the imagination can this great city, with its unparalleled assets, sink under the weight of the current wave of unwarranted negative publicity attributed to certain segments of the financial community."

Far from anemic, Beame said, the city was a huge and dynamic economic force, with $100 billion a year in business transactions, $80 billion in taxable real estate, and the capacity to generate $7 billion in local tax levies annually. That the banks would turn back such a customer could only be the result of unwarranted fear. "Our total revenues," he went on, "are six-fold, six times, greater than the annual cost of debt service. The city provides constitutional and legal guarantees of repayment for our note holders and our bondholders. The underwriters of our obligations know that, and they know our assets are better than most others, and that is why I cannot understand the 'scare' statements regarding the city, its assets, and its obligations," said Beame.[33]

The mayor acknowledged the need to trim the size of city government, given its deficits, and announced an immediate $125 million spending reduction, to be followed, he said, by a 4,000-person reduction in the payroll. Still, he had failed to make good on promised budget-cutting staff reductions in 1974, having removed only 1,000 employees from the city's 330,000-person payroll since he was elected fifteen months earlier.

The banking community was therefore skeptical.

"It would have made one hell of an inaugural," wrote Fred Ferretti, the *Times* City Hall bureau chief, of the speech in *The Year the Big Apple Went Bust*, his detailed book chronicling that roller coaster year. "As it was, it was about fifteen months too late."[34]

Standard and Poor's suspended its "A" rating on the city's General Obligation bonds, which financed the city's construction program, citing its "rapidly deteriorating ability to raise money in the capital markets," coupled with the possible "inability or unwillingness of the major underwriting banks to continue to purchase the city's note[s] and bonds." However, Moody's reaffirmed its "A" rating, arguing that the city, with so many underlying assets that could be sold or leveraged, remained a secure and sound place for investment. But Moody's was alone in its judgment among credit rating services.[35]

Its access to the credit market blocked, mired in deepening recession, its all-important real estate tax collections plummeting, Beame's New York was caught short. A report by the nonpartisan Congressional Budget Office would soon describe the city's bind: "The existence of this large long-term debt and the magnitude of the . . . [city's budget] deficit mean that New York must borrow every month or so regardless of how unattractive market conditions may be to 'roll over' the part of its short-term debt coming due and to finance its monthly shortfall between current revenues and expenditures. The only alternative would be to repay the principal and interest due out of current revenues. [But] ... that ... would absorb roughly half of the city's annual tax revenues, leaving little to support essential public services."[36]

Beame and Carey joined forces, making their first joint pilgrimage to Washington, D.C., on May 13 to appeal directly to President Ford, who agreed to see the two leaders on the advice of his presidential counsel, John O. Marsh Jr.[37] The New Yorkers asked Ford to extend the credit of the United States to the city for ninety days to support additional local borrowing totaling about $1 billion. This cost-free and temporary federal guarantee would give the New York State Legislature time to act on Beame's request for increased local taxing authority to balance the city budget for the upcoming city fiscal year slated to begin July 1, they reasoned.

The tense, one hour and forty minute meeting of the two New York officials and their aides in the White House's ground-floor Cabinet Room—attended by Ford advisers Alan Greenspan, chairman of the Council of Economic Advisers; treasury secretary William Simon; White House chief of staff Donald Rumsfeld; Rumsfeld's deputy Dick Cheney; Vice President Rockefeller; and other key advisers—did not go well from the perspective of the New York supplicants, though they would tell the press afterward that the president and his cabinet had lent them a sympathetic ear. At one point, Vice President Rockefeller had turned to Carey and, pointing across the table to state comptroller Arthur Levitt, wryly and perhaps cavalierly said, "Why don't you get the money from him—he's got all the money you need."[38] Referring to Levitt's role as the trustee of the state's billions of dollars in public employee pension funds, Rockefeller was contending that the national government was not in fact the city's rescuer of last resort, as Beame and Carey were suggesting. Needless to say, Carey didn't appreciate Rockefeller's off-hand remarks, since Rockefeller must have known that Levitt was resistant to investing state pension funds to help the city; his position was well-established. Rockefeller's comments were delivered, Carey remembered, with almost smug self-satisfaction, and were decidedly unhelpful.

President Ford's formal, written response to the meeting came out the next day. The "Dear Abe" letter confirmed Carey's and Beame's worst imaginings, as it flatly denied their request for federal help for New York. It was prepared by White House aide James Cannon, a former special assistant to Rockefeller in Albany turned director of the White House Domestic Council, although Cannon had recommended to Ford that he instead leave the door open to aiding the city if it made progress toward self-reform. Under the harder line chosen by Ford, the letter stated that "the city's basic critical financial condition is not new, but has been a long time in the making without being squarely faced ... [and] ... a 90-day Federal guarantee by itself would provide no real solution but would merely postpone, for that period, coming to grips with the problem."[39] A curtailment of "less essential" city services was needed, wrote the president, along with an evaluation of whether the city could transfer some expenses to the state, as well as whether the state could provide guarantees or loans. "Fiscal responsibility is essential for cities, states, and the Federal Government," the letter lectured. "I know how hard it is to reduce or postpone worthy and desirable public programs. Every family which makes up a budget has to make painful choices. As we make these choices at home, so must we also make them in public office, too. We must stop promising more and more services without knowing how we will cover their costs." He concluded by stating that William Simon and Federal Reserve Board chairman Arthur Burns would monitor the city's situation "very closely."

Simon became Ford's public point-man on New York. A former bond trader with Salomon Brothers on Wall Street who had once chaired then comptroller Beame's Technical Debt Advisory Committee—but had never in those years of easy credit waved a red flag about the city's debt levels or financial practices—he emerged in his role as treasury secretary as a tough, moralistic critic of city leaders and what he termed their long history of unchecked spending and borrowing. On May 14, 1975, in Simon's second scolding statement in just four days, he declared that New York City should regard Ford's response as a signal that "it take extremely difficult political actions . . . to put its fiscal and financial house in order." He added that granting federal assistance to one city under financial duress would only create "extremely dangerous" precedents requiring the federal government to throw a lifeline to other imprudent municipalities with significant budgetary imbalances. As he would write his 1978 book *A Time for Truth,* "American taxpayers could not be drained to fill New York's bottomless pit." He believed the effects of a city default would be short-lived and containable.[40]

Carey, though, responded quickly and forcefully to the Ford letter at the annual black-tie dinner of the Brooklyn Democratic organization held at the Waldorf Astoria Hotel in Manhattan the next evening, inveighing against "this Republican administration, the Ford and Rockefeller administration." He said the president reflected "a level of arrogance and disregard for New York that rivals the worst days of Richard Nixon and his band of cutthroats . . . Have they no heart," he asked. "Have they no understanding of our city's problems? Must a city riot?"[41]

Carey and Beame soon offered a joint retort.

"In light of this development, the alternatives facing our country's greatest city are both few and horrible," they said in a public statement. "To balance the city's budget by cutting services over and above the drastic cuts already announced, as suggested by the Republicans, will seriously jeopardize the social stability of 8 million people and will call upon their mayor to place the safety and health of the citizens at risk. More hospitals, more schools, more firehouses will have to be closed. Police protection will have to be substantially reduced. The remaining services will be both inefficient and thin, beyond all contemplation and beneath what the citizens have the right to expect. The president should know, as do his colleagues in the State Senate, that by their calculated inaction they are driving a great city into default. This may appear to them to be the correct political choice—to make New York City an object lesson for the nation. But we maintain what may be politically advantageous now"—for Ford was gearing up to run in the 1976 presidential primary—"will ultimately prove disastrous to the people. Every municipality in this state and nation will become vulnerable to this political/financial pincer and more and more, New York City and other cities will have public and social policy decided in bank boardrooms."[42]

Not surprisingly, the debate over the fiscal crisis of New York was turning sharply partisan and ideological: liberals vs. conservatives, Republicans vs. Democrats, supposedly right-thinking Midwest conservatives vs. allegedly free-spending Northeast liberals, Ford vs. Beame and Carey, the City of New York vs. much of the rest of New York.

Warren Anderson, a long-serving Binghamton Republican and the state senate majority leader, summarily rejected Beame's request for additional local taxing authority worth $400 million and state aid worth $200 million. Sounding suspiciously like the White House, Anderson declared that city leaders must "must stop delivering more services than [they] can afford to give," and sent word that any assistance would require that City Hall first accede to massive layoffs and a four-day work week for city workers, a hike in the thirty-five-cent subway fare, and tolls on the city's free East River bridges to Manhattan.

Legislative approval of Beame's proposed aid package without dramatic restructuring would be "totally imprudent and really a severe disservice to the long range well being of the city and its people," said Anderson, as it would "give the city a few more taxes to impose, a small increase in aid, and a set of magic mirrors to make everything—gimmicks, taxes, and all—look like the budget crisis was over, at least for a year. The city's real problem lies not in its budget deficits, but in the almost total loss it has suffered in investor confidence in its bonds and notes, both long term and short term." The Senate majority leader attributed the confidence gap to a legacy of "trick or treat municipal budgeting."[43] In a meeting with reporters, Anderson likened the city requests to a junkie's need to satisfy his addiction to heroin: Do you really help him by giving him more?

Beame floated the Anderson-recommended four-day work week to Victor Gotbaum, the head of District Council 37, the catch-all union for about one-third of the city workforce. Not surprisingly—least of all to Beame himself—Gotbaum rejected the idea outright.

On May 29, Beame gave another televised speech, unveiling two proposed city budgets, one balanced with hoped-for state aid, and the other a "crisis" plan with far deeper cuts to city day care centers, fire battalions, libraries, drug treatment programs, and 38,000 personnel, among them thousands of police officers, firefighters, sanitation workers, and jail officers. Beame blamed Anderson as well as the city's seven Republican state senators, and of course President Ford, though he was ultimately dependent on all of them for assistance. On top of the layoffs he included in his crisis budget were 3,000 additional dismissals that he said were already in the pipeline, and another 10,800 jobs to be cut by agencies not directly controlled by the mayor, including the Board of Education and the Health and Hospitals Corporation.

"Without recourse to additional aid, we must move from programmed recovery to shock therapy," declared Beame, describing his planned austerity measures as "the largest tax levy savings ever in this city."[44]

The mayor concluded with words of suspicion: "What is ironic, puzzling, and astonishing about this situation is that instead of being encouraged by the unprecedented actions taken by our administration to move the city to a sounder financial position, the financial community institutes its bank embargo. Why is this taking place? Why has the financial community created an atmosphere of doubt and uncertainty about New York City's securities at this point in time? Who started the whispering campaign to denigrate our financial integrity—a whispering campaign that has manifested itself in roaring headlines and handwringing editorials?"

Weisman and other reporters were reporting that, whisper campaign or not, the city's revenue shortfalls were dramatic and probably worse than even Beame's crisis budget conveyed, for all the fudging and finessing of the figures over the years had been more extensive and therefore consequential than many people suspected.

Given the increasing scrutiny by the banks, the days of masking costs or pushing them into out-years were over, and there was, of course, no surplus to fall back on. On May 19, three commercial banks and one investment house refused to buy $280 million in city notes needed to sell by the following day.[45]

On May 31, just after Beame had unveiled the "crisis" budget in an attempt to spur state action, the city expected to fall short by $84 million of the $174 million needed to cover its biweekly payroll. A $752 million debt fell due on June 11, just the latest payment deadline stemming from the total

$4.5 billion in short-term notes and $9.4 billion in long-term bonds the city then had outstanding. On June 25, a $249 million payment was due on a BAN; by June 27, the city was required to pay $2.7 million in interest on long-term indebtedness. And on and on it went, piles of bonds and notes coming due in a cruel but not unexpected cascade.

Beame had struggled to keep the word "bankruptcy" out of the press, to stop that kind of negative terminology from damaging investor confidence in the city. He suggested that the banks were collectively embarked upon an insidious effort to protect their profits at city expense in the most difficult times. "We were told we couldn't use the term 'bankruptcy' when we asked him questions at his weekly press conferences," said George Arzt, who reported for the *New York Post* from Room 9, the crowded City Hall press room. "We tried to find ways around it and instead used words like 'fiscal deterioration' and 'budget woes' in questioning the mayor."[46] But there was no avoiding the reality. The city simply lacked the money to pays its debts, and lacked the credibility to borrow. It was sliding toward bankruptcy.

During May, 1975, in his first major move to confront the city's problems head-on, Governor Carey appointed a "blue ribbon" advisory group from the private sector, including Simon H. Rifkind, the former federal judge and a partner in the white-shoe law firm Paul, Weiss, Rifkind, Wharton & Garrison; Richard R. Shinn, head of Metropolitan Life Insurance; Donald B. Smiley, chief executive of R.H. Macy and Company; and, of course, Felix Rohatyn.

Not long after, in their own bit of hands-on fact-finding, Carey and Rifkind, whom the governor revered, paid an unpublicized visit to City Hall to interview Beame's first deputy mayor and dear friend James Cavanagh. They hoped to learn more about the city's money management techniques. The meeting in Cavanagh's office confirmed what the bankers, who were now making their complaints known to the governor's business advisers, had been saying all along.

Carey recalled that Cavanagh, sixty-one, an amiable, white-haired man, began by delivering a somewhat meandering introduction to the city's budget process when Rifkind interrupted him with a pointed question: "Where are the books?"

"What books," answered Cavanagh light-heartedly, as Carey recalled it.

"Accounts payable, accounts receivable—where are the city's books?" said Rifkind.

"But you don't understand how we do it, judge," the deputy mayor responded. Then he dipped his hands into his shirt and pants pockets for illustrative effect and described the city's borrowing programs. "We have these TANs, which come from here, then we get these RANs from here, and these BANs come from here. That's how we do it: we issue the notes and we get the proceeds, then we roll them over to keep things going," said the deputy mayor.

"Show us the books," insisted Rifkind.

"You see, that's just it—we can't issue any books right now," said Cavanagh. "First, we need to know how much revenue is actually coming in . . ." The city, he said, had seasonal needs for money, not a deficit.

"My God, my good man," interrupted Rifkind, in Carey's recollections of the episode. "You don't have any books!"[47]

At the state budget division, Peter Goldmark raised the idea of creating a state tax-exempt corporation to sell bonds supported by specially diverted city tax revenue, and discussed it with Rifkind, Rohatyn, Shinn, and William Ellinghaus, president of New York Telephone. Together, with others in the Carey administration, they devised an approach that the governor felt would, if successful, provide the city with immediate and desperately needed funds to pay off its maturing bonds, breathing room to straighten out its budget, and a path back into the credit market—all within perhaps three months' time.

The tax-exempt vehicle was to be called the Municipal Assistance Corporation for the City of New York, or MAC, a vehicle designed to retire the city's short-term debt and convert it into long-term obligations with a lower interest rate. In its design, the basic apparatus Goldmark suggested and the mechanics worked out by Rifkind were not much different from the city's now-contested Stabilization Reserve Corporation, or even the Project Finance Agency, which had been used to ease the Urban Development Corporation back from its brush with default. But there was one major difference: MAC, at least as initially formulated, was to enjoy extensive authority to circumvent the mayor's power when it came to managing the city's finances and balancing the city's budget in the coming years. But Beame's ally in Albany, the assembly speaker Stanley Steingut, made sure the legislation creating the MAC board did not go that far, nor supersede the budget authority of the mayor, the city council, and the city Board of Estimate.

So it was that intense statehouse negotiations preceded the advent of MAC. The banks, looking for an avenue by which to influence the impervious Beame administration, indicated they would be willing to roll over $285 million in notes to keep the city out of default that June in exchange for their support for the creation of the MAC board. Warren Anderson insisted that New York City sales and stock transfer tax revenues supporting the MAC bonds be funneled through the state-controlled board instead of through the city to ensure that the revenues would be viewed by investors as safe, sound, and well out of City Hall's political and budgetary reach. When Beame and the city council offered some resistance to giving the MAC board the right to audit the city's finances, Carey offered the city a $200 million state advance as a salve within the bill, and the objection to auditing was dropped.

"We're trying to keep the patient alive so we can treat him," Rohatyn told reporters as the amended MAC legislation headed toward passage.[48]

Rohatyn was asked at a press conference before the vote whether default was likely.

"We just cannot accept that this is an option we can live with," he said, but quickly added, "I want to emphasize again that MAC is no guarantee. It can possibly, hopefully, get you over the eleventh of June. It can buy you a couple of months. It can take some short-term debt off the city and create a climate and a series of perceptions that might enable the city to get itself back into the marketplace—which is going to be the ultimate test of this thing."[49]

Approved by the Legislature in the early morning hours of June 10, the bill creating the entity that Carey dubbed "Big Mac" was signed—"with relish," he pronounced—the day before the city's outstanding issue came due for repayment. The legislation called for immediate "bridge" loans to the city with the involvement of banks and the state, as well as advances of scheduled state aid, thus affording the city a narrow escape from default the next day.

Rohatyn assembled a team of financiers from Lazard Freres to advise the state's new public benefit corporation, while attorneys from Rifkind's Park Avenue law firm Paul, Weiss, Rifkind, Wharton & Garrison served as Big MAC's legal team, led by an incisive young attorney, Peter R. Haje. Under the bill, the MAC board was authorized to raise up to $3 billion in the credit market to aid the city through the summer and fall months. MAC, as the reliably quotable Rohatyn said, was the city's "only visible means of support."[50]

Clearly, the state was assuming a risk on behalf of Beame and the city by creating the Municipal Assistance Corporation. Though backed by diverted city revenues, the state's involvement through MAC in the future survival of the city put its own standing in the municipal bond market on the line.

The MAC board was created, principally, to advocate on the city's behalf to creditors, since purchasing MAC bonds was a way to help New York avoid default. But MAC's powers were ultimately advisory. While it could hold back cash proceeds from bond sales from the city as a form of political pressure, review every city expenditure and revenue item, and set limits on short-term borrowing, it lacked the power to manage the city budget directly.

It could not impose a wage freeze, tinker with a proposed budget, or reject one directly. So Beame could live with the MAC board's demands for information and results if he had to, and undoubtedly the city's note repayment deadlines meant he had to. (The act required the city to provide the MAC board with periodic reports on municipal expenditures and operations, and the mayor would have to certify that his annual budget proposals were "feasible" and in balance, and that conditions of the new law were being satisfied. It also stipulated that if the city failed to live up to its requirements under the act, the board could issue a "determination of noncompliance" notifying the state and the public that the city was not fulfilling the terms of its contract.)[51] "Somebody's always looking over my shoulder," the mayor postured. "The Citizens Budget Commission looks over my shoulder. The *New York Times* looks over my shoulder. The *Daily News* looks over my shoulder. The State Comptroller looks over my shoulder. What's new about that?"[52]

In addition to appointing Rifkind and Rohatyn to the MAC board, Carey named as chairman Thomas Flynn of the accounting firm Arthur Young and Company, former U.S. Housing and Urban Development Secretary Robert Weaver, and Donna Shalala, a professor of political science at Columbia's Teachers College. Beame received appointments, too, and named William Ellinghaus of New York Telephone, Francis Barry of the Circle Line, John Coleman, vice chairman of the New York Stock Exchange, and George Gould, an investment banker with Donaldson, Lufkin & Jenrette. They met twice a week in Manhattan and began coordinating their work with the Carey administration, bankers, leaders of the city unions, and top city officials. The board members agreed that all their votes would be unanimous, to maintain a united front.

Even as the MAC legislation became law, social tensions in the city persisted, contributing to investors' enduring skittishness about all things New York. The city's labor unions, having denounced the bankers as greedy elites, took aim in June at Beame's crisis plan for tens of thousands of municipal layoffs. MAC executive director Herb Elish, a former sanitation commissioner for Mayor Lindsay, negotiated with union leaders and urged a cooling-off. Nevertheless, some ten thousand city workers rallied in front of First National City Bank's Wall Street headquarters to protest the bank's refusal to help the city in its financial crisis. Five days later, about twenty-five thousand people demonstrated against cuts in the education budget. Meanwhile, the Patrolmen's Benevolent Association and the Unified Firefighters Association drafted scare leaflets whose cover bore a hooded skull and the words "Welcome to Fear City—A Survival Guide for Visitors to the City of New York," an alarmist warning that crime and violence were "shockingly high" and advising tourists to stay off the streets after six PM, avoid public transportation, and be aware of fire hazards, given the mayor's firefighting reductions.[53]

"A new low in irresponsibility," responded Beame, and he sent the city's lawyers to court to restrain the police and fire unions from handing out the leaflets, resulting in the unions halting their distribution.

As June ended, the city's ten thousand sanitation workers went out on a two-day wildcat strike, leaving the city soon stinking from the accumulation of forty-eight thousand tons of garbage and billowing acrid smoke from the burning of trash by merchants. An editorial in the *Wall Street Journal* called for the National Guard to collect the city's garbage. Highway workers picketed vital arteries during rush hour, causing further chaos, and three of the city's drawbridges attended by union workers were left up, unattended.

The sense of havoc grew as the Fire Department reported that twenty-six fire companies had already been disbanded and dismissal notices had been sent to sixteen hundred men. Firemen staged a sick-in. Hospitals warned of the effect of massive staffing reductions in the offing. Beame stood with the unions this time, much to the dismay of bankers and their principal Republican ally in Albany, the bespectacled Warren Anderson. Beame asked legislative leaders to approve additional city taxes to save jobs. "Anderson doesn't give a god damn what we do," Beame said. "He's in a world by himself."[54]

The mayor flew to Albany the evening of July 2 and met with Carey at the Executive Mansion shortly after ten PM. Another deal with Anderson was in the works, aides explained. In exchange for $150 million in additional state education funds the senate majority leader was then seeking, the state senate would give the city authorization to raise $330 million through expanded local taxing powers. An exultant Beame returned to the city, saying the new funds would allow sanitation men to return to work, and dismissal notices sent to two thousand policemen and 750 firefighters could now be retracted.[55]

By now, the MAC board had pulled together its first financial package, scheduling the sale of $1 billion of bonds backed with city revenue, one of the largest single offerings in the history of the municipal bond market. MAC sent out "road shows" of underwriters and state officials to market the bonds around the state and country. Two hundred and twenty banks and securities houses responded by signing up to buy some, and Standard and Poor's rated the offering an A-plus. The sale went ahead and was declared a success. But it had not been an unqualified triumph. The bonds plummeted in price, some by 10 percent, despite an interest rate of 9.5 percent, among the highest in the history of the market. In addition, 145 dealers who had been solicited to buy the MAC bonds had said no.[56] Rohatyn years later contended that Beame's reflexive decision to rescind the city layoffs had hurt the initial MAC sales a great deal, damaging faith in the city's ability to reform itself. "He just didn't have the stomach for it," said Rohatyn.[57] By August, when MAC was getting ready to issue a second billion-dollar series of well-secured bonds, $50 million from that first MAC bond offering still remained unsold. Rohatyn and others began pressuring City Hall for more dramatic actions to repair investor confidence.

MAC in turn began to get tougher with the city, prodding officials for deeper cuts to improve the market's perception of the bailout bonds. Robert W. Bailey, in his trenchant 1984 analysis of the financial debacle, *The Crisis Regime,* observed that MAC's role shifted markedly at this point from primarily serving as an advocate for the city to the credit market, to principally advocating on behalf of the credit market to the city. One telling sign: the MAC board began transmitting bond sale proceeds to the city in smaller and smaller increments rather than in larger lump sums, the better to ensure that Beame cut the budget.

Though the Carey administration's topmost goal had not changed—to rescue the city from a default and bankruptcy—its tactics were becoming difficult to discern from those advocated by the banking community, even as he faced criticism from the right for moving with insufficient speed or toughness, and from the left for increasingly hardball tactics.

Carey replaced Thomas Flynn with the more hard-line Ellinghaus as the MAC board chairman, while Rohatyn, having pushed for the change because of perceptions that Flynn was too accommodating toward Beame, became the influential head of MAC's financial committee. At the board's July meetings with city officials, bankers, and union officials, Ellinghaus and Rohatyn together pushed for an unprecedented wage freeze, something the president of the United Federation of Teachers and later the American Federation of Teachers, Albert Shanker, a towering figure in the municipal labor movement and public education, predicted would trigger a citywide teachers strike. Herb Elish began by negotiating for the wage freeze with the Board of Estimate, city council, and the unions. But the city had yet another payment deadline looming that it could not meet: $792 million in notes due August 22. The money from the first MAC bond series, according to Goldmark, who was now poring over the city's financial ledgers in addition to the state's, enabled the city to cover its costs only through August 10. "We are becoming deadline junkies," Assembly Speaker Steingut at one point complained to journalists.

While Shanker maintained his union's usual adversarial posture, his some-time rival, Victor Gotbaum, and pension consultant Jack Bigel began to see the possibility of a city bankruptcy as all too real, not the usual budget-season posturing. They grasped that labor contracts with the city would no longer hold any legal weight in the event of a bankruptcy, and hard-won gains in wages and benefits would be null and void. The credit market's less than strong reception of the MAC bonds was also weighing on them, not to mention the Ford administration's obstinate posture, while Rohatyn was emphasizing that in Congress, the lack of sympathy toward New York was bipartisan.

The underwriters of the second MAC bond issue scheduled for August soon dropped a bombshell letter to the MAC board, implicitly faulting the Carey administration and the board for nibbling at rather than biting the bullet, and demanding, once and for all, quick and far-reaching city cutbacks to "restore the total fiscal condition of New York City in a manner that will rebuild investor confidence across the country—confidence that has significantly eroded in the last six months, and on an accelerating basis in the more recent months." What the market was really saying, said letter writers Wallace Sellers, vice president and division director of the Municipal and Corporate Bond Division of Merrill Lynch, and Thomas Labrecque, executive vice president of the Chase Manhattan Bank, was there is "country-wide apathy to New York City's problems . . . a strong perception by investors that the city continues to operate in a 'business as usual' mode, and a perception by investors that the State of New York is not taking the lead in seeing that the city's problems are solved, but is only reacting when forced to do so." Brimming with impatience, the letter called for "an immediate, dramatic, and credible program putting a firm, Spartan control on the total expenses of the city, which is endorsed and visibly supported by the governor and the legislative leaders, and implemented by the mayor and the MAC board."[58] David Rockefeller of Chase then released a rare public comment: "The facts of the matter are now clear to everyone. What is desperately needed is concrete action now."[59]

At MAC's biweekly meeting in Manhattan in late July, Allen Thomas, an attorney in Rifkind's firm, stated that research was under way to figure out what might happen if the city defaulted or went bankrupt. Rohatyn said an "extreme negative view might require some thought of introducing into Congress federal bankruptcy legislation" to prepare for that eventuality.[60]

Carey called on the unions to accept the wage freeze, while the MAC board forced Beame to agree to a deadline of midnight July 29 for a deal with the unions on a major retrenchment program. The mayor received a politically and personally distasteful menu of options, including the salary freeze, a transit fare hike, City University cuts, and a change in employee work rules to ensure greater productivity. The MAC trustees also said Beame must seek an aid advance from the state, a state takeover of certain city functions such as the courts and jails, a switch to a regular accounting system, high-interest loans from the banks, and federal guarantees to insure future MAC bonds and city securities.

As objectionable as these options were for Beame, he embraced the recommendations almost as if they were his own, and added in a few more for good measure, such as a proposed increase in the 5-cent Staten Island ferry fare, which had been in place since 1898. The mayor said he would seek the wage freeze in the city council if the municipal unions refused to submit to one voluntarily, and assailed his agency commissioners for misleading him in an effort, he said, to avoid laying anyone off.

State officials visited Washington for a second set of meetings, to no avail, and Ellinghaus reported that the Treasury's Simon "gave them no encouragement along the lines of federal insurance on corporation or city obligations."[61] The New York Telephone executive added that the Fed's Burns told them that "it would be almost impossible for the Federal Reserve to make a loan inasmuch as the city does not have the necessary security as required by law." Levitt, the state comptroller, declined to invest any state employee pension funds in MAC bonds, which private investors unfortunately took as a further justification for their wariness.

In midtown Manhattan, at the Americana Hotel, the press camped out in the carpeted lobby as Gotbaum and Bigel held marathon contract talks with other union leaders and city and state officials, along with Ellinghaus and Rohatyn, forming a tossed salad of competing interests—labor and business, city and state, conservative and liberal. The issue was the wage freeze, a litmus test of whether city and state officials could control labor costs. Both sides were nervous and uncomfortable, no doubt. When Rohatyn spied one of the union leaders wearing a sidearm, he asked, "Is this the way you guys always do business?"[62] But frequent and close contact over the days and nights of negotiation dispelled many myths each side held about the other. "I always thought the city union leaders wore 'black hats,'" commented Ellinghaus years later, "but I found out that the unions knew more about what was going on than many of the city officials did, and in many cases wore 'light-colored hats,' like the rest of us."[63] Rohatyn, for his own part, never imagined that he would become close friends with Gotbaum, or the best man at the labor leader's 1977 wedding. Likewise, Rohatyn was singularly impressed by the encyclopedic knowledge of city-labor history and the understanding of financing brought by Jack Bigel, a veteran labor battler in New York City, whom he described as "tough as a boot . . . and the closest thing to a real Marxist I ever met."[64]

The Americana talks produced an agreement worked out chiefly by Elish, Rohatyn, Ellinghaus, Bigel, and Gotbaum, who headed the city unions' Municipal Labor Committee, allowing a voluntary wage increase deferral, short of a full-out wage freeze. Civil servants making less than $10,000 a year would give up 2 percent of their raises in their pending contracts until the city achieved a balanced budget; those earning between $10,000 and $15,0000 would give up 4 percent, and workers making more than $15,000 would surrender the entire 6 percent raise that had been granted by the city. Gotbaum and Bigel asked for but did not win guarantees that future layoffs and staff reductions would be based only on attrition.[65]

Hugh Carey and four of his brothers singing "Bill Bailey, Won't You Please Come Home" at a mirthful moment in Albany during Carey's governorship. (left to right) John, Martin, Hugh, Denis, and Ed. *Courtesy of the Carey family.*

Left: Denis Carey, Hugh Carey's father, wore stylish hats as the proud owner of Eagle Petroleum, and refused to declare bankruptcy after the Great Depression—and the monopoly practices of the great oil and railroad titans—clipped the once-successful company's wings. *Courtesy of the Carey family.*

Right: The wedding day picture of Hugh Carey and Helen Owen Carey. *Courtesy of the Carey family.*

The young Carey brothers and their parents pose for a portrait in the family home in Park Slope, Brooklyn: (standing left to right) Hugh, Denis Jr., Martin, and Ed, with (seated left to right) John, Denis Sr., George, and Margaret (their mother). *Courtesy of the Carey family.*

**HUGH L. CAREY**

60 Rutland Rd., Bklyn.

Student Council Vice-pres. 4; Azarias Society Vice-pres. 4; "Lance" Editor 4; Class Basketball 1, 2, 3, 4; Class Pres. 1, 2; Debating Team 1, 3.

Hugh Carey's high school yearbook photo, ca. 1937. Carey attended St. Augustine's Academy and High School in Brooklyn. *Courtesy of the New York State Archives, NYSA_ 13708-83_B8_019.*

Hugh Carey (right) with an Army colleague, ca. 1942. *Courtesy of the New York State Archives, NYSA_13703-83_B8_023.*

Congressional candidate Hugh Carey (left) at a John F. Kennedy campaign stop. *Courtesy of the Carey family and the New York State Archives.*

Congressman Carey with senators Hubert H. Humphrey and Robert F. Kennedy.
*Courtesy of the Carey family and the New York State Archives.*

Congressman Carey on Air Force One with President Lyndon B. Johnson. *Courtesy of the Carey family and the New York State Archives.*

The last congressional campaign postcard (1972). *Courtesy of the Carey family and the New York State Archives.*

Carey with his family in Prospect Park, Brooklyn, for a gubernatorial campaign photograph (1974). *Courtesy of the New York State Archives, NYSA_13703_82_B5_007.*

Carey campaigns for governor in 1974 at Nathan's Famous restaurant with sons Kevin and Thomas. *Courtesy of the Carey family and the New York State Archives.*

Governor Carey taking his first oath of office, administered by Charles D. Breitel, Chief Justice of the State Court of Appeals. Governor Carey took the oath at 10:30 PM on New Year's Eve, 1974, so that his youngest children could witness the ceremony before they went to bed. *Courtesy of the New York State Archives, NYSA_13703-82_B3_8152-012.*

Carey swears in Judah Gribetz as his gubernatorial counsel (1975); New York City Mayor Abraham Beame and former mayor Robert Wagner are to the right. *Courtesy of the New York State Archives, NYSA_13703-82_B3_8155_009.*

Governor Carey and Nelson Rockefeller at a meeting in 1975. *Courtesy of the New York State Archives, NYSA_13703-83_B8_027.*

Governor Carey and New York City Mayor Abraham Beame at the mayor's office (1975). *Courtesy of the New York State Archives, NYSA_13703-82_B1_002.*

Frank Sinatra joins Carey at a Friar's Club dinner honoring Sinatra in 1976. The crooner campaigned for Carey when he was running for governor. *Courtesy of Hugh Carey and the New York State Archives, NYSA_13703-82_B1_001.*

Carey attends NAACP executive director Roy Wilkins's retirement dinner in 1977. Among those who showed up were former New York City mayor Robert Wagner, New York City Mayor Abraham Beame, New York Secretary of State Mario M. Cuomo, Governor Carey, Roy Wilkins, and New York State Comptroller Arthur Levitt. *Courtesy of the New York State Archives, NYSA_13703-82_B1_023.*

Carey announces Secretary of State Mario M. Cuomo as his running mate in the 1978 campaign for a second term in Albany. *Courtesy of the New York State Archives, NYSA_13703-83_B9_11349_009.*

The governor speaks with construction workers during a 1978 campaign stop. *Courtesy of the New York State Archives, NYSA_13703-82_B6_001.*

Two well-known wits: Carey and Bob Hope trade one-liners in the Red Room (1977). Hope's wife Dolores is seated to the right. *Courtesy of the New York State Archives, NYSA_13703-82_B4_10380_052.*

The 36<sup>th</sup> anniversary of the Warsaw Ghetto Uprising at Temple Emanu-el in New York City (1979). *Courtesy of the New York State Archives, NYSA_13703-82_B7_019.*

Carey shakes hands with Senate Majority Leader Warren M. Anderson after delivering his 1980 State of the State address. *Courtesy of the New York State Archives, NYSA_13703-82_B1_8024_025.*

Governor Carey receives the Olympic torch for the 1980 Winter Olympics, which took place in Lake Placid, N.Y. *Courtesy of the New York State Archives, NYSA_13703_82_B5_80116_008.*

A press conference with the transit task force in 1980. Looking from left to right in this photo are, among others: Felix Rohatyn, Governor Carey, New York City Mayor Ed Koch, Richard Ravitch. *Courtesy of the New York State Archives, NYSA_13703-82_B7_008.*

Governor Carey at St. Patrick's Cathedral on the day of the St. Patrick's Day Parade in 1981, with (left to right) Terrance Cardinal Cooke; the parade grand marshal, Joseph P. Kennedy; and Carey's son, Paul. *Courtesy of the New York State Archives, NYSA_13703-83_B10_022.*

Governor Carey at the unveiling of the portrait of former governor Franklin D. Roosevelt by J. S. Perskie (1981). Roosevelt's son, Franklin D. Roosevelt Jr., was in attendance. *Courtesy of Hugh Carey and the New York State Archives.*

With His Holiness Pope John Paul II. *Courtesy of the Carey family and the New York State Archives.*

Peter Goldmark (Director of the State Budget) and Governor Carey converse at the economic summit held at Topridge, Marjorie Meriweather Post's Adirondack Great Camp, on October 23–24, 1977. *Courtesy of the New York State Archives.*

Hugh L. Carey receives Doctorate of Humane Letters, *honoris causa*, during the 2008 commencement ceremonies at Wagner College. Standing left to right: Jay P. Hartig, Chairman of the Board of Trustees, Hugh L. Carey, and President Richard Guarasci.

President Gerald Ford in mid-May, 1975. *Courtesy of White House Photograph Courtesy Gerald R. Ford Library.*

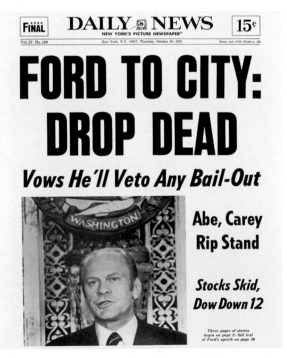

Ford never used the words "drop dead," but he nevertheless vowed to veto any bill intended to keep New York from defaulting on its outstanding obligations. *Courtesy of New York Daily News.*

City and state officials debated the constitutionality of breaking exist-ing labor agreements to achieve the agreement. Finally, though, the state attorney general Louis Lefkowitz announced at his office in the north tower of the World Trade Center that the mayor did have the authority under his home rule and police powers to impose a unilateral wage freeze. Decreasing their wages in a time of crushing inflation was hardly acceptable to working people. At a city council hearing, Beame was denounced by some city work-ers for caving in to the bankers, who, according to articles by investigative reporter Jack Newfield in the *Village Voice,* had precipitated the fiscal crisis by quietly "dumping" their city securities and were now forcing the city's workforce and citizenry to pay for the ensuing financial collapse with their jobs, wages, and public services.

Beame's program now called for full-scale retrenchment, and a full-scale retreat from many of the political values he stood for.[66] With the wage freeze included, his austerity program was worth $500 million, including the MAC-demanded fifty-cent subway fare, cuts in city funding for the City University of New York, a slash in capital spending, the elimination of several city departments, and many bookkeeping reforms. Beame demanded an end to reduced "summer hours" for workers (a legacy of the years before air-conditioned offices) and the contractually allowed day off from work to "recover" from donating blood. He sought to curb the management practice of allowing selective employees to accrue overtime in their final year of city service in order to inflate their pension.

"There is nothing I have done in public life," he said, "that has been more bitter than recommending these slashing economies that affect each and every one of us."

After the announcement, MAC rushed out with its own recommenda-tions for these and other city cutbacks. It was widely hoped that the feds, and the financial community, would take note.

One evening, as these pressures mounted, Beame phoned the home of Howard Rubenstein with some news. A public relations expert, Rubenstein had handled publicity for Beame's successful race in the 1973 Democratic primary runoff election against the popular, left-leaning Herman Badillo of the Bronx, and had even helped write Beame's acceptance speech and given him a victory ride back to his home in Belle Harbor on election night. The son of a crime reporter for the New York *Herald Tribune* and the owner of a small public relations firm, by the time of the gathering fiscal crisis he was an informal intermediary and familiar face at City Hall.

Beame told Rubenstein he planned to resign rather than bow to another, now-brewing Carey plan to undermine him further. He choked back tears as he talked. His push for retrenchment was, to him, an overwhelming, corporate-led attack on a disciplined political system that had led the way in providing gainful employment and public services over his three decades as a loyal Democrat, a devastating assault on him, the party, his principles, and a way of life.

Rubenstein, in a low voice, asked Beame if he had told his family. Beame said that he hadn't broached his resignation yet with his wife, Mary, but his son, Buddy, agreed with him that he would be better off quitting than acceding to any further political humiliation.

"You really ought to speak to your family first," cautioned Rubenstein.

The next morning, Rubenstein's phone rang; it was Beame. The mayor said he had given the matter some more thought overnight.

"I'm not resigning," he said.[67]

6

# "We Confront, therefore, a Formidable Dilemma"

*Carey pushes through the Emergency Financial Control Board to ride herd on City Hall, and cobbles together more than $2 billion in stopgap assistance, but a restive, powerful union leader threatens to pull out of the arrangements, bringing New York City to the brink of bankruptcy.*

In the summer of 1933, New York City Mayor John O'Brien, a former judge, faced demands for budget cuts from the J. P. Morgan Bank and other financial giants. The Great Depression was going full tilt. New York's former governor, Franklin D. Roosevelt, had been elected president that November amid the widening national economic catastrophe. Brushing aside the laissez faire economics of the free-wheeling 1920s and former president Herbert Hoover, the new commander-in-chief quick-stitched a series of economic stimuli in his first one hundred days in the White House. The unprecedented safety net was properly aimed at the millions of luckless citizens thrown out of work, their investments and savings up in smoke. It was not designed with the particular intent of buoying up local and state governments caught in the same cyclone.[1]

As governor, Roosevelt had pulled the plug on the political career of New York City Mayor Jimmy Walker, a beloved Tammany Hall figure despite, or because of, his happy complacency about widespread city corruption, bureaucratic sloth, and social despair. Directed to answer charges arising from Judge Samuel Seabury and a state legislative investigation that found that he had accepted hundreds of thousands of dollars from individuals with business ties to the city government, "Beau James" resigned from office and fled to Europe for a lengthy holiday. O'Brien won a special election to complete the last year of Walker's second term—1933.

Upon taking office, O'Brien, a bear of a fellow given to discursive speeches about his cherished legal profession, faced heavy pressure from the banks to get the city's crumbling financial house in order. The city had debts of at least $330 million, with $227 million due for repayment before the end of 1933, and not nearly enough revenue coming in to cover them. O'Brien at first recommended a few tax increases, but a furious outcry from business leaders ensued and he withdrew his proposals. The clock ticked toward the city's loan repayment deadlines as O'Brien offered up a modest tax on Wall Street stock transactions, but the Stock Exchange ensured the proposal's quick demise, threatening to relocate to New Jersey.

By September, 1933, O'Brien was all but begging the bankers to provide more loans to the city to keep it from defaulting on its debt payments, something thousands of small municipalities already had been forced to do, and throwing untold numbers of people out of work. The national financial barons of New York, their aims supported by then governor Herbert Lehman (the son of one of the three founders of Lehman Brothers investment bank), agreed to resume lending if the city instituted a five-year program of municipal cutbacks and discrete taxation. The plan became known as the "Bankers Agreement," as the city's leaders, with their backs against the wall, had little to say about it.

The agreement required the city to set aside a dedicated stream of tax revenues to ensure the repayment of bank loans, with a 10 percent fine for late payments. As an added protection, the banks insisted on passage of a city tax on public utilities.

If anyone doubted that bankers, not elected leaders, were calling the shots, Mayor O'Brien shelved a tax he wanted to impose on savings banks and insurance companies, and at the same time bowed to the demands of real estate developers, another major bank client, by freezing property taxes for four years. "The bankers," wrote the *New York Times,* "had taken ample precaution to safeguard the money they had already lent, as well as the funds they proposed to lend."[2]

O'Brien's successor, former congressman Fiorello LaGuardia, united the city's liberals and WASPs under a banner of reform. From his first day in office in 1934 to his last in 1945, the hard-charging Republican maverick battled the Tammany Hall–influenced state legislature and the Democratic political machine's many city government fiefdoms to make government more professional, more responsive, and capable of implementing programs to modernize the metropolis. As a tireless, unabashed populist, he was successful ini making the city less dependent on the bankers, and he derided them as "greedy" for trheir "unconscionable" interest rates. Toward that end, in early

1934 he headed straight up to Albany to press Governor Lehman and the leaders of the state legislature for temporary control of the city's taxing, hiring, and spending. Albany, not surprisingly, threw up roadblocks. In those years, despotic powers and commercial monopolies were much feared and decried, rarely more vocally than by LaGuardia, "the conscience of the Twenties" in historian Howard Zinn's phrase. His opponents turned the tables, cynically accusing LaGuardia of betraying his populist rhetoric and engaging in a naked power grab. Tammany's leaders had plenty of other reasons for resisting. Even amid the Depression's roiling seas of unemployed and impoverished, Albany's politicians, of both parties, remained committed to a ruthless patronage system, with government serving no higher purpose in their eyes than as a cash cow. LaGuardia's philosophy, however, embraced a restive, socially progressive agenda, viewing government as a blunt tool for civic change and social betterment. LaGuardia, born of a Italian-Catholic father and Italian-Jewish mother, deeply empathized with the struggles and aspirations of the working class, much in the manner of another storied son of American immigrants, former governor Al Smith. Both helped to inspire and set the stage for the New Deal reforms that Roosevelt, though an entitled, Dutchess County, New York, aristocrat, forged into existence during the financial meltdowns of the 1930s. Regulating Wall Street, saving farmers, supporting workers, and fundamentally reining in the self destructive urges and tendencies of unfettered capitalism were part of their legacy, as well as Roosevelt's.

LaGuardia's legendary, foot-stomping impatience only got him so far with the dukes of the state legislature in his first year in office, and so he was forced soon to do something unnatural for him—compromise—and acceded to a Tammany-promoted temporary 2 percent city sales tax, while successfully winning legislation that exempted food and medicine, and winning, too, higher taxes on large inheritances and politically connected utilities. As he proceeded to institute unprecedented city layoffs and agency consolidations across a graft-ridden municipal apparatus, he gained a measure of independence from the requirements of the bankers. When the Depression eased, the lending markets signaled a renewed willingness to do business with the burgeoning city. Enhanced by LaGuardia's assiduous courting of Roosevelt during the New Deal, and his alliance, however uneasy, with the powerful city parks commissioner and master builder Robert Moses, the city rode out the hard times. There soon arrived more favorable currents, fueled by preparations for World War II. The resulting economic expansion and prosperity continued with few serious interruptions all the way until roughly the time Hugh Carey, a teenager during LaGuardia's finest years at City Hall, became governor at middle age.

In mid-May of 1975—more than four decades since the 1933 Bankers Agreement—Morgan Guaranty Trust, First National City Bank, Chase

Manhattan Bank, and Salomon Brothers refused to buy $280 million in city notes then up for grabs. Carey summoned Richard Ravitch, who had not long before guided the Urban Development Corporation through a default, to his office in Manhattan.

Ravitch was met there by David Rockefeller of Chase, Walter Wriston of First National City (later Citibank), and Elmore Patterson of Morgan Guaranty. The governor showed up from a lunch wearing a dark blue three-piece suit. Sunlight poured through the windows of Carey's office with blinding intensity. With much formality and no apologies, the bankers proceeded to explain to Ravitch and Carey that there was no more room for negotiation: The market for city securities was oversaturated; the city's credit was no good; they were no longer willing to buy or sell New York City bonds and notes, and that was that.

Then they departed.

Carey asked for a reality check. What are they saying, he asked Ravitch?

"It means," Ravitch summarized, "that without an infusion of cash the city will soon go broke."[3]

A month later—June 10—the state MAC bond was born, approved by the state legislature at the Carey administration's arm-twisting, with the nearly $1 billion raised in the first of three planned bond sales used by New York City to redeem short-term notes and meet other obligations falling due and otherwise impossible to pay. Carey and his advisers envisioned that the two additional MAC bond offerings scheduled through September would bring in enough cash to allow the city to refinance and stretch out its short-term debts, balance its budget through aggressive cutbacks, and, it was hoped, win back the confidence of the lenders.

While the bankers had been supportive of the MAC legislation, they shared with Carey's private sector advisers their belief that Mayor Beame was not up to the task of balancing the city's books. The mayor, to be fair, presided over a $12 billion budget in which many spending commitments were locked in by local, state and federal laws. Federal aid for popular programs was slowing. In addition, Beame faced continuing resistance from the semi-independent City University of New York, the Health and Hospitals Corporation, and the Board of Education, three huge entities over which the mayor's office legally lacked direct control. The unions, too, were not eager to compromise over their hard-won contractual gains of the past fifteen years or so, during which the municipal labor movement hit its stride. Department heads, meanwhile, seemed to have no shortage of ingenious ways to avoid mayoral budget-cutting directives. And Beame had to work any cuts through the reflexively self-protective city council and the borough presidents who sat with him on the powerful land-use panel, the Board of Estimate.

Increasingly, as 1975 wore on, Carey felt that the mayor was blind to the implications of the banks' decision to stop marketing or purchasing the city's securities, particularly the short-term notes on which the city had been relying so heavily to pay its way as tax collections fell and budget shortfalls grew.

Carey grew irked, too, by city officials' failure to reach a consensus on the size of the gap between operating expenditures and revenues (one taking into account the years of tucking current expenses under the long-range capital budget despite accounting standards that dictated otherwise). The financial community demanded a realistic budget shortfall estimate, as did the MAC officials, but Beame seemed in no great rush to comply. For Carey, as long as the ultimate goal was getting the city back into the market, Beame appeared to be more of an obstacle than a help, in part because he was so unpopular with the bankers, as was his deputy and friend, James Cavanagh, and his budget bureau chief, Melvin Lechner.

Felix Rohatyn and other representatives of the MAC board of directors visited Washington on July 25 and met with treasury secretary William Simon, Federal Reserve chairman Arthur Burns, and L. William Seidman, Ford's economic adviser. Later, commenting on the meeting in a memorandum to Ford, Simon said that he was "encouraged" that MAC and the state were spearheading a city wage and expenditure freeze, a transit fare increase, and budget cuts for the City University, which, in a break with tradition, were to be covered by the introduction of tuition. These were all "steps in the right direction," declared Simon. But, Simon quickly added, "I am not convinced, however, that these actions will restore public confidence quickly enough to allow MAC to sell its bonds immediately. I believe something more must be done to convince the public that the reforms at the city level will be real and permanent. One possibility might be to place decision-making authority in the hands of MAC's board and not the mayor. That's a pretty drastic step and would require state legislative action, but I wouldn't rule it out."[4]

The MAC board convened with officials from the Treasury, Federal Reserve, and White House about two weeks later, raising the issue of whether Washington would support federal guarantees of all New York City debt paper for a limited period of time to ensure that future investors in the city's securities would be repaid. Though this was a cost-free proposal, federal officials stood opposed to it, or to any type of federal assistance for the city, for that matter.[5]

If federal guarantees were off the table, Carey's hopes for the MAC initiative suffered an equivalent blow when he learned that only one-quarter of the $960 million in financing raised from the second of three planned MAC offerings had come directly from the municipal bond market despite a record-setting 11 percent interest rate (so high that Rohatyn had worried that investors would interpret it as evidence of underlying weakness and risk). The majority of this second series of MAC bonds were sold through directly negotiated purchases among banks, state aid advances, and the employee pension funds of the city's teachers, police, and firefighters unions, which—crucially, for none of this would have been possible without the unions' voluntary participation—agreed to buy the bonds in order to participate in the MAC-led bailout out of their beleaguered employer. While the city was able to cover $791 million in expenses falling due, the governor and the MAC board were forced to conclude that the market's appetite for what the state had to sell on a suspect city's behalf was weakening. Thus, the third planned MAC bond sale slated for September was put on hold. A city default now seemed unavoidable and inevitable. A letter to Carey by a Big MAC trustee, summarizing the predicament, set the stage for far tougher action by the state.

"The Municipal Assistance Corporation," the letter signed by William Ellinghaus of New York Telephone began, "was created by the state legislature in June, 1975, after the city failed to market its debt obligations in the public market. It was intended at that time that MAC would raise 3 billion dollars in medium- and long-term bonds during the summer, providing the city with enough time to take visible and decisive action that would demonstrate that it was clearly on the road to fiscal stability and prepared to re-enter the market on its own. The city was simply not considered a good credit risk at that time. In spite of the clear security of the MAC bonds, however, the July financing of $1 billion was accomplished only with difficulty. The August financing of 960 million dollars was even more difficult. Because of the confusion surrounding many of the mayor's efforts," Ellinghaus, a Beame appointee to the MAC board, went on, "and in spite of his repeated assurances that he is doing all in his power to put the city's fiscal house in order, the message from the marketplace is clear. The investing public apparently lacks confidence in the city's management and its ability to regain its solvency. There is a pervasive perception that city efforts at fiscal and management reform are not credible.

"For this reason, the cash necessary to meet the maturing obligations of the city and operating expense requirements for September and beyond cannot be raised through the sale of MAC bonds. Default is now an imminent prospect that must be faced with the utmost urgency and seriousness. Therefore it is the unanimous decision of the Board of Directors of MAC that emergency action of a new and decisive kind is necessary if the financial obligations of the city are to be met and if default is to be avoided."[6]

The letter was a private one to Carey. Before making it public, Carey made it known that his administration and key members of the state legislature were trying to create a five-member board to oversee the city's financial management, with powers stronger than those of Big MAC. Beame, of course, objected, despite having rattled bankers' nerves by failing to submit a three-year city financial plan to the MAC board by an agreed-upon deadline of August 25, which was also the date of Ellinghaus's letter. Carey and Beame, according to Fred Ferretti's *The Year The Big Apple Went Bust*, met behind closed doors in a suite at the Waldorf Astoria Towers, in what was ostensibly a bid by the governor to make a last stab at achieving a compromise with Beame, minimizing their political estrangement, and avoiding a nasty showdown. That evening, with reporters and TV cameramen clamoring to get a view of them, the two men emerged from their talks to announce a tentative agreement: in return for a $1 billion state loan to the city (with repayment to be due in a year and payable through a future issue of MAC bonds), Carey would appoint a deputy state comptroller for city affairs to lead a *three*-member financial board consisting of just Carey, Beame, and State Comptroller Levitt. "We're not giving up home rule," Beame declared triumphantly, and Carey did not contradict him.[7] But the lead banks mentioned by Carey as part of this agreement, Chase Manhattan Bank, Morgan Guaranty, and First National City, reacted to the news by telling Ellinghaus and Rohatyn that they opposed buying $1 billion in MAC bonds if the credit market showed no interest in participating in what would be a cornerstone of the deal. Moreover, the bankers wanted a five-member panel in order to dilute Beame's influence.

Carey withdrew his proposal as the MAC board and Carey administration officials—Rohatyn, Goldmark, Gribetz, Burke, Berger, and others—continued working on and soon completed a 111-page proposal that involved the creation of an "Emergency Financial Control Board," the administration's most sweeping response to the crisis thus far, subject, though, to negotiation with legislative leaders. The *Wall Street Journal* meanwhile published an editorial calling on New York City to declare voluntary bankruptcy in order to reorganize its debts and obligations, including its labor contracts and pensions.[8] Rohatyn called the editorial devastating, as it came on the eve of the special session, and feared it would harden Republicans in the state senate and the banking community against the bill, perhaps fatally so.[9]

Still, as planned, Carey called the state legislature into special session, and he was characteristically detailed, purposeful, and persuasive, describing a state of emergency akin to a flood or a hurricane and presenting an omnibus "Financial Emergency Act" that would create a board with the sweeping powers to approve or reject New York City's yearly estimates of anticipated revenue, its planned expenditures in the aggregate, collective bargaining agreements, and long-term financial planning (of which there had been virtually none)—in short, whatever was needed to ensure the city moved aggressively toward achieving a balanced budget. The panel, as designed, effectively would make the governor, and therefore the state, responsible for putting the city's financial house in order. It placed the state's financial credibility in the market directly on the line, much as the state's advances of aid and loans to the city had done, but much more extensively and overwhelmingly this time.

The bill also cobbled together $2.3 billion in aid from a wide variety of sources to keep the city from becoming insolvent at any time through December of 1975.

Having met on convivial terms with most of the state lawmakers on whose votes the Financial Emergency Act now depended (like the former congressman he was, he was in the habit of inviting lawmakers over to the Executive Mansion for drinks and dining), Carey's address to the legislature framed the city's financial crisis in measured, compelling tones, imparting accurate information about the risks at hand, and, respecting the existence of other points of view, suggesting what he felt needed to be done.

"I have convened your Honorable Bodies in Extraordinary Session to share with you and to seek your counsel and support for prompt action to deal with a dire financial emergency," Carey began solemnly. "The city of New York is on the brink of financial collapse; an unparalleled disaster looms over it. The city's inability to raise funds needed to pay debts as they come due and provide essential municipal services without interruption are at stake, and the state is hardly insulated. The doors to the capital markets have been closed to it directly and now also indirectly. New York City's financial failure threatens to paralyze vital governmental functions, endangering the health, safety, and welfare of the more than twelve million people in the city and region. If not quickly and decisively constrained and resolved, this crisis portends a severe financial risk for New York State, and perhaps for the nation as well."[10]

Carey went on to describe the recent months of activity by state officials and MAC: the formation of a business advisory committee to improve city management; the establishment of a ceiling on the size of the city's budget; a moratorium on additional city taxes to cover an accrual of shortfalls; dismissal of thousands of municipal workers; elimination of thousands of open positions from the city's budget; a freeze on new hiring; a negotiated deferral of a wage increase for civil servants; an increase in the subway and bus fare and the Staten Island ferry fare; a reduction in the budget of the City University and a consequent increase in some students' fees, encroaching on CUNY's tradition of free tuition; a slashing of the city's capital budget; and the impending appointment of a deputy mayor for finance (it would be JC Penney senior vice president Kenneth S. Axelson, whose selection was urged by the state and came after consultation between Beame and the bankers).

"It was our hope," Carey said, "that all these steps, coupled with MAC's financing efforts, would enable the city to market its own securities by this October. But this hope has not been realized, thus making the prospect of default more imminent and the need for immediate state intervention inevitable and crucial if we are to stave off the dire consequences certain to follow a default . . . I must in candor alert you, as MAC has alerted me, that these measures contain certain risks to the state. If all elements of MAC's proposed plan were enacted, they would produce financing to New York City for the next three months. We have no assurances that at the end of this period capital markets will be open again to New York City, or to MAC. Should that be the case, the continuing inability of the city and MAC to obtain financing for New York City's debt and municipal services would impair the soundness of the financial plan and, in consequence, at a measureable level, the credit of the State. There are no commitments or understandings for private financing of the order required for a long-term solution. New York's commercial banks have indicated that they are prepared to participate in financing portions of the plan but in very limited amounts.

"I have been in close contact with Federal officials in efforts to enlist federal support for the city's emergency," Carey added. "This week I met once again with President Ford to apprise him personally of our desperate situation and of the alarming economic disorder that the financial fall of New York City would cause throughout the nation, and of the need for federal cooperation in the state's efforts to avoid such a disaster. The President and other federal officials were understanding and sympathetic, but offered no commitments. We confront, therefore, a formidable dilemma. There are major risks in any choice we make. Our most prudent course is to weigh the risks and follow the path that minimizes them."[11]

While Beame, through Assembly Speaker Stanley Steingut, had watered down the earlier MAC legislation, the pressure this time to accommodate the Carey administration fully was overwhelming, with default threatening and neither the banks nor the federal government coming forward with help, and with many state legislators less than eager to bail the big, bad city out this time, or at least wanting to have as little to do with it as possible. Steingut moved to get his legislative battalions in line. To have blocked what was now the second major phase of Carey's response to the city's fiscal crisis would have risked incurring much of the blame if the engines of the city government came to a standstill. The negotiations over the city's fate, with billions of dollars of private and public capital at stake, were "a game of Pass The Pistol,"[12] in Goldmark's description, in which the banks, union leaders, and elected officials at every level and from both parties cooperated despite divergent views and interests. "The city is drowning, and we have tied ourselves to them irreversibly," Goldmark said at the time to many people and in many ways, making the case for Carey's enormous policy gamble. That gamble involved lashing the city and state together—state strength and city weakness. Goldmark went on to warn that the state would default within thirty days of a city bankruptcy, for the city's costs of supporting its one million welfare recipients would likely have to be picked up by the state in the event of a default (as it was during the Great Depression in Grand Rapids, Michigan, the small city where Gerald Ford was born). Moreover, banks and other institutions and individuals that traditionally invested in the city's notes and bonds would likely shun New York State paper as well. Bondholders would not discriminate between city and state securities; they would simply go in search of other tax-shelter investments. The result, which Carey viewed as the paramount moral, political, and human failure—bankruptcy—would therefore unfold for both "child" and "parent," for both city and state.

In the statehouse, Warren Anderson, the white-haired majority leader of the state senate, who had spoken out earlier in the summer against any new and costly save-the-city plan, also found himself under increased political pressure to approve the Carey measure. Interestingly enough, his fellow conservative Republicans in the New York banking community were working with Big MAC to keep the city going and their New York City holdings whole, and were even helping to lobby federal officials for assistance. They wanted the Carey bill to pass, and made it clear to Anderson that they wanted the senate leader to take up the cause. He took the cue, and for that reason, as well his own judgment that the city's managers could no longer be trusted to balance the budget, he pushed for a strong state hand in the city's financial affairs, and as powerful a control board as possible.

In preparing for a vote on the huge and daunting package, Carey had asked leading municipal union officials and their knowledgeable and influential pension consultant, Jack Bigel, to meet with him in Albany. Helped by his aides, the governor succeeded in eliciting from them a pledge to support the legislation and use their organizations' pension funds to purchase large sums of MAC bonds—the very bonds the New York banks were eschewing as too risky and even potentially worthless in the long run because of the city's problems. The union leaders' willingness to play along was a huge development, crucial to the future success of MAC. To achieve their assistance, Carey warned labor leaders such as Victor Gotbaum and Barry Feinstein that in the event of a city bankruptcy filing, union contracts would be null and void. At the same time, however, Carey acknowledged that the unions were taking an enormous gamble with their members' retirement money. There was no other way to characterize it.

"Buying the MAC bonds was a matter of self-preservation, was how Carey put it—and by that point it made a lot of sense," remembered Al Viani, who was director of research and negotiations for Gotbaum's District Council 37 union (while Gotbaum was also the head at that time of the Municipal Labor Committee, an umbrella policy-making group for the union leadership of the city). Given that virtually all of the city's labor leaders were extremely worried about the survival of their contracts and about the collective bargaining process itself, the foundation of labor power in the city,[13] said Viani, they acceded to or agreed with Carey's reasoning and, in essence, they "shot craps with the assets of 350,000 pension fund members"—in Bigel's description later on—by investing in New York's future solvency.[14] (Actually, the unions were also rolling the dice with the government's money, since the city, as a public employer, was legally obligated to pay workers' pensions no matter the condition of their unions' pension funds.)

While no one could say for certain how serious or far-reaching the consequences of a default of the city would be, it was universally agreed that any bond repayment failure would certainly require the city to file for bankruptcy to protect itself from creditors demanding immediate repayment and to preserve its remaining assets. There would be enough aggrieved vendors and suppliers, municipal employees, retired city workers, and welfare recipients—and their respective attorneys—to fill Yankee Stadium many times over. The bankruptcy case could last for a decade, perhaps two. The bankruptcy judge who would hold the city and its assets in receivership would effectively be its unelected mayor, working to determine which debts would be repaid, when, in what order, and to what degree. It would meanwhile fall to the court to arrange that essential services were delivered, and to what extent—a huge task given the complexity of the city government and its many units, from police to fire safety to education to hospitals, and on and on.

Still, the prospect of insolvency did not stir universal fear among state and city Democrats, some of whom felt a bankruptcy court would be fairer to a city-in-retrenchment than a state control board. The liberal Howard Samuels was among those who did not sound especially worried about the possibility of a city-in-receivership. Many were distrustful of the state legislature and would have preferred to see a federal judge placed in charge. Meanwhile, conservative magazines and newspapers had a field day, cheering the prospect of a city bankruptcy, hopeful that the city's fiscal breakdown would weaken its municipal unions and liberal philosophy. New York Republican U.S. senator James Buckley echoed this view. It often fell to financial expert Felix Rohatyn to describe what a New York City bankruptcy might really mean, and his point was that it wasn't worth finding out. At a Manhattan gubernatorial news conference, when Carey was asked whether bankruptcy

was as serious a peril as some maintained, Rohatyn stepped to the micro-
phone and said that in his opinion, a large-scale municipal bankruptcy was
"like stepping into a tepid bath and slashing your wrists—you might not feel
yourself dying, but that's what would happen." The morbid observation was
picked up widely by the press, carried by papers that were finding Rohatyn
to be a crucial source for boiling down the unfolding developments, both
political and financial.

"I had a conviction," recalled Carey years later. "If the city went down,
the state would go with it. Not everyone agreed with me."[15]

Under the Carey administration's historic bill, virtually all the city's
regular fiscal decision-making powers and processes were to be suspended
for at least three years. The new control board would be given the authority
to decide how much the city budget was to be cut each year, though not
how such reduced spending levels would be achieved. The board would be
permitted to order reductions in overall spending, reject collective bargaining
agreements, and prohibit borrowing by any agency of the city government. It
would be given access to all city records and the right to initiate the removal
of and even criminal charges against intransigent city officials. At Warren
Anderson's insistence, it would also have a professional staff and executive
director, make managerial recommendations, and develop and approve the
city's first-ever long-range financial plan to balance the city budget by the
beginning of the 1978 New York City fiscal year.

If MAC had impinged on Mayor Beame's political turf and legal authority, what was about to be proposed went a long way toward gutting it.

In return for Beame's submitting to temporary state financial oversight
and overall-spending limits, the Carey administration's legislation offered him
a huge pile of money, enough to ensure the city could pay its bills for another
four months. The total $2.3 billion would be scraped together from bank
loans, city and state pension funds, state borrowing, prepaid real estate taxes
elicited with discount incentives, the city's sinking fund (a pool of money
set aside to repay bond issues), and a state insurance fund. MAC, in turn,
would be reauthorized to issue up to $5 billion in bonds, greater than its
initial $3 billion limit. Revenue-sharing funds, which usually flowed from
the state to the city, would be set aside for the sole purpose of guaranteeing
that investors in future MAC bonds would be repaid.

Carey still hoped for federal assistance. But he knew that even if President Ford suddenly supported a bill to provide emergency assistance to the
city—a doubtful prospect, since the president faced a potentially strong 1976
primary challenge from the more conservative Ronald Reagan, and because
anti–New York political rhetoric was flourishing in many heavily Republican
states—then the Congress would require two or three more months to get it

approved. So not only did the city lack congressional support, it also didn't have that kind of time to wait. It was already too close to the edge.

Yet the legal and financial edifice that MAC and the Carey administration had created and placed before the state legislature for approval was something of a house of cards, since a failure by any single financing source to participate in creating the $2.3 billion bailout fund could lead to the cancellation of other parties' contributions, and the structure's collapse. New York State Comptroller Arthur Levitt was already signaling his disinclination to provide the requested $125 million in state pension funds. Partly for that reason, the legislation included a special section providing for an "orderly default" if events dictated one. Under it, no creditor lawsuits could be filed for thirty days while the city, along with the control board, created a plan to continue essential services. Noteholders who filed suit could be paid only after ninety days.[16]

The risks presented by the proposed legislation are "real and substantial," Carey had acknowledged in opening the legislature's special session, but "a choice of default holds the prospect of inestimable harm for an indefinite time, not only to New York City but to the state and the nation as well . . . injurious for years to come . . . This opinion is shared by numerous eminent authorities of unqualified and respected judgment in national and international finance whom I have consulted, including several former U.S. secretaries of the treasury and former officers of the Federal Reserve system, all of whom unequivocally advised me that default must be avoided. Inexplicably, offices in the federal administration do not seem to share that view. I have received little indication that they as yet truly appreciate the gravity of the city's situation, or its profound implications for our state and nation. The experts I consulted warned that default would indefinitely close the capital market to New York City and to MAC. If the city cannot borrow, the state will be called upon to meet the full or a greater share of the costs of insuring the continuity of the city's municipal functions—both for services for which the state contributes part of the costs, as well as for those fully funded with city revenues. The state would be faced with the shutdown of construction projects, worth over $1 billion and affecting thousands of workers, financed by its authorities and public benefit corporations. Projects now under construction could not be completed, and the holders of outstanding securities issued for such projects would call upon the state to fulfill its moral obligation pursuant to the law. The 'faith and credit' of the state would be adversely affected by these uncertainties, disruptions, and dislocations, raising the costs of borrowing for state purposes. The ability of other cities, counties, and districts throughout the state to borrow would be similarly impaired, again raising the probability of calls upon the state to make available its credit and resources for assistance."

Carey's opening address had further laid out the risks.

"Other states and municipalities throughout the nation will not escape the shocks and waves emanating from a New York City financial collapse," he said. "This picture is not mere speculation. The failure earlier this year of the New York State Urban Development Corporation to pay a bond anticipation note on the date of maturity caused immediate and substantial increases in the interest rates paid by several other public authorities and corporations. Other municipalities, school, and sewer districts throughout the state have faced greater difficulty borrowing and are paying higher interest as well. These likely results of a default are unthinkable and unacceptable. Instead, I choose to follow a route of more limited risks presented in the program before you. My conscience and my sense of prudence and public responsibility lead me to a judgment in which I ask you to join me, to exert the limit of our energies and powers to avert the catastrophe of a default. Faced with these choices, it was my obligation to reach a decision that I believed to be in the best interest not only of New York City, but of all the people of the state. I did not make the decision lightly. But on balance I am confident the choice I have made is morally right."[17]

At the moment Carey was opening the legislative session, city officials were scrambling to make sure that paychecks due employees of the sanitation department and 36,000 welfare recipients were backed by sufficient cash deposits. City comptroller Harrison J. Goldin ordered the payments held back, and city budget director Melvin Lechner solicited the trustees of the city's five municipal pension funds for help. They all came up with $100 million from their retirement accounts to buy MAC bonds so the proceeds could be shifted to the city treasury in time to meet the latest payroll. That evening Lechner announced, "The city is solvent, today."[18]

The Albany debate proved predictably acrimonious. Blame was cast all around for the city's predicament. Anderson expressed discomfort with appropriating any state funds to help so incorrigible a city as New York, speaking for many upstate legislators and voters who saw nothing in it for upstate communities hobbled by the loss of industry, soaring unemployment, and rising inflation, problems dating back at least to the Arab Oil Embargo of 1973, which had sent gasoline prices sky-high. Anderson, who approved the formation of the MAC board only after winning an increase in school aid around the state, pressed for substantially more city oversight as a condition for supporting the Financial Emergency Act's stopgap assistance for New York City. If the state was going to put its "faith and credit" behind the city, he said, the new control board should have a greater number of seats to ensure state influence.

Tough questions also arose from the legislature's Black and Puerto Rican Caucus, which recognized, as did other liberals, Carey among them, the weakening pull of liberal forces dating as far back as the New Deal. Leveling false charges that the state was engaged in a conspiracy to bail out the bankers, many observers nonetheless perceived, correctly, that the needs of lenders and of capital were increasingly taking precedence over those of governments and their poorer citizens. "We have reached the point where if a liberal can't be a realist, he won't be able to do much more than talk philosophy," Carey, a pragmatist at heart but decidedly oriented toward the public interest since the beginning of his political career, declared.[19]

To try to ensure state senate approval, Anderson began marshalling support from Republican state senators downstate—Republicans whose constituents often lived or worked in the city and would be the most directly harmed by a bankruptcy. He knew he had a better chance with them than he did with the senators from upstate communities in which anti–New York City feelings ran strong. Anderson's maneuverings were successful, as were those of his counterpart, Steingut. On September 8, the Financial Emergency Act passed 80 to 70 in the Democratic-led Assembly (with not a single Republican supporting the bill, and without the help of eight upstate Democrats, who were given leave to vote against it). In the state senate later that evening, the final tally in favor of the bill was 35 to 26 (one upstate senator reportedly hid in a first-aid room so Anderson couldn't put the arm on him during the marathon debate). Carey, waiting in his office on the floor below, signed the measure at 4:47 in the morning.

The governor, initially reluctant to support the idea of placing the city under a state control board, which was driven hardest by Anderson, became its ex officio chairman and, unmistakably, "the financial guardian of the city," as the *Times* called him. The seven EFCB members—up from the original five, at Anderson's behest—would, in addition to Carey, include Levitt, Beame, and Goldin (giving the city comptroller a seat at the table equal to that of the mayor). In short order came three Carey recruits—William Ellinghaus (who would leave MAC, his chairmanship there filled by Rohatyn), American Airlines chairman and president Albert V. Casey, and Colt Industries Inc. president David I. Margolies. The law also provided for Comptroller Levitt to appoint a special deputy for the city who would serve as the control board's operating director and monitor the city's compliance with the legislation. A member of Levitt's staff, Sidney Schwartz, was named to the post in mid-September. But the bankers wanted still more—they wanted heads to roll at City Hall because, even stripped of much of his budget authority, the mayor still exerted political pull, and could get in the way of slashing economies to show the credit market and the Ford administration that the city was worth their future aid and investment.

It was often left to Carey to explain to the sometimes politically naïve bankers something that Beame well understood, but which they did not.

Though they would probably have been thrilled to see Beame resign, if he did quit he'd be succeeded under the city's governing charter by none other than the city council president Paul O'Dwyer, whose left-wing outlook would be even more noxious to the financial men.[20] By early December, though, Beame would be forced to serve up a sacrificial lamb to the banks and fire his friend and deputy Jim Cavanagh. The directive was delivered by Carey's counsel, Judah Gribetz.

Even before the mayor's crushing political and personal defeat—with Cavanagh soon replaced by city planning department head John Zuccotti, someone in whom the financial community had a great deal more trust and confidence because of his business orientation—the creation of the Emergency Financial Control Board scrambled the city's political process and traditional lines of influence. Jack Newfield and Paul DuBrul of the *Village Voice* called it a "revolution in the governance of New York City," and so it seemed to many participants in the city political arena. When the city's teachers went on strike after returning from summer vacation to find that class sizes had ballooned and many schools faced chaotic conditions because seven thousand school employees had been laid off, it was not clear to anyone who effectively wielded the real influence to settle the matter—the Carey-run EFCB or the Beame-run City Hall.

The strike was a harbinger of things to come. The teachers union estimated that to rehire all the teachers laid off as a result of Beame cuts in school funding would cost $220 million. The union's president, Al Shanker, realizing that the city didn't have that kind of spare change to spread around, saw that City Hall was in no rush to negotiate an end to the dispute: As long as the walkout continued the teachers didn't have to be paid, so the city was effectively realizing a badly needed budget savings.

Normally, when there's a strike, Shanker said, "the governor calls, the mayor calls, the mediator calls. Everybody wants to settle it. This was exactly the opposite . . . Nobody would talk to us . . . We could have stayed out for two years. They were not interested in opening the schools."[21]

After having been outvoted by his pro-strike union members, Shanker pushed for a settlement, and in a matter of days he announced a deal with City Hall to hire back some of the laid off teachers by using the wages forfeited during the strike, plus a small salary hike for all. "We've gotten the most we can possibly get," including a plan for holding down class sizes and hiring back 2,400 of the 4,500 laid off teachers. Shanker pleaded to his rank and file: "A strike is a weapon you use against a boss that has money. This boss has no money."[22] His appeals struck a chord. The union membership called off the strike after five days by a vote of 10,655 to 6,695.[23]

But the UFT's deal with City Hall then failed to hold up. On October 7, it was rejected by the Emergency Financial Control Board, which declared it out of line with the new budget-balancing imperatives and a bad precedent for upcoming contract negotiations with other city unions.

Shanker, a shrewd tactician with connections all the way to Washington, lashed back, refusing on October 15, 1975, to commit the city's Teachers Retirement System to its earlier agreement to purchase $225 million in MAC bonds under the Financial Emergency Act, and thus imperiling the entire bailout package.

The fearless and unyielding liberal leader had shut down the city school system with wrenching strikes in 1967 and 1968, adding to his mystique as a powerful labor leader. In Woody Allen's 1973 science fiction comedy "Sleeper," Allen's character wakes up two hundred years in the future to find out that civilization was destroyed when "a man by the name of Albert Shanker got hold of a nuclear warhead." In October, 1975, Shanker really did hold in his hands the power to cause a devastating chain reaction. Participation by all of the city unions' pension funds was a linchpin of the EFCB legislation: if any of the union funds withdrew their commitments to purchase MAC bonds, other components of the financing package would fall through. At the very least, $250 million in state loans to the city and $60 million in bond rollovers by the banks were contingent upon the buy-in of the teachers union.

On the day Shanker pulled out of the arrangement, Beame handed over to the control board the city's three-year financial management plan, in compliance with the Financial Emergency Act. The submission, which the board would approve after a hurried rewriting of its initially confusing and incomplete summary pages by Goldmark and two assistants from the state budget division, included in its final form a statement of how much more money the city budget would have to set aside to service its debt (significantly more, as it happened). It included a conservative estimate of anticipated revenues, a request for advances of state aid, and a proposed shift of certain city costs and responsibilities to the state. To achieve a balanced budget within three years, the financial plan also signaled a series of slashing cuts aimed at the city services upon which the middle and lower classes most of all depended: the City University of New York, the municipal hospital system, the Mitchell Lama middle-class housing program, and many other social services, including drug treatment, job training, and neighborhood action programs initiated in the 1960s with infusions of federal aid. In the absence of federal assistance, there seemed few practicable alternatives. An immediate sharp rise in local taxes might have only furthered the exodus of companies and middle-class residents fleeing during the recession. Some voices called for immediate increases in workforce productivity, but these were contractual issues requiring labor-management negotiation. And of course, the state and federal taps were all tapped out for the moment. "We can take no pride in the plan," Mayor Beame said, "because it places a higher priority at this time on the grim economic realities confronting the city, rather than upon the needs of our citizens. Unfortunately, this is a course that must be taken at this time in the interests of our economic survival."[24]

That evening, Carey attended Cardinal Cooke's annual Alfred E. Smith Dinner at the Waldorf Astoria, where an aide approached the dais and whispered something in his ear. He rose, shook hands all around, and made his way out of the ballroom midway through the ceremony to his official state car; he was driven to his midtown office. There, Felix Rohatyn, George Gould (Rohatyn's replacement as MAC finance chairman), and MAC board member Robert Weaver (former secretary of Housing and Urban Development in Lyndon Johnson's administration) were already calling members of the teachers-union pension fund board to try to get them to change their minds, all to no avail. Carey got on the phone and called the state's legislative leaders, and Arthur Levitt and Ford administration officials. Beame, too, was notified, and soon, the Board of Estimate and city council leaders were seen pulling up after midnight at Gracie Mansion to meet with the mayor. In the predawn hours of October 17, a Friday, city and state officials realized that they had only until the end of the day to meet the city's payroll and other debts, and no money to do it unless the Financial Emergency Act aid package came through. Beame even phoned the White House and asked to speak to Ford. His call was brushed aside. President Ford was sleeping, he was told, but be assured, his aides were monitoring the situation. *Click.*[25]

One of the people Carey got in touch with early on was Richard Ravitch, as both Ravitch and his wife, Diane, author of a well-received 1974 history of the city's school system, *The Great School Wars*, were close to Shanker. As in Congress, it was often personal contacts that carried the most weight in Carey's calculations; his mental Rolodex was vast and his connections ran deep, both in New York and Washington; he was quick to summon the names, dates, and acquaintances to help him with any particular problem. Shanker, he knew, had been trying to get Diane Ravitch appointed to a seat on the state's Board of Regents.

"You *gotta* get Shanker to change his mind," Carey told Ravitch after awakening him at his Park Avenue apartment with a call.[26] Carey then phoned other aides.

"We knew that Shanker didn't play with phony cards—we knew what kind of power he had and that he was determined to use it," recalled Carey. "Tough guy, nothing scared him, but I found that he was a reasonable guy, too."[27]

It was still dark out when Ravitch got Shanker on the phone and then went to see him. They talked for nearly two hours. It was morally wrong, the union leader insisted, to commit retirees' contributions in order to protect the wages of current employees, and would violate his role as a fiduciary of the payroll contributions that school employees made toward their financial security in retirement.

Maybe so, countered Ravitch, but if the city went broke, there will be untold human suffering—for example, no one would then extend credit to the city's hospitals or child care institutions. What possibly could a bankruptcy court judge do about that?

Furthermore, argued Ravitch, the union's contracts would matter little or not at all in a bankruptcy court proceeding. The contracts would be tossed out as creditors' claims came to the fore and were worked out.

The two friends parted at four in the morning.

"I'll call you," Shanker said.[28]

Ravitch went home and telephoned Carey: Shanker was unbowed, Ravitch relayed, but perhaps open to further talks.

Sometime after seven, Ravitch went to Carey's office, where he found David Burke and Judah Gribetz working on the next frantic improvisation. The city had until three o'clock on Friday afternoon, the closing time for commercial banks, to lay claim to the union's contribution and keep the omnibus Financial Emergency Act from crumbling, taking the barely solvent city down right along with it.

Gribetz was a cautious and trusted Carey adviser, suitably protective of the governor and an invaluable counselor as a huge flood of bills and other paperwork requiring legal vetting coursed through the executive chamber that year and beyond. Burke, too, was essential to the daily functioning of the Carey team, helping translate the values and views of the governor and put them into action when others couldn't grasp their import.

Burke in particular helped Carey sort and think through his instincts and utterances in real time. He also relayed to Carey significant staff proposals and insights, and fought for relevant concepts even when the governor's initial reaction to them was negative or—sometimes—explosive. Burke counseled Carey, closely, incisively, and often wisely on the political strategies that helped shape the state's response to the fiscal crisis, including the uses for advisers from the business world such as Felix Rohatyn, the creation of the MAC board, the EFCB, and finally the pursuit of federal aid. While Burke's name appeared on no paper and his voice was not heard at press conferences, he and Carey shared a strong bond. They were both progressive Democrats who had ties with and admired the Kennedys. Burke's behind-the-scenes touch with staff, bankers, and federal officials, was light, yet often effective.

By the fall of 1975, however, even the most able Carey hands were hostages to fast-racing events. Burke asked Stephen Berger at the Department of Social Services to lead an informal committee of state agencies that might be called upon to step in on behalf of vulnerable populations, such as city hospital patients and welfare clients, in the event of a city bankruptcy. Not surprisingly, this went unpublicized. Berger recalled that he put together a proposal to issue partial-payment welfare checks. State budget officials considered issuing IOUs. But these were the kind of draconian measures Carey hoped never to have to employ.

At City Hall in lower Manhattan, reporters alerted by their night city desks to Shanker's brash move arrived early to Room 9, down the hall from the mayor's office. Many took up a betting pool, wagering on whether the city would again cheat disaster; most bet that it would not, recalled George Arzt, who worked for the *New York Post*. Holders of city notes began showing up at tellers' windows in the Municipal Building to redeem their investments ahead of a crash. They were asked to come back a few hours later, for the city lacked sufficient deposits to pay off their notes at that moment, with the state aid package unavailable and suddenly in doubt.

City lawyers meanwhile drew up a bankruptcy petition for possible filing with the federal court in the worst case; a police car waited, idling, outside City Hall for fast delivery of the dreaded document.

It was as early as the spring of 1975 that Mayor Beame had consulted with Charles Seligson of the law firm Weil Gotshall, who had served in the transition team after Beame's election and was perhaps the city's most respected expert on bankruptcy. But after Seligson died in September, 1975, Seligson's partner, Ira Millstein, an antitrust and trade regulation specialist, became the city's bankruptcy counsel and strongly advocated keeping the city out of bankruptcy at all costs. Millstein was now in the hot seat.[29]

"So many people were talking glibly about putting the city in Chapter Nine, Ten or Eleven. It would have been totally unmanageable," Millstein told Paul Hoffman for his book *Lions of the Eighties: The Inside Story of the Powerhouse Law Firms*, noting that the federal bankruptcy law had been drafted in the 1930s as smaller cities went into default and was "inappropriate" for a city the size of New York. It was estimated that New York City's bond- and noteholders alone numbered 160,000 individuals and institutions across the country. A bankruptcy filing by a city as huge as New York could bring chaos. "But as a lawyer," he said, "it was my duty to prepare for it."[30]

Millstein worked through the night with the city's in-house lawyers to prepare a streamlined bankruptcy petition and got the mayor's signature on its bottom line in case it had to be presented to a bankruptcy judge. Bernard Richland, who headed the city law department, put the petition in his briefcase and there it stayed as the day's events unfolded. At the same time, city lawyers obtained from state supreme court justice Irving Saypol—the former U.S. attorney who had prosecuted Julius and Ethel Rosenberg—an order outlining the city's view of its expense priorities in the event of a default. Topping the list were not the bondholders, as the state and federal constitutions arguably required, but rather essential public services, followed by the city's payrolls and then, and only then, payments to holders of city debts. The state judge signed the papers at his home.

"We were simply acting as lawyers and trying to dream up the parade of *horribles* if things got crazy," said Millstein. "The city money was in a variety of banks. We did not have an anti-setoff provision to prevent the banks from seizing the money to satisfy their own claims, and we did not have any mechanism to stop that from happening. There was a question under the state constitution as to whether payroll checks to city employees could be honored if there were insufficient funds in the bank to meet both the city's debt and the payroll. There were rumors that the sanitation men would walk off their trucks if they didn't get paid. Only a judge could postpone debt service and permit the payrolls to be met . . . We drew the simplest petition we could. Nobody had ever done anything like this in the history of the world. This was bottom-line desperation."[31]

Beame said in an interview with the *Times* some years later that he phoned Victor Gotbaum during the day and asked the union leader to purchase more MAC bonds if Al Shanker reneged on his required payment under the Financial Emergency Act. Gotbaum, though, wanted to see what Shanker would do first; he is even said to have bullied Shanker to participate, threatening to throw him out the eighth-floor window of the teachers union president's Park Avenue South office if he refused.[32] Beame, for his part, also called the head of the sanitation workers union, John DeLury, seeking a similar assurance of eleventh-hour assistance if needed. DeLury agreed, according to Sid Frigand, the mayor's press secretary, though Carey didn't know it, and no commitment was made to Beame in writing. "He had that in his pocket, and was not as nervous as a lot of us were," insisted Frigand, recalling the mayor's round of calls.[33]

Nonetheless, Frigand drafted a mayoral press release to be released only in case of a default. It began, "I have been advised by the comptroller"—Harrison Goldin, a Beame critic and rival who had supported the creation of the EFCB and gained a vote on the panel equal to that of the mayor—"that the City of New York has insufficient cash on hand to meet debt obligations due today. This constitutes the default that we have struggled to avoid."

Shanker, unaware of the full range of attempted countermeasures in flux, phoned Ravitch's home and left a message with one of his children.

Ravitch returned the call soon thereafter.

"I want to meet with you and Carey" was all Shanker told him.

"Just tell me where," replied Ravitch.[34]

Shanker got in a cab and headed over to Ravitch's apartment, where trade union leader Harry Van Arsdale and former Mayor Robert Wagner soon arrived to join the discussion. Gribetz, too, arrived, as did Carey, with Simon Rifkind. Some used the building's back staircase in case any reporters had gotten wind of the secret meeting and tried to waylay them.

There wasn't much food in Ravitch's refrigerator, so the nervous host pulled out a stack of matzoh from a cupboard and set it on a table. A tense, four-hour discussion ensued.

It was after one o'clock when Shanker relented: "OK," he said. "I'll do it," and got up to leave.

"I simply think he realized that it would have been a catastrophe if he hadn't," Ravitch said, many years later.[35]

Shanker never mentioned the sensitive topic of the in-limbo teachers contract during the conversation, but Carey knew it was on his mind and took Shanker aside, offering to try to have the contract dispute mediated by someone favorably disposed toward labor. In the governor's recollection, the gesture may have made all the difference.

Whatever the case, in the wake of his concession Shanker headed downtown to UFT headquarters, and Carey went out to a lunch at the 21 Club. Ravitch, alone again in his apartment, was seized with worry, realizing that in less than two hours the banks closed, and Shanker's staff might not have enough time between now and then to deposit the $453 million the city needed to meet its bond and payroll obligations by the end of the afternoon.

Ravitch placed a series of calls to the state's banking commissioner, John Heimann, to the clearinghouse association of national banks in New York City, and to the federal comptroller of the currency, asking them to find a way to keep the doors of certain banks open till five o'clock. Carey, Rohatyn, and others also made calls. Finally, it was arranged that the state-chartered Manufacturers Hanover, the city's pay agent, would keep its doors open till five. The Federal Reserve Bank also extended its hours.

In the end, the unprecedented extension of hours proved unnecessary. As promised, the teachers union showed up before the standard three o'clock bank closing time with a check from its pension fund. New York City had avoided default with only hours to spare, its closest brush with financial collapse in its history, or ever since.

Shanker spoke to reporters shortly after 2:05 PM about his decision. It was not universally popular with his members, but he said the pressure to buy the MAC bonds had come not from the governor, or from the mayor, but from the *situation*. And in his paid column, "Where We Stand," in the *Times* that Sunday, Shanker wrote, "If the city goes down, you don't have a system," and added that default would have meant "economic, social, and political catastrophe."[36] Still, the union's wings were clipped. It would take seventeen months for the EFCB to approve the 1975 teachers' contract, and, what was more, the union went on to lose fifteen thousand teachers and classroom aides, or 20 percent of its membership, during the ensuing three years of austerity measures mandated by the control board.

At his apartment later that afternoon, Ravitch was relieved but visibly exhausted as his wife returned from her job at Columbia University. Eager to prepare a dinner for some of her former college classmates coming to visit, she spied matzoh crumbs strewn on the floor, and did not hide her displeasure.

She turned to her husband for an explanation.

"Diane," said Richard Ravitch, pleadingly. "You can't believe what went on here today, and you wouldn't if I told you."[37]

# 7

# The Battle of Washington

*President Ford <u>doesn't</u> tell New York City to "Drop Dead,"
as an instantly famous headline asserts, yet does vow, all the
same, to veto any bill intended to insulate the errant city
from a default, forcing Governor Carey to navigate
the political minefield amid stiff resistance from the
White House and Congress.*

More than a month before the city teachers union president Al Shanker had his last-minute change of heart and gave New York City a reprieve from fiscal ruin in mid-October, 1975, President Gerald Ford was being urged by one his best-known subordinates, Vice President Nelson Rockefeller, to extend a helping hand to the city before, not after, it defaulted on its debts and obligations. Initially somewhat resistant to supporting the cause of Abe Beame and Hugh Carey, Rockefeller came to the city's defense at the moment when Carey was preparing to convene the special session of the New York State Legislature to push through the Financial Emergency Act containing $2.3 billion in city assistance and the game-changing Emergency Financial Control Board. Rockefeller, speaking to reporters on September 5, 1975, disclosed his fear that New York City could go bust, and announced that this unparalleled event would have "very serious implications in terms of the ability of our municipalities to sell bonds. The repercussions would be hard to estimate because this has never happened in modern history and certainly not in the largest city in our country. Therefore, it is very serious, and very tragic."[1]

Then, in early October, with the city still struggling to meet its huge short-term debts together with its payroll and other current expenses, Rockefeller took action internally, urging Ford to approve federal loan guarantees for the city, and thereby separating himself most noticeably from two of the president's senior financial advisers—Federal Reserve Board chairman Arthur Burns and treasury secretary William Simon. Burns and Simon each were contending at the White House that a Big Apple default would have little effect on the nation's banking system, municipal bond market, and overall economy. Their assessment comported with the views of political advisers who wanted President Ford, by nature a laid-back and understanding leader, to show Republicans in advance of the 1976 presidential primary that he could and would be tough toward a liberal Democratic city that so many of them viewed as synonymous with financial profligacy, excessive taxation, crime, poverty, and even sin.

Carey's creation of the MAC board and then the EFCB were calculated to impress Ford, who four months earlier, in a May letter, had admonished Mayor Beame for the city's affordable mass-transit fare, for what he called the exceptionally generous wages and pensions of the city's employees, and for the amenity of free tuition at the City University of New York. These and other socially beneficial costs had, in many ways, helped lift the city's working poor and immigrant population into the middle-class mainstream. But from the vantage point of Ford and other conservatives, and given the relentless pressure from the recession, these and other public expenditures now appeared most unwise and imprudent, and no doubt promulgated for self-serving reasons by politicians and their allies in labor, welfare advocates, and other constituencies. Just as bad, according to the president's sense of fiscal propriety, had been the eagerness of the big banks to underwrite more and more debt with little apparent concern for their municipal client's ability to repay the loans and redeem the bonds over time.

The first question for Carey and his circle was whether the issue of New York's worthiness for federal assistance would be treated as a matter for traditional political debate and negotiation in Washington, or would be relegated instead to an arena dominated and defined by those who, like William Simon, argued heatedly against helping the city for largely ideological and moral reasons. Deserving of help or not, Carey felt the city could not survive without an infusion of federal aid, even with the passage of the Financial Emergency Act. State officials estimated that the city would only be able to meet its expenses until December 11, 1975. With the state doing all it could possibly do, and with the city acceding to stringent economies under the gaze of the EFCB, only the federal government possessed the power to protect the nation's largest city—and, the governor argued, the country too—from the economic consequences and international fallout that he contended a New York City fiscal breakdown would trigger.[2]

The differences of opinion about "the New York question" within the White House went largely unnoticed by the press, but they were substantial. James Cannon, who headed the president's Domestic Council, and his deputy, Richard Dunham, had sent Ford a memo over the summer countering

Simon's strident public and private opposition to providing aid of any sort to the city. The pair argued for a moderate approach, urging Ford to state publicly that the city's strained and straitened circumstances were not unique but in fact were common to "most major cities in the nation" ("Boston, for example, has considerably increased its borrowing in the last few years to cover deficits," they noted). They internally recommended that Ford create a Domestic Council/Economic Policy Board to keep an eye on the fiscal problems of all big cities. Their reasoning was strategic: "By generalizing the study to include all major urban areas, we can continue to monitor closely the New York City situation"—as Ford had prescribed back in his May letter to Beame—"yet avoid the political problems inherent in any direct attempt to pressure the city toward fiscal reform . . . Nothing would play more into the hands of the unions and the city administration, which could claim—to a highly responsive audience—that the Ford administration was threatening and bullying the city into actions designed to harm the low and middle classes."[3]

In a reflection of the wide range of advice reaching the president, treasury undersecretary Edwin H. Yeo III also sent Ford a memo a bit later in the summer describing the likelihood of a New York City default from, as he put it, the city's perpetual overspending, the failings of the MAC board ("an impotent and divided group"), and Carey's "increasingly obscure role" and unwillingness to take charge of the situation. What was needed, Yeo stated, was federal legislation to foster a "suitable bankruptcy procedure," a "review of civil disturbance arrangements," and a rescue plan for the "20–25 or more smaller banks [that] could become insolvent." Carey, who was not privy to these recommendations, learned after one trek to Washington with David Burke that Simon was unavailable to see him but that Yeo would be able to receive the governor and his people at his office located outside Washington, D.C. Carey took the apparent snub in stride, finding a shred of humor in it.[4]

"Hi ho, hi ho," he chimed over and over as he returned to Albany, Burke remembered, "it's off to Yeo we go!"[5] He would not, and did not, concede defeat easily.

In August, Ford asked the Treasury Department to prepare a draft statement articulating his view that the city had not yet done enough to solve its own problems and detailing the kind of steps it needed to take. But the formal statement of his position—a much-needed statement of clarification as well as a possible starting point for negotiations with city and state leaders—never emerged. At the very least, it would have represented a step away from the all-or-nothing commentaries that Simon was putting out, in which he warned that providing aid to the city under anything but "punitive" and "painful" terms would leave the federal government fielding an unmanageable and unwelcome flood of similar requests for help from municipalities that also didn't want to rein in their spending and mend their ways.[6] At the same time, Alan Greenspan, chairman of the president's Council of Economic Advisers and an ardent admirer of philosopher Ayn Rand's ideas embracing laissez-faire capitalism, believed along with Simon that the federal government should not play a role in keeping the city from defaulting. But Ford economic adviser L. William Seidman, whose principal charge was to curb runaway inflation, appeared more amenable to the view that a default posed a risk to the nation's recovery.

The evening of September 2, three days before Carey's speech opening the state legislative special session, Ford, Carey, the state comptroller and many of their advisers gathered under an elegant chandelier around a huge oval table in the White House cabinet room.[7] Carey also was permitted a private, roughly forty-five-minute conversation with the president, a "heart-to-heart" in which, as the governor told the press afterward, Ford indicated that he would consider helping the city if the state continued to take strong measures to put the city's house in order. White House press secretary Ron Nessen had a different take on it. He insisted at a news conference that, despite rumors to the contrary, there had been no change in the president's firm opposition to federal aid to bail out the city, though of course, he added, the president's door would always remain open to the good governor from New York.

According to Carey, speaking years later, the meeting was pivotal in his fight to rescue New York, for Ford told him that while he would like to help the city, he couldn't, given the antipathy that most Republican members of Congress harbored toward a federal aid program, not to mention the similar sentiments of many Democrats.

"You've had a great time running around Washington seeking help, but I know that you know that you don't have the votes," Carey recalled Ford telling him. He told Ford that while Congress wasn't on his side, he planned to see a mutual friend of theirs, Arizona Representative John Rhodes, the Republican minority leader in the House and on the Banking, Finance and Urban Affairs Committee, to turn things around.[8] And off he went. Just in case Carey was getting to his old congressional colleague, the president received a position paper from William Simon about a week later casting aspersions on the governor.

"In recent weeks it has become clear that avoiding a default is less important to the governor than his own political future," the Treasury secretary wrote. Carey was putting forth in Albany an "unworkable plan . . . designed to shift the blame elsewhere: either to Washington or the banks," Simon contended.[9]

Carey decided to seek the help of Melvin Laird, the powerful former Republican congressman from Wisconsin and Nixon administration secretary of defense, who was then traveling the world as a senior representative for *Readers Digest* (among other things, his job was to keep the magazine's postal rates steady in foreign countries where it had large numbers of subscribers). Carey was on friendly terms with Laird, who had helped Ford become the House minority leader, a post which, as fate would have it, helped lead to Ford's abrupt swearing-in as the disgraced Richard Nixon's presidential successor in August of 1974.

"Can you help me? What should I do?" a rather desperate Carey remembered asking Laird when he reached him by phone from Albany shortly after the passage of the state bill creating the Emergency Financial Control Board—something which had by no means softened Washington's opposition to helping the city avoid bankruptcy definitely and for the foreseeable future.

Laird told him to fly down to Washington and "bring your golf clubs." He also told him to bring a hundred dollars.

"I didn't know how many 'coupons' I had with Laird," recalled Carey, "but I thought I'd take a whack at it." So he went.[10]

Laird was waiting for Carey as he touched down at Dulles Airport. He had a silver limousine furnished with a prominent bar and invited Carey to join him inside for the luxurious ride to Burning Tree Golf Course and its beautiful, exclusive greens.

"Do you have the hundred dollars on you?" Laird asked as Carey climbed in.

"I do," Carey nodded.

"OK—here's the plan," Laird quickly explained. "We're going to play, and I'm quite sure that I am going to beat you, and then you're going give me my hundred dollar winnings in the clubhouse." And that's how it happened, with the New York Democrat only too happy to pay up in full view of Laird's appreciative, partisan chums. "He wanted me to be humbled in front of all his Republican pals," Carey said with a laugh.

The stunt done, they discussed Ford's intractability.

"Here's your problem," Laird said. "Jerry's been told by somebody that when New York City collapses, Chicago may become the financial center of the U.S. Your friend Daley"—Chicago Democratic Mayor Richard Daley—"heard this and that's why you're not getting any votes out of Illinois in Congress." He was referring to the large Illinois congressional delegation, which included Senator Adlai Stevenson III, an influential member of the Banking Committee.

"Who's doing this?" Carey asked.

Laird leaned in. "Well, Rummy comes from Illinois," he said, referring to Donald Rumsfeld, Ford's chief of staff and a former congressman from the state. "Rummy—he's your problem!"

Carey was taken aback. "I know Don. He's no enemy of mine." But he said he'd go see Rumsfeld, though Laird had other ideas for the governor: "You know Daley, don't you?"

"Yeah, I once did him a small favor," said Carey, referring to his role in a congressional site visit to one of Chicago's federally subsidized poverty programs in the 1960s, which concluded with a finding that the city's programs were properly run and not money pits, as some had charged.

"Then you'd better collect," Laird advised.

Carey said he went to see the storied boss of the Chicago political machine and learned that some bankers had indeed been telling him that the Windy City stood to become the nation's financial capital if the Big Apple went under. The governor used all his considerable gifts of persuasion and gab to disabuse Daley of the rather fanciful notion, while Stevenson's staffers at the same time were hearing from Felix Rohatyn and others at Lazard Freres that New York City was working mightily to mend its ways with active state support.

Carey and the state's lobbyist in Washington, James Larocca, soon called upon the former New York governor W. Averell Harriman to help take Carey's case for federal assistance to Senator William Proxmire of Wisconsin, who, all-importantly, chaired the Senate Banking, Housing, and Urban Affairs Committee. In part out of his friendship for Carey, but also because he felt that letting the city go bust would harm Ford politically, Laird faithfully followed up the Burning Tree outing with a flurry of phone of calls and visits to Washington movers-and-shakers to change Ford's mind. "I had several discussions with Jerry Ford because I thought his was a very dangerous position to have, not only in New York but around the world."[11] He also got in touch with Rumsfeld. "I said, 'Rummy, you're making a hell of a mistake here. We can't let New York go down the drain," Laird recounted to author Dale Van Atta for the 2008 biography, *With Honor: Melvin Laird in War, Peace, and Politics*. According to the account, Rumsfeld yielded to Laird's persistence. Although Rumsfeld hadn't been deeply involved in the White House discussions about New York City, he had seen the advantages for Daley's Chicago if New York City went bankrupt.

Laird also imported West German chancellor Helmut Schmidt when Schmidt stopped at the *Readers Digest* headquarters in Chappaqua, New York, while on his way to the International Monetary Fund conference in Washington, asking him to remind Ford about the importance of New York City's survival for the global economy. The opportunity arose at the October 3 meeting when Ford asked the German official, "How's the Bundesbank? How's the mark?" Schmidt responded, "Mr. President, never mind the Bundesbank or the mark. If you let New York go broke, the dollar is worth"—and here Schmidt used the German word for excrement—*"scheisse!"*[12] Schmidt said publicly that a default by New York City would have a "domino effect, striking other world financial centers such as Zurich and Frankfurt," and cited the heavy impact of two 1974 bank failures involving the Herstatt Bank of Cologne and the Franklin National Bank of New York.

The trepidations of the leader of one of America's most important postwar allies apparently did not go unnoticed by the leader of the free world or key influencers.[13]

On October 8, Fed chairman Burns modified his earlier position, stating that the impact of a New York City default might not be so minimal. He told the Joint Economic Committee of Congress that "protracted congressional debate will keep the markets uncertain and in turmoil" and if Congress were inclined to bail out the city, "I wish you would do it quickly."[14] At the same time, a dealer in tax-exempt notes and bonds was far more blunt, telling *Business Week* that "New York is like a disease that is contaminating all insurers, there is total panic in the credit markets; the city has taken the state down with it, and if the state goes, others will follow."[15]

Soon, Ford was asked at a news conference for his view on the various bailout bills pending in Congress (and going nowhere). He said that despite his reservations about this kind of legislation, it would be "very premature to make any comment." Here, then, was a signal, clearly, that Ford was not completely closed to helping the city avoid default. In response to a follow-up question, he added, "Unless they come in with a balanced budget, unless they get some state aid from the State of New York by some means or other, I am just very reluctant to say anything other than 'no' until I see the fine print, until I see what New York City has done."[16]

All this time Carey was keeping up the pressure on his cohorts and colleagues in the Congress and working to coordinate his red-flag warnings about the dangers of default and the state's commitment to a balanced city budget with those of bankers, bond dealers, and other governors and mayors who were testifying before several congressional committees. Mayor Beame also sounded the alarm, and managers of the city's purchasing department called New York City's now-nervous suppliers around the country and urged them to contact their congressmen about the need to help the city. Lew Rudin, who with his brother, Jack, headed one of the city's oldest real estate dynasties and in 1971 founded the Association for a Better New York, defended the Big Apple against its many detractors. This kind of extensive, nationwide lobbying was orchestrated to a large extent by the politically masterful Carey. It was helped not only by his familiarity with the ways and means of Washington, but by his skillful blend of tough confrontation and gentle negotiation.

"I come to you today with as great a sense of urgency as any governor has ever felt in the history of this country," Carey told Senator William Proxmire and his Banking Committee on October 9, a day after Ford's potentially significant news conference. "As a former member of Congress," the governor said, "I know full well how frequently you are asked for financial assistance, for tax breaks, and for the means to enhance wealth and credibility. I come today on a very unique mission—to tell you that the default of New York City will cause not only the bankruptcy of the state and city of New York, the devastation of seventeen million people, but unforeseeable national consequences of such an adverse and sizeable nature that we have no choice but to prevent them." He touched on the stringent steps his administration had helped to bring about: the wage freeze, "in a city with the strongest municipal unions in the nation"; a freeze on new capital spending, "in a city with the largest construction industry in the nation"; a new state fiscal control board "in the financial capital of the world" which "completely controls New York City's access to money"; the rescue of the state Urban Development Corporation from default; a New York State government hiring freeze, resulting in 5,800 fewer employees; and one of the most favorable collective bargaining settlements in state history, holding 140,000 employees to a 3.5 percent raise. "Now, I must tell you, as a state, we have done all we can to help New York City. New York State cannot guarantee the securities of New York City. We have neither the resources nor the power . . . Now we seek recognition from the federal government for what we have done. We need and deserve federal assistance. We are not asking for a handout or a bailout. We are asking for a sensible solution—a limited guarantee of the securities issued by the Municipal Assistance Corporation, the state financing agency for the City of New York."[17]

On October 11, Vice President Rockefeller publicly pulled away from the Ford administration's official stance, and radically so. Speaking at a Columbus Day event in Manhattan, the vice president urged Congress to take immediate action. "Time is of the essence and the resolution of this immediate New York City situation is crucial . . . it will be a true test of the responsiveness of our congressional system as to whether the Congress can act in time to avoid catastrophe."[18]

Beame and the state Emergency Financial Control Board were negotiating a required three-year financial plan; it came to include an unspecified "thousands" of city layoffs on top of the twenty-one thousand city workers dismissed earlier in the year, extremely deep cuts to the city's capital budget, and the continuation of the controversial Beame-instituted city wage deferral through the life of the plan. Meanwhile, New York State's entanglements with the fiscally troubled city began to endanger materially the state's own bond offerings and ability to borrow, which is to say its very ability to survive the city crisis. One public authority of the state, the Housing Finance Agency, faced the possibility of default because it didn't have $90 million to redeem notes and those of a subsidiary due to mature on October 15; another authority, the Medical Care Facilities Finance Agency, was rescued only after New York City's Board of Estimate approved the temporary transfer of city funds from one city budget line to another—essentially an accounting maneuver, not an actual increase in overall city spending.

*Time* magazine's October 20 issue illustrated how far the city had sunk with a cover depicting Mayor Beame as a genteel hobo wearing a tattered top-hat, shaking a tin cup and pleading, "Brother, Can You Spare $4 Billion?"

The Congress remained unmoved, even after the city's harrowing near-calamity involving Al Shanker. Tip O'Neill Jr., the majority leader of the House, a proponent of aiding the city, said that, even after Carey's impassioned plea before the Senate Banking Committee and before Thomas Ludlow Ashley of Rhode Island and Carey's other former colleagues on the House Banking Subcommittee, legislation providing aid to the city was well short of the votes needed for approval. "If there were a vote today, I would have to say that New York would not prevail," O'Neill said.

As he would write later in his autobiography, Ford remained torn between his concern about the impact a default would have on city residents and their schools, hospitals, and fire and police protection, and his desire not to let city leaders and lenders off the hook for their years of fiscal irresponsibility.

In the end, the president reconciled these competing forces tugging on him by proposing a bill that would add a "Chapter 16" to the federal Bankruptcy Act in order to allow an insolvent municipality to file a petition with the U.S. District Court in New York stating that it was unable to pay its debts as they matured, and authorize the court to issue an automatic stay of creditor's lawsuits. The bill, Ford believed, would allow a gentler, "orderly" bankruptcy, and keep the city's remaining operating funds from getting tied up in years-long litigation. The court could authorize the sale of debt certificates secured by future city revenue, providing a short-term source of funds to carry on "essential services."

"The bankruptcy option," wrote Charles J. Orlebeke in a definitive study of the Ford White House during the city fiscal crisis, "appeared to offer [the president] both a morally satisfying and administratively feasible path."

But when, in a speech to the National Press Club on October 29, the president publicly proposed his bankruptcy bill, delivering his first formal statement on the New York crisis since his May letter to Beame, his tone and message were noticeably harsh. In the fateful speech, Ford ignored the Herculean efforts that Carey and Beame had made over the past six months. He termed the city's fiscal mismanagement "unique among municipalities through the United States," and alluded to "a steady stream of unbalanced budgets, massive growth in the city's debt, extraordinary increases in public employee contracts, and total disregard of independent experts who warned again and again that the city was courting disaster." Ford furthermore denounced "scare talk" used by New York politicians and bankers—"the blatant attempt in some quarters to frighten the American people and their representatives in Congress into panicky support of patently bad policy"—and he added: "The people of this country will not be stampeded. They will not panic when a few desperate New York City officials and bankers try to scare New York's mortgage payments out of them."

The city's "high wages and pensions . . . its tuition-free university system, its city-run hospital system, and welfare administration," as Ford saw them, meant the city must be held accountable for its profligacy, and make its own inevitably painful solutions. Ford also said the city's political leaders had nonetheless shown that they could not be trusted to do so. An unearned and undeserved bailout by Congress would, he said, set a "dangerous precedent," as it signaled that the federal government would provide "immediate rewards and eventual rescue for every other city that follows the tragic example of our largest city."

To allow the city to go on spending more than it could pay for would set a hazardous precedent for the whole country.

The city, Ford said flatly, must face its "day of reckoning."

"I can tell you, and tell you now," he pronounced, "that I am prepared to veto any bill that has at its purpose a bailout of New York City to prevent a default."[19]

Ford's speech derailed some of the inroads that Carey had been making in the Congress. On October 30, Senator Proxmire's committee approved, 8 to 5, loan guarantee legislation for the city, and the House banking committee followed suit. Ford's statement stopped the momentum cold in its tracks.

More broadly, Ford's line in the sand marked the beginning of a change arising in American political life, one that would be expressed in the angry citizen property-tax revolts a few years away. California voters in 1978 would approve Proposition 13, which deprived that state of increased taxes to pay for its systems of transportation, education, sewerage, and potable water, in an antitax movement that helped set the stage for the election of Ronald Reagan—the conservative former governor of California—as president in 1980, and his inaugural address in January, 1981, in which he declared, "Government is not the solution to our problems—government *is* the problem." In 1975, the debate over New York's fate offered an early clue to the antitax fervency that was soon to gather to a gale force, although few then could have imagined how successful that ideology would be, the vast social inequalities it would foster, or how ferocious and long-lasting would be the public and political backlash against unions, government, and public regulation of private industry and Wall Street. These first gusts emphasizing the finite nature of the public purse—which liberalism, in its view of government as the principal vehicle of opportunity and advancement, had never really defined—eventually turned into cyclonic winds in the 1980s as corporate interests and influence rose, dominated, and flourished.

Ford's immediate need to court the right-wing of his party in the face of a Reagan challenge was a crucial factor in his giving New York the cold shoulder. He made up his mind that fall, too, to exclude from his reelection ticket Vice President Rockefeller, known as a liberal Republican and inextricably identified with his home state of New York, selecting instead the conservative Kansas Senator Bob Dole as his vice-presidential running mate.

Felix Rohatyn recalled that he and Carey watched Ford deliver his National Press Club speech on a television in the governor's Manhattan office and were "thoroughly depressed" as they sat down afterward for a late dinner at Elaine's, a watering hole on Manhattan's East Side. A newsboy walked into the casual bistro favored by Manhattan notables at about ten o'clock, hawking the early edition of the *New York Daily News,* and no one could believe their eyes. The front page headline in 144-point type, soon to be seen by millions of readers, screamed: "FORD TO CITY: DROP DEAD," followed by the explanatory words: "Vows He'll Veto Any Bail-Out."[20]

Powerful and unsettling—and instantly famous—the headline was an "unfortunate overstatement," as James Cannon put it years later at a Hofstra University forum on the fiscal crisis, for Ford had never actually uttered the words "drop dead."[21] And he did not harbor malice toward its citizens.

Ford himself was deeply stung. As late as 2001, five years before his death, he approached David Burke at a gala dinner honoring the ex-president with the John F. Kennedy Library's "Profile in Courage" award for having delivered his controversial pardon of Richard Nixon, and told the former Carey aide: "I want to get one thing straight: I never said 'New York City drop dead.' I never said that," Burke recalled.

The headline, though, reflected that he was, in fact, "prepared to veto any bill that has at its purpose a bailout of New York City to prevent a default," as he had put it. It arguably cost him New York's forty-one electoral votes in the close November, 1976, presidential election that followed against Democrat Jimmy Carter of Georgia, after Ford's defeat of Reagan in the primary. Melvin Laird said years later that the headline was exceeded only by Ford's pardon of Nixon in the level of damage it caused his popularity and chances in the 1976 election. "That headline caused him a lot of harm, almost as much harm as the pardon did."[22]

According to Rohatyn, Carey glared at the headline before him at Elaine's and pronounced: "Now we're going to win." It seemed to everyone sitting at the table that he was right and that Ford would not be able to withstand the heat. Yet Carey worried privately about political fallout.[23] Despite what he told his dinner companions, he felt the headline might cause Ford to harden in opposing a New York aid package so he wouldn't appear to waffle or flip-flop at a critical moment, with the eyes of the country and the world upon him. Still, he felt that Ford would remain true to his word of September 2 and support federal assistance if Carey could bring Republicans (as well as many reluctant Democrats) around in Congress.

Carey put the pressure on all the same, exploiting the headline's national publicity, pointing a finger of accusation at Ford and the Republicans for promoting the city's demise at the risk not just of the city itself but of almost everyone. Speaking to a gathering of the AFL-CIO in upstate New York, the governor was indignant, saying it "isn't fair when the President of the United States hauls off and kicks the people of the city of New York in the groin."[24] On the first of November he delivered a blistering statewide radio and television address, emphasizing that the threat of a default had already raised the cost of borrowing in many cities and states. Knowledgeable and well-organized, he further declared that the "Ford formula deliberately unravels every step we've taken to solve our own problems," as the easier bankruptcy option he proposed would scare off prospective investors in municipal bonds. "Who would risk his funds knowing that the government could avoid repayment simply by slipping into bankruptcy?" the governor asked. Carey also accused Ford of effectively running for reelection at the expense of the city's millions of residents, with his "simplistic, self-defeating plan . . . designed more to appease the Republican Party's Reagan wing than to help New Yorkers."

If the city defaulted, Carey stated, the holders of the city's $14 billion in outstanding bonds and notes would conservatively lose $6 billion in the value of those securities. "That money will be written off on tax returns, and that means $2 billion less in federal tax payments." He added that it would be left to the U.S. Treasury to pay the cost of unemployment insurance and welfare assistance when businesses owed money by the city, including those "in communities such as Grand Rapids, Michigan"—Ford's hometown—went under, while there likely would be "tremors and collapses in local governments around America, including agencies of New York State." Even so, Carey acknowledged that Ford was correct in describing the city's fiscal irresponsibility. But he said the blame belonged to many, mentioning "city officials and interest groups; banks that did not ask the hard questions; a state legislature and hand-picked vice president"—Rockefeller—"that specifically authorized every fringe and pension benefit and every unwise borrowing Mr. Ford now attacks so righteously; and presidents who diverted tens of billions of dollars to foreign dictatorships and senseless war, and who plunged our economy into its worst crisis in forty years."

Carey's blistering declaration alluded to a "skeptical, hostile" Congress and the antipathy that New York City aroused in many quarters.

"Our city," he conceded, "is often abrasive and arrogant, sometimes cold and unfeeling, always challenging. For a lot of reasons it has incurred the scorn of some of our countrymen; because of our pace and tone of voice, because of the colors of our skins and the accents in which we speak, and our tradition as a magnet for the disaffected, the dispossessed. What we're hoping to buy" from the White House and Congress "is time to finish the job we've started. We don't want to be bailed out. We don't want to be a ward of the federal government. I ask Mr. Ford not to work against us to make New York bankrupt. I cannot believe that the specter of temporary political gain will lead him into driving a city into bankruptcy and risking the loss of taxpayers' dollars . . . If the financial structure of government is shaken, Mr. Ford will be accountable to all the people."

He had faith in the president, Carey concluded. "I spent more than a decade with Gerald Ford in Congress. We disagreed about many things. But I always found him a man ready to negotiate and compromise for a practical result."[25]

Later that day, a study released by the Joint Economic Committee of Congress found that default would hamper recovery from the recession by swelling the ranks of the unemployed by three hundred thousand nationally and depressing the gross national product by as much as 1 percent in 1976. Here was more fodder for Carey's argument. In another study soon to follow, two experts on municipal financing meticulously spelled out that a rise in interest costs to cities and states owing to the threat of a city default was already topping $180 million.[26]

At home and internationally, Carey's position drew great praise, and Ford's address heavy criticism. The *Times* of London termed Ford's statement barring federal aid to the city an "act of monumental folly." But at home, Carey still faced enormous obstacles, with House Speaker Carl Albert, an Oklahoma Democrat who supported aid to the city, noting that his constituent mail ran 8 to 1 against aiding the city. Even so, the tide of public sentiment seemed to be turning at last. Three national polls taken after Ford's National Press Club speech signaled this much-sought shift. One of them, a Harris poll conducted November 2–4, found that 69 percent of 1,549 persons surveyed favored assistance for the city if it didn't cost taxpayers outside the city any money, and as long as officials balanced the city budget. Only 18 percent of those polled opposed federal support, even though 82 percent felt the city was at fault for not living within its means.[27] After months of hoping against hope for federal aid, the wind appeared to be at Carey's back. In what could only be unintended praise for Carey, even Simon would write, in his political memoir, that the "pressure from all sides was enormous. The fear campaign and blackmail from all groups had their effect."

Missing from Ford's "orderly bankruptcy" legislation was any real specificity about the "essential services" the president promised to provide the city's citizenry in the event of a default, or how they would be administered. And Simon, in the wake of the speech, followed up on this point with Ford, asking him to define "essential services": "Is education an essential service, for example?" Or, for that matter, day care, outpatient clinics, jail guards, school lunches? The situation was more complicated than the president's formula had allowed, and meant inevitably that the federal government would become entangled in the messy business of running the city, something Ford, a proponent of federalism, wanted to avoid, seeing it as contrary to his belief that national authority should be devolved as much as possible to the states.[28]

Carey took his lobbying act on the road in early November, warning political and business leaders from St. Louis to Los Angeles of the ominous economic ramifications that a city bankruptcy portended for them, and of "the chaos of bankruptcy." As the governor grew more and more confident, Ford misspoke. During an appearance in San Francisco, the president defended his bankruptcy option and added that the city-on-the-bay deserved credit for having rebuilt after the 1906 earthquake from its own resources. "The reconstruction of San Francisco," he said, "was not a federal bailout." In fact, as some commentators were quick to point out, quake-devastated San Francisco got a great deal of federal financial aid, and additional reconstruction capital came from New York City commercial banks.[29]

Carey in a way reverted to his former role as an infantry battlefield planner, plotting his moves carefully as he sought to minimize hazards and casualties, and pushed forward on his path of risk. During one reprieve on Shelter Island, Carey gathered his thoughts, and walked "thirty or forty times" around the pool at advance chief Tom Regan's adjacent house without saying a word. Regan, ever loyal, shadowed him through the paces, even as Regan's wife observed and found the whole scene bewildering and perplexing. "She'd say to me, 'What the heck is he doing?'" recalled Regan, who stood in awe of Carey's intellect. "Let him be, I said. The man is *thinking*."[30]

As he had told Ford he would do, Carey repeatedly visited and called Arizona congressman John Rhodes, asking for advice on how to turn the tide in Congress. "John," Carey said, "how can we get the votes from your side?"

Said the Republican, "I'll tell you. If you let the bankruptcy bill come out with a bailout provision, then I can get you the votes."[31]

According to Carey, Rhodes advised him to provide House Republicans with political cover by marrying New York City aid provisions with the essential elements of the Ford bankruptcy amendment. Then, he said, Republican opponents of New York City from the farm fields of Kansas to the rocky shores of Maine would be able to tell their constituents that they were supporting bankruptcy, while omitting that they were also supporting aid.

It was, and remains, a common Washington dodge.

Carey then went to see Brooklyn representative Emanuel Celler, the dean of the New York congressional delegation and chairman of the House Judiciary Committee, and Rhode Island congressman Thomas Ashley, chairman of the Subcommittee on Banking, both of them Democrats and Carey friends from way back. Celler let the bankruptcy bill out of his Judiciary committee for debate, while Ashley released a bill that would provide seasonal loans to the city for three years. Then, on November 11, Rohatyn, Burke, Rifkind, and Gribetz went to Washington and met with Simon, Seidman, and Burns. The Carey entourage asked whether the president might now be willing to support federal assistance short of the city going into default, given that new city and state taxes were soon to be imposed and the city's debt was to be restructured as a result of pending Carey administration efforts in the state legislature.

Ford's financial advisers said Ford would support federal aid if the state approved such steps as outlined.

Carey had first hit on the debt restructuring plan earlier in the month in the wood-paneled offices of Simon Rifkind. At the time, the two men were munching on pastrami sandwiches, figuratively and literally chewing the fat.

"I didn't realize it, but Judge Rifkind had been a campaign volunteer—what we now call an advance man—for Governor Al Smith when he ran for president," Carey recalled. "All the hatred that Smith endured in the Deep South during that campaign: well, Rifkind was there. And then I spoke about how my father was saved from foreclosure on one of his mortgaged properties during the New Deal."[32]

Carey said his reminiscences about his late father got Rifkind talking about a famous Great Depression case, *Home Building and Loan Association v. Blaisdell*, in which the U.S. Supreme Court upheld an effort by the State of Minnesota to prevent banks from seizing and selling private homes on which they held a mortgage after the homeowners fell behind on their payments. Although Article 1, Section 10 of the U.S. Constitution prevents any state from "impairing the obligation of contracts," the high court ruled that Minnesota's act was legal and valid during an "emergency." New York State subsequently passed a bill, also validated by the court, which allowed distressed homeowners to withhold the payment of principal on all or part of their mortgage as long as they stayed current on interest, taxes, and insurance bills.

"Judge," Carey asked Rifkind, "I know we're not in a Great Depression, but what kind of public emergency would justify my doing that sort of thing now?"

"Oh," said the elder Rifkind, "fire, flood, natural catastrophe."

"What about a *financial* emergency depriving people of their livelihood?"

"If you invoked special authority under that kind of situation, it would be a matter of contest in the law," Rifkind answered. "You'd be challenged."

"OK," said Carey. "But if we passed a moratorium on city payments to bondholders, how long would it take for someone to challenge it and get a ruling from the courts?"

"Oh, we'd be in court for a year," replied Rifkind.

"That should do it," said Carey. "That's what we need right now—time."

"My man," Rifkind replied. "We'll try it."[33]

So the Carey administration put together a bill and pushed for the controversial debt moratorium as structured by Rifkind, which the state legislature passed on November 14 with the help of Senate Majority Leader Anderson, Republican, and Senate Minority Leader Manfred Ohrenstein, Democrat. The Moratorium Act, fondly recalled by Carey as the "Pastrami Agreement," affected three city note issues totaling $1.6 billion. Holders of those short-term notes, including many banks and individuals, had two options under the new law: They could swap their city securities for long-term MAC bonds, redeemable in ten years at 8 percent interest, or retain their note holdings and accept a suspension of payments on the principal for three years, or longer if the Legislature chose to stretch out the moratorium even further. They would receive interest on their holdings, but at a reduced rate.

The act's passage was yet another striking example of the exceptional working collaboration, however reluctant at times, that had developed among long-established adversaries—bankers, bond counsels, business people, union leaders, city and state politicians, Republicans and Democrats, upstate and downstate elected officials—and characterized the broad, Carey-led response to the crisis. "We may be creating the first commune in the U.S. on such a large scale," Rohatyn said then, only half-jokingly, speaking of the way long-estranged interests found common cause in rescuing the city. Holding together this shaky edifice was Hugh Carey and the confidence, and sacrifices, he was able to cajole from others.

The Moratorium Act effectively authorized postponing and reducing payments due to banks and other creditors who had invested in the city's short-term securities. Since, practically speaking, it represented a kind of default—even a "sham default," as critics called it—it satisfied Ford, who had vowed that he would not provide aid to the city until it had suffered adequately and defaulted because of its poor management. The moratorium was scheduled to begin on November 25 under the bill, but the Flushing National Bank, a small lending institution in one of the city's boroughs, Queens, challenged the measure with a lawsuit. The suit cited Article I, Section 10 of the U.S. Constitution.

With Thanksgiving approaching, Ford was in France for a Western economic summit in Rambouillet. At the request of Rohatyn, Arthur Burns, who was increasingly worried about the impact of a default on the international banking system (a Federal Reserve study released November 13 showed that 346 banks across the country held state and city securities in "significant" amounts, in half the cases exceeding 50 percent of their capitalization), told Helmut Schmidt and French president Valery Giscard d'Estaing in Ford's presence that Ford was quite possibly on the verge of putting New York City into bankruptcy. "The foreign leaders looked at Ford and said you have to be joking—it would be seen as the bankruptcy of America." recalled Rohatyn, who said he thanked Burns afterward.[34]

Republican members of Congress got the message, too, fearing that default might hurt their own states, and so leaders began telling the president, "I guess we have to do something," according to James Cannon.

Ford moved closer to a change, but first Carey had to begin driving through the state legislature $200 million in new taxes, something he and his aides finally managed to do in a late-night session on November 25, after days and nights of deadlock. The deal provided for an average 25 percent increase in the city's personal income tax levy on local residents, a 50 percent surcharge on the state's estate tax come April 1, 1976, and higher state taxes on cigarettes and certain personal services, such as those provided by barbers and beauticians. Carey worked for and obtained the support of Republican minority leader Perry Duryea to ensure passage in the assembly, as that chamber's black and Hispanic legislators, all of them Democrats, stood strongly opposed, citing the heavy impact of recent budget cuts on government employment and services on low-income constituents and communities. Still, Assembly Speaker Stanley Steingut had the support of most of his fellow Democrats in his chamber. In the state senate, Warren Anderson brought thirteen other Republicans with him in support of the tax package, and it was approved, 31 to 27, with the majority of Ohrenstein-led Democrats in the chamber voting for it.[35]

Legislators from the suburbs surrounding the city, in rancorous talks, blocked a proposed ten dollar increase in the city's automobile-use tax, replacing it with an increase in a bank tax. In addition, Carey ended another impasse by agreeing to take political responsibility for the tax hikes. But under a corollary agreement with Anderson, who was concerned lest Ford be blamed for the local tax increases that his administration was demanding, the EFCB was empowered to certify the need for the higher levies before they would be imposed. That maneuver spared both the governor and the legislature from direct blame for hiking taxes.

Amid the deal-making in the state legislature, Carey asked the city's five municipal unions—on top of their earlier agreement to purchase $2.5

billion in MAC bonds with their pension funds—to roll over another $1.2 billion in city and MAC notes that they held in order to ease repayment pressure on the city. Trustees for the city's retirement system contended that this was asking too much, and dug in their heels by refusing to purchase $860 million in city- and MAC-issued securities. Carey changed their minds, however, when he agreed to indemnify them from any future lawsuits alleging a breach of their fiduciary responsibilities.

Meanwhile, the banks stepped up, agreeing to extend maturities at a low rate of interest on about $550 million of city notes and $1.1 billion of MAC bonds in their portfolios.

Signs that Ford was ready to announce an aid package were evident as the flurry of activity in Albany got under way, as it was in keeping with the president's earlier demands for pain, sacrifice, and "self-help" by the city and state. Rhodes, the Republican leader in the House, came out in support of limited federal aid for New York City on November 11, a pronounce- ment that signaled that the president and members of his party were now willing to help. Two days later, White House officials contended that the Moratorium Act was tantamount to a declaration of voluntary default, and added that the state and city were jointly facing up to their years of fiscal irresponsibility.

Ford delivered a nationally televised press conference November 26, calling on Congress to approve new legislation to make $2.3 billion in direct federal loans available to the city on an annual basis for up to three years.[36]

It was a huge turnaround. Clearly, Carey had won the day. Ford asked Congress to amend the federal bankruptcy laws all the same, "so that if the New York plan fails, there will be an orderly procedure available" to deal with the unsatisfied claims of its various creditors and to reorganize the city's debt.

Federal administration officials indicated that seasonal loans were in their eyes preferable to loan guarantees for city borrowing because the former afforded federal officials more control as the city moved to implement badly needed reforms. "Governor Carey has taken full responsibility for the total package," Ford said, and he added that the loans and the commitment to repay them represented a "courageous stand" on the governor's part.

The House approved the historic bill by a tightly controlled 213 to 203 vote, with many Republicans from outside New York given license to vote Nay, but not so many as to change the desired outcome. The Senate approved it by a vote of 57 to 30, with conservatives labeling the measure a bottomless pit for American taxpayers, and proponents warning of the city's looming payment deadlines while complaining that the assistance might not be sufficient to stave off a bankruptcy in the future. Ford signed the measure into law without ceremony on December 9, 1975, allowing the city to avoid defaulting on more than $644 million in debt and payroll obligations for which it had neither sufficient funds nor any notion of where to get them. The final version required the seasonal loans to be repaid at the end of each city fiscal year—June 30—at an interest rate 1 percentage point above the prevailing Treasury borrowing rate, thus allowing the Treasury to realize a profit, some $30 million by the summer of 1978, when the last loans would be repaid. To ensure the city met the conditions of the loans, the city's familiar nemesis, treasury secretary Simon, was selected to monitor compliance.

"Bankruptcy for New York City is now behind us," Carey declared, hailing the president's decision. "Talk of collapse and chaos now should disappear."

But Carey's sense of relief and satisfaction turned out to be short-lived, simply because the city, while solvent, remained underfunded and forced to slash jobs and services to an unprecedented and draconian extent to balance its budget. "The pain is just beginning," warned Rohatyn, correctly anticipating the impact of the federally required, state-enforced retrenchment. Carey's choice for executive director of the EFCB in mid-1976 was Stephen Berger, who replaced Herb Elish. Described by critics as the governor's "hatchet man," Berger rode City Hall hard to chop its operating and capital budgets. The public hospital system had to shed thousands of employees, including its president, Dr. John Hollomon, a veteran of the Selma marches with the Rev. Martin Luther King Jr., after he tried to resist the EFCB's cost-slashing demands. The chairman of the City University's board of trustees, Alfred Giardino, quit in protest, citing political pressure to end CUNY's 129-year-old egalitarian tradition of free tuition at the city colleges (a shift Carey supported while at the same time pushing through the legislature legal changes that allowed the state to increase aid to the beleaguered system, and to assume the full cost of running its four-year colleges). The cutbacks ultimately affected every neighborhood of the recession-battered city, and sent parks, subways, schools, roads, police and fire services, and libraries into a downward spiral—a decline that would take at least two decades to reverse.

Then, too, a year after the "Pastrami Agreement," the state's Court of Appeals under Chief Justice Charles J. Breitel, formerly legal counsel to Republican governor Thomas Dewey, struck it down, calling the Moratorium Act a violation of the state and national constitutions and an abrogation of the contractual obligations under which the city had pledged its faith and credit for the repayment of bond principal and interest.

The court's decision came as a shock and a jolt to the city's and state's efforts. Indeed, Mayor Beame, visiting Jerusalem, placed a one-word note in a crevice of the Western Wall—"HELP."

Still, Court of Appeals Chief Judge Breitel's majority opinion balanced the contractual rights spelled out in the U.S. Constitution with Rifkind's courtroom arguments that ending the moratorium would be disruptive to the city and state in the extreme.[37] Under the ruling, bondholders were indeed constitutionally entitled to payment, both principal and interest, as anything else would undermine the legal underpinning of the municipal bond market. But the opinion added that the note holders did not have to be repaid immediately, as that would be "unnecessarily disruptive of the city's delicate financial and economic balance." He appreciated that the state or city needed some time to pay their debts.

When the ruling hit, Carey hastily assembled his advisers, including Rohatyn, who had played such a prominent and central role in keeping the city afloat.

John Connorton Jr., an assistant counsel to the governor, recalled the meeting.

"Hugh Carey was a force of calm and reassurance, telling us that we were simply not going back to Washington to ask for more federal aid," he said. "He told us we were going to have to find a way to take care of this ourselves."[38] And eventually they did, through a series of complex financing efforts negotiated with the state legislature.

"Carey had one of those strange psyches," said Peter Goldmark. "The greater the pressure, the bigger he got."[39]

# 8

# Thus Passes the Glory of the World

*After the city's cash crunch recedes, default looms for the state, while other battles also come to the fore.*

New York City's sorry reputation in the municipal credit market in the final weeks of 1975 did not stop at the city limits. Even in the wake of Congress's approval of seasonal loans for the city, the market—fickle and opportunistic—became suspicious of all varieties of "New York" debt issuances, including those of the state. The New York State budget might have been in decent shape, especially compared to the city budget, but the state's and the city's bonds shared the label "New York." And in light of the city's brush with near-bankruptcy, that was a brand more likely to inspire dread than confidence among investors.

So at the end of 1975, the market, rather than giving the Carey administration credit for leading the financial bailout of the city, moved in the opposite direction, effectively punishing the state for its ties and continuing involvement with the infamous city. The New York banks were particularly wary of four financially shaky statewide public authorities—the State Dormitory Authority (SDA), the Housing Finance Agency (HFA), the Medical Care Facilities Financing Authority (MCFFA), and the Environmental Facilities Corporation (ECF).

These four organizations, which were then developing a total of $2 billion in construction projects with state "moral obligation" bonds—the now much-questioned financing instruments on which the Urban Development Corporation defaulted in February of 1975—were forced to pay higher and higher interest rates in the latter months of 1975 until the big New York commercial lenders finally stopped investing in them altogether. That sent the large authorities on a UDC-like slide toward default.

Here, then, was a dangerous aftershock of the New York City cash-flow debacle—a new crisis just as serious in its implications, if not more so, as the city's fiscal crisis had been, but an episode that would draw far less public attention, not only due to its arid fiscal complexities, but also because this time there would be no lecturing President Ford, no indignant Abe Beame, nor even an alarming *Daily News* headline of national note to personalize the drama. Besides, fiscal crisis fatigue was afflicting the New York public and media, and, too, 1976 would be a year rich with far more colorful spectacles for New York: the nation's bicentennial celebration would be centered in New York Harbor, and Democrats would chose to hold their presidential nominating convention in Madison Square Garden. The notion that one of the oldest and most important large-state governments in the land might crumble must have seemed absurd and far-fetched, particularly since Washington had just recently given in, granting the city its substantial, life-saving treasury loans.

Yet if any of the endangered state authorities had ended up reneging on their debts to bondholders, then the credit market might have then stopped participating in many or even all of the Empire State's borrowing arrangements, repeating the kind of boycott that had touched off the New York City fiscal crisis. The state government would then face a possible bankruptcy. If that occurred, then the statewide constellation of local governments, not to mention their school, fire, sewer, and water districts, equally dependent on the state's capacity to borrow and circulate billions of dollars in aid in April, May, and June of each year—the first quarter of the state's fiscal year and the last quarter of the local governments' separate fiscal years—would screech to a terrible halt. Without this "spring borrowing," the routine internal circulation of state revenue and aid to localities, it was doubtful any local unit of the government would be able to pay its debts. All could face collapse, the recently rescued New York City government included.

Peter Goldmark, the state budget director, must surely have felt as if he was handed a live grenade when, in late 1975, Carey assigned him the task of keeping the four imperiled "moral obligation" authorities afloat, and the chain of financing linking the state and local units of government from snapping.[1] Immediately, Goldmark raced to ensure that the bonds of the HFA and SDA coming due could be redeemed. He succeeded initially on December 15, 1975, when the Carey administration found $200 million in the State Insurance Fund, which existed to support the Workers' Compensation Fund for state employees injured on the job. Carey signed the bill appropriating this aid at 11:20 PM, forty minutes before the agencies' deadline for repayment.[2] The city of Yonkers, too, with 175,000 residents, just north of the Bronx, teetered on default, forcing the state legislature to give it $4 million on the cusp of a January 2, 1976, deadline of the same kind; the small, poorly managed city was placed under the temporary yoke of a state financial control board, headed by Comptroller Levitt.[3]

Goldmark created a task force of deputies that determined that $2.6 billion—equivalent to roughly one-fifth of the entire state operating budget—would be needed by April 1, 1976, to provide a sound, long-term basis for keeping the four authorities alive and enabling them to regain a receptive audience for future bond sales. Scraping together such a sum required turning to large, medium-sized, and small banks outside the city holding the agencies' "moral obligation" securities, since the New York powerhouse banks were still too spooked by what had happened in New York City to step up on behalf of any more shaky public entities. Goldmark set out to convince the out-of-state banks to trade in their holdings for what were arguably more dependable longer-term bonds with revised repayment deadlines, extended well into the future. His ultimate objective was to spare the imperiled authorities the burden of having to pay back investors according to the original contractual terms under which the outstanding bonds had been issued—conditions that the authorities could no longer honor because they had neither the money nor the credit.

The names of the financial institutions holding the authorities' paper were not considered public information at the Fed, even for state budget officials. Goldmark, though, patched together a complete list based on information teased from the Federal Reserve Bank of New York, then headed by Paul Volcker. He called it his "black book." It included about 150 banks in all.

Goldmark and his assistants then fanned out, meeting personally with the presidents of each of one of these widely scattered banks. Some, like the San Francisco–based Bank of America, the most important commercial bank in the country outside New York, needed no arm-twisting to "hold and roll" their notes—the bank had already shown a willingness to take carefully considered risks on the future growth of California, and probably, too, wanted to show up its bigger and better-known New York competitors. But many smaller banks, said Goldmark, had to be reminded, pointedly, that they would recoup only a fraction of the value of their original investments if any of these agencies was allowed to go bankrupt.

To secure the cooperation of the most reluctant of the bank presidents, Goldmark vowed to "name and blame" any who declined to refinance their moral obligation bonds.

"Here's the plan, you have to participate, or the whole thing is in danger," was the gist of what the New York budget director told them. Still, during the big road show, one chairman of a state-chartered bank almost comically fell asleep as Goldmark delivered his intense sales pitch, while another tried to walk out in the middle of a meeting; he returned to his chair when Goldmark snapped at him, reminding everyone in the suite that he had come thousands of miles for the chance to talk to them, with a great deal at stake.[4]

For those bankers who wanted assurance that their industry peers would assume the same level of risk as they themselves were being asked to shoulder, Goldmark improvised a "pledge card" for each bank chairman to sign. Though little more than an unofficial security blanket, the card offered the needed psychological effect.

In the race to cobble together the total $2.6 billion bankroll required to keep the agencies in business, Goldmark and his team also approached several insurance companies, and these executives were almost invariably amenable to pitching in, while members of his staff prevailed on the U.S. Department of Housing and Urban Development to insure $260 million in HFA projects so that the mortgages could be sold to private investors. At the same time, several construction projects that had been enthusiastically initiated by the HFA and other authorities when their credit with the banks was good were now suspended or sold to private developers or county governments for eventual completion, raising $400 million.

From a variety of state funds yet another $400 million was extracted for Goldmark's hastily and brilliantly improvised kitty.

Still needed, though, was the key consent and participation of the New York State comptroller, Arthur Levitt, long a critic of moral obligation bonds. Levitt, as sole custodian of the state's $12 billion pension fund assets—the Policemen's and Firemen's Retirement System and the State Employees Retirement System—faced an internal lobbying push, since Goldmark set up an informal "Committee to Manage Arthur Levitt" to prod and pressure the state's most experienced and senior public official.[5] One member of the effort, Frank Smeal of Morgan Guaranty Trust, who had been involved with the state's efforts to stem the city's fiscal crisis, convinced Arthur Burns to tell Levitt that the four authorities must not be allowed to go under, for the collapse of the "moral obligation agencies" could close the municipal credit market to New York State as a whole and send it into bankruptcy. He added that the public authorities' survival, or collapse, was in Levitt's hands.[6] By implication, Levitt's estimable record of public service would be tarnished, to say the least, if he let the agencies, and by possible extension the state and its millions of people, suffer a mortal blow.

Levitt relented, allowing the pension funds to invest $400 million in whatever Goldmark was selling. As a result, the budget director was able to negotiate a separate, $418 million purchase by still another holdout, the New York State Teachers' Retirement System. The diverse elements of the $2.6 billion plan were reminiscent of the Financial Emergency Act of September, 1975, and perhaps just as precarious. They were considered amid the acrimonious budget negotiations of the winter of 1976 between the governor and legislative

leaders, who strongly objected to the administration's plan to rely on cuts in
local aid rather than tax increases to fill the gaps in the state's proposed budget.
During one of many cliffhanger moments in the talks, administration officials
hastily dispatched New York State troopers to round up assembly members
who had adjourned without passing a technical bill necessary to prevent the
collapse of the State Dormitory Authority by the end of that day, a Friday in
mid-March. The prideful lawmakers greatly resented being treated as fugitive
lawbreakers as they were tracked down in motel rooms, parking lots, bars,
and restaurants as far as forty miles down the New York State Thruway and
led back to the Albany statehouse in the predawn hours. "The police dragnet
was only one in a bizarre series of events surrounding an Assembly session
that hovered for hours between the comic and the surreal and left one aide to
Stanley Steingut shaking his hand and muttering: 'After 200 years of democracy,
it's come to this,'" reported the *Times*.[7] And it came to this: Having been
reassembled to correct one technical flaw that could have brought down the
entire rescue package, the legislators had to fix still another—a defect in the
Housing Finance Agency reserve fund triggered by a tenant rent strike at the
vast Co-op City housing development in the Bronx. The funds were finally
appropriated March 31, hours from an HFA default deadline, after senate
Republicans won assurances that the Co-op City tenants would be required
to make good on their rent arrears at the strike's end.

The marathon statehouse negotiations also produced a new Public
Authorities Control Board to oversee the projects of the Housing Finance
Agency, State Dormitory Authority, Medical Care Facilities Financing Authority, and Environmental Facilities Corporation, and how much they would be
permitted to borrow. This panel grew out of a Carey-initiated commission
to investigate the collapse of the Urban Development Corporation and, in
part, from the thinking of one of the panel's participants, John Heimann, the
state banking commissioner. A majority of the new board, which consisted
of the governor, the assembly speaker and the senate majority leader, could
now reject a state authority's capital project. This put the governor and
legislature more in control when it came to public authorities, long viewed
by critics as unaccountable.

In the final analysis, the so-called "build-out" of the four authorities—an
initiative described at its inception by skeptics as "a tissue of hopes, dreams,
and aspirations"—was successful in keeping the agencies from defaulting.[8]
The state's moral obligation bond, a legacy of the Rockefeller era, was soon
replaced by a more acceptable bonding instrument, which similarly allowed
the state to initiate major capital projects without first seeking voters' approval
through a ballot referendum.

"It is difficult to do justice to the combination of frustration, sense of
risk, taut nerves, short tempers and, withal, statesmanship and achievement,
that characterized both executive and legislative efforts in the struggle to

contain the crisis, and prevent it from overwhelming the state as well as the city," wrote Robert Kerker, a long-time state budget examiner, in an authoritative book on the history of the executive budget in New York State published in 1981.[9]

## Insinuations

Always there were turbulent cross-currents—unrelated to the state's fiscal crises.

In the middle of 1975, an article appeared in the Cox newspapers containing unattributed assertions that Carey had used his influence while in Congress to obtain oil-export licenses for the benefit of his oldest brother's New England Petroleum Corporation. Carey was incensed when his press aide showed it to him. Ever since Watergate, politicians were guilty until proven innocent in the eyes of a jaded citizenry. So Carey took the highly unusual step of writing to U.S. Attorney General Edward H. Levi to request an investigation of these anonymous allegations, which he felt may have been planted in the press to blunt his possible candidacy in the 1976 Democratic presidential primary. An investigation was opened, and Carey appeared, voluntarily, before a federal grand jury, and denied under oath the newspaper article's claims. In February, 1976, the *New York Times* carried a most unusual article on its front page referring to a letter that Levi wrote to Carey putting the entire matter to rest. The headline on the front page of the *Times* read: "U.S. clears Carey of aid to Brother on Oil Deals," though there had never been a formal complaint.[10]

More ominously, in late December, 1975, just as Goldmark was beginning his mad scramble to keep the four state authorities from collapsing, Carey confronted an even more disquieting matter of insinuation. This time the instigator of the aspersions was Maurice H. Nadjari, a powerful New York State special prosecutor.

Nadjari's position had been created under Governor Rockefeller because the Knapp Commission, established by Mayor Lindsay, had found widespread corruption in the New York City Police Department (helped by a police whistleblower, Frank Serpico, whose courage was memorialized by Peter Maas's three-million-selling biography and the film based on it) and throughout the state's criminal justice system. Nadjari's office had the power to investigate cops, city and state officials, judges, even district attorneys. And he did, beginning in 1972. The hundreds of targets of Nadjari's undercover investigations included such big fish as the city's cultural affairs commissioner, the former head of the city Tax Commission, a retired judge of the U.S. Customs Court, and the Queens County district attorney.[11]

As he had a flair for public relations, many of his arrests and accusations appeared in the press, raising the profile of his office, and attracting a lot of applause, including from the editorial pages of the *New York Times*. He was a highly popular figure with the public.

But in 1975 many of his cases were overturned on appeal, raising eyebrows in the legal profession in New York. In November of 1975, New York State Supreme Court Justice John Murtagh, who supervised Nadjari's cases, said that the special prosecutor had been "wholly without authority" to bring a case alleging theft and fraud against the city cultural affairs commissioner. Nadjari's case to the jury had teetered on "contempt" because Murtagh had warned him that it fell outside the boundaries of the Rockefeller executive order creating his office, the judge complained.[12]

Carey was never much of a fan of Nadjari's brand of undercover work, but for the governor—who some Washington press pundits were calling a possible candidate for president or vice president in 1976—seeking to topple a figure of Nadjari's independent prominence, press contacts, and power was not necessarily advisable, politically speaking. Still, at a dinner December 4 at the Executive Mansion—five days before President Ford signed the legislation providing breakthrough federal loans to New York City—Carey broached with Judah Gribetz, David Burke, and Robert Morgado, the director of operations, the powder-keg notion of having Nadjari replaced. Carey believed that Nadjari, overall, engaged in questionable tactics and strayed well beyond the constraints of his mandate in ferreting out wrongdoing. They talked about replacing him with Robert Morgenthau, then the Manhattan district attorney. Gribetz mentioned the idea to Morgenthau the next day. Carey and Morgenthau, a fellow Democrat, would meet in a few weeks.[13]

The governor's qualms about Nadjari were in part idiosyncratic. He was still disquieted by a 1968 investigation of his Shelter Island friend and neighbor, Queens County Supreme Court Judge James Roe Jr., conducted by the Suffolk County district attorney's office when Nadjari worked there as an assistant prosecutor. That investigation led to Roe's indictment on a charge that arose from a traffic offense. During the course of the trial, Roe boarded a small plane with his two sons, traveling by air in part to avoid any additional unpleasant encounters with local traffic cops. The plane crashed at Flushing Airport, killing Roe and seriously injuring his sons. The next day, he was exonerated by the judge presiding over the case. Although Nadjari maintained he was not involved in the Roe investigation, to Carey the matter was deeply personal, and the investigation of his friend represented to him the kind of unwarranted and defective prosecutions that he felt Nadjari conducted as a special prosecutor, and which violated his sense of fairness and how he believed the system should work.[14]

On December 23, 1975, Carey went public with plans to transfer Nadjari's state investigative mandate to DA Morgenthau's portfolio. Nadjari, however, would not accept this judgment quietly. He gathered the press and announced he had been zeroing in on corruption by top state Democrats; he alleged, albeit somewhat indirectly, that Carey was trying to squelch the inquiry by pushing him out. The governor's hand, Nadjari suggested, was being compelled by "improper influences" and "self-motivated" persons who were targets of his probe.[15] It soon emerged that he was investigating the alleged sale of judgeships by Patrick J. Cunningham, the head of the state Democratic Party installed by Carey.

Now the press had on its hands a kindled fuse, with the state's special prosecutor apparently suggesting, however indirectly, that a cover-up existed at the state's highest levels of political authority. A *Daily News* headline blared on page 3: "Nadjari Hint: Dirty Hands on that Ax."[16] At a further press conference at his office in the World Trade Center, Nadjari cast more suspicions toward Carey, suggesting possible gubernatorial misdeeds reminiscent of Watergate. Nadjari didn't provide particulars, but at least from a PR standpoint, he succeeded in shifting the public focus from his own conduct while in office, to Carey's current motives in trying to get rid of him.

While the office of the special prosecutor was created by a governor, it was the attorney general, Louis Lefkowitz, who was technically responsible for appointing the person to head it. Carey therefore needed Lefkowitz's permission to name Morgenthau as Nadjari's replacement. At the second of two meetings on the issue, Lefkowitz flatly refused.[17]

In the much same way he had responded to the Cox Newspapers article containing anonymous allegations, Carey then demanded Lefkowitz instead name a special deputy attorney general to investigate Nadjari's accusations about him. This time Lefkowitz agreed, choosing the soon-to-retire state Supreme Court justice Jacob Grumet to conduct a formal inquiry. The judge was a Republican, like Lefkowitz, so Carey was raising the ante. But according to Gribetz, the governor felt deeply that the integrity of not only his reputation but that of his office and the courts were at stake. " 'I don't care who Louis picks—justice is on my side,' " Gribetz recalled Carey telling him when they grappled privately over the risks.[18] Grumet's inquiry marked the first time in New York State history that a governor had called for an official state investigation of himself.

In the end, Carey's political instincts, respect for the judicial system, and "love of the law," as Gribetz put it, won the day. Grumet's investigation, which took six months, cleared Carey of the many doubts about him stirred up by Nadjari, including the major one—that Carey had sought Nadjari's dismissal in order to stop an investigation into the alleged sale of judgeships in the Bronx by the state Democratic Party chairman Patrick Cunningham.[19] While Carey and Cunningham were political allies and social friends, Grumet found that Nadjari's facts just didn't add up. For while Nadjari stated that Carey had acted to dismiss him after the governor learned in mid-December about the Cunningham investigation, the report by Grumet established that Carey had actually decided to fire Nadjari more than a week before. "There is no evidence," Grumet's report read, "to support the charge or allegation that the governor's decision on December 4, 1975, to replace Mr. Nadjari was the result of any 'improper influences.' I also find that there is no evidence to support the allegation by Mr. Nadjari that an investigation pending in his office 'triggered' his proposed dismissal."[20] Still, while Grumet's inquiry was going on, Nadjari remained in office, owing to Lefkowitz's decision that he could stay on for at least an additional six months—until late June, 1976, that is. Lefkowitz's decision effectively gave Nadjari a platform from which to embarrass the Democratic Party before the National Democratic Convention at Madison Square Garden. A Nadjari-empaneled grand jury did subpoena Patrick Cunningham in mid-May, 1976, in its search for evidence of the possible sale of judgeships on the criminal court bench. But the case was eventually dropped.[21] Lefkowitz dismissed Nadjari with the release of Grumet's findings, ending the special prosecutor's clean-government crusade of nearly four years.

At the Carey administration's request, Nadjari was replaced by John Keenan, a Republican prosecutor who had worked for Morgenthau at the DA's office; a vetting of the law indicated that the sitting DA, Morgenthau, was not permitted to hold the dual role of special prosecutor. In taking over the special prosecutor's role, then, Keenan replaced a number of the attorneys in the office still sympathetic to their former boss. "He had been investigating anything he could see, and much of it didn't have anything to do with his mandate," Keenan commented many years later.[22]

"Everything that Maurice Nadjari alleged about the governor turned out to be demonstrably untrue, and there's no other way to put it," said S. Michael Nadel, first assistant counsel to Carey. "But the details of it consumed twenty to twenty-two hours of every day for almost six months of several peoples' lives who worked for the governor."[23]

Despite Carey's exoneration, the epic fight left its scars and heavily damaged Carey's chances of ever emerging as a major candidate for national office. But such flame wars are part of the life of a governor, especially one as forceful as Carey was across his eight-year tenure.

## Willowbrook

In 1965, New York senator Robert F. Kennedy toured the Willowbrook Center for the Developmentally Disabled on Staten Island, which had six thousand residents. Emerging from the facility, Kennedy branded it a "snake pit."

Seven years later the television personality Geraldo Rivera surreptitiously filmed and then aired scenes of overcrowded rooms, filthy and naked residents, and their overwhelmed caretakers.

Governor Rockefeller sought to reduce Willowbrook's population, but the process was slow and unsuccessful in part because of the high cost of providing decent alternative places for the residents to live. Meanwhile, former residents of other types of large state institutions—those housing the mentally ill—were being released more and more often on new tranquilizing medications and drifting toward the relative anonymity of New York City's subways and streets. The old, senile, and infirm, for whom institutionalization was deemed inhumane, took up residence in cockroach-infested, unsupervised single-room occupancy hotels in Manhattan; many became prey to a new and abusive cottage industry of proprietary nursing homes, prompting Carey to name Charles Hynes, an independent prosecutor, to investigate their often-greedy owners, to widespread and lasting effect.

Carey had made the education and care of the developmentally impaired a central part of his record in the Congress, and shortly before his inauguration as governor, he had followed in Kennedy's footsteps to Willowbrook, which by then had 4,600 wards. He asked his then newly recruited budget director, Goldmark, to negotiate with Willowbrook plaintiffs and their lawyers, who had filed a lawsuit to close the institution.

Out of it came a nationally influential agreement ordered by the governor: a forty-page, single-spaced consent degree of April 1975 issued by the state supreme court. The consent decree required transfer of all but 250 of the institution's residents to small group homes by 1981, a process that required concessions to communities uncomfortable with having the developmentally disabled in their midst. Clarence Sundram, an assistant counsel to the governor, drafted a key compromise requiring community input before a group home could be established in a residential neighborhood. Carey's social services commissioner, Barbara Blum, worked to make sure that the consent decree was satisfied in practice, as did Thomas Coughlin, a former state police sergeant whom Carey named as the head of a new autonomous state office for the developmentally disabled after meeting him during a visit to a well-run educational center for this population in upstate Watertown where Coughlin had helped bring about new programs.[24] A year after the 1981 deadline set by the consent decree, Willowbrook's population was far thinner, at thirteen hundred residents. It took four years before Carey's drive to create more humane and adequately staffed community residences for virtually the entire Willowbrook population was accomplished. The agreement also set the stage for the downsizing and reform of the state's massive institutions for the mentally ill.

Though Sundram was in his late twenties and not politically connected, Carey chose him to be chairman of what became a nationally influential

State Commission on Quality of Care for the Mentally Disabled, given the knowledge and experience he gained on the ground during the Willowbrook episode. "The accomplishments of the past twenty-five years are nothing short of astonishing," Sundram, who had early on spent time at Willowbrook as Carey's representative and been horrified by what he saw, wrote a quarter century later. Looking back at the consent decree, Sundram added, "Almost the entire agenda of the most visionary advocates has come to pass, from the decline of institutions to the growth of community services, to the passage of new laws around the nation, such as the Americans with Disabilities Act of 1990."[25]

Others felt much the same, viewing the case as the turning point in the treatment of the institutionalized. Scholars David and Sheila Rothman, in their definitive study of the episode, *The Willowbrook Wars,* said that reducing the Willowbrook population could not have been achieved but for the "personal commitment" of Goldmark to a state program that he and other state officials genuinely believed in, and, of course, Carey's willingness to acknowledge years of state complicity by signing the decree in the first place.[26] John R. Bartels, the Republican justice who presided over the federal court's supervision of former Willowbrook patients for eighteen years, looked back in 1993 and remarked: "The retarded have really overcome, and social justice has prevailed."[27]

## Capital Punishment

Hugh Carey also emerged, in the spring of 1977, as a nationally known opponent of capital punishment. Though as reticent and self-effacing about his World War II service as many other members of his generation, he nonetheless cited, in defending his unpopular position, his unforgettable encounter with the Nordhausen slave-labor camp in Nazi Germany and his military regiment's efforts to rescue the barely living and bury the dead, the bodies stacked with ghoulish efficiency in the orderly piles he observed. His awareness of the dangers of unfettered state power undoubtedly contributed to his decision to veto a stream of bills from 1977 through 1982, all with the aim of reactivating the death penalty in New York. He felt that no government had the moral right or should have the legal power to take a life, citing the dangers of executing the wrongly convicted, and questioning the deterrent value of capital punishment.

When Carey delivered his first veto of death penalty legislation in the spring of 1977, crime was very much on the minds of voters—it was arguably the No. 1 political issue, driven by fear, high-profile murders, tabloids, and TV news.[28] There were, in fact, an average of seventy-five felonies each hour in New York City, an all-time high, and the issue animated a stampede of candidates for mayor in 1977.[29] Polls showed huge support for a return of capital punishment, and some of the Democratic candidates, including Mayor Abraham Beame and Manhattan congressman Edward I. Koch, got on the bandwagon, reversing their previous positions in order to embrace the cause of the death penalty.

Carey, however, was willing to remain decidedly unpopular for opposing the restoration of the death penalty, even when his own reelection campaign was approaching in 1978 against a formidable Republican opponent. He insisted in an interview years later that even if he had been overridden by the state legislature and ordered by a court to sign a convict's death warrant, he would have refused.[30]

"I have spoken plainly on the penalty of death in our criminal justice system," Carey stated in that first death-penalty veto message he served up, one consistent with all those he issued in the ensuing years to state legislators, and which David Burke, for one, called his finest moment, a model of political courage and conscientiousness. "On numerous occasions I have reiterated the arguments that stand against it—it is no proven deterrent to crime . . . ; it leaves no room for human fallibility; it lowers all of us who abide by the law and the Judeo-Christian tradition of preserving and perfecting human life and dignity. In my view, for a government to sanction the death of a man or a woman is not only an admission of our inability to cope with the worst among us, it also admits the possibility that there are times when the government has the power to act violently and kill its own people—a power that throughout the ages has never elevated a society or been known to protect any minority."[31]

## The "Four Horsemen"

Carey's opposition to the use of violence was not limited to the death penalty debate. He became known as one of the "Four Horsemen" of Irish American politics, pushing, with Tip O'Neill, Pat Moynihan, and Ted Kennedy, for constitutional, nonviolent means to achieve a united Ireland, and condemning, starting with a collective statement on St. Patrick's Day, 1977, NORAID, the membership organization accused of operating as an American front for the Irish Republican Army, as well as the IRA itself. Given their stature as U.S. elected officials, their peace effort influenced Irish opinion in both the United States and abroad, provided encouragement to American business leaders and others who similarly favored peaceful solutions but were wary of speaking out, and contributed to President Jimmy Carter's human rights-based policy toward Ireland and the Northern Ireland peace process.

"Those fascinated with death as a political weapon," Carey said in a lecture at the Royal College of Surgeons in Dublin that April in reference to the Irish Republican Army and its violent campaign to reunify the country of his ancestors, "are surely as sick as people can be . . . So I will speak to death—and its brother, violence—only to condemn it in my own land and yours . . . To what end then do the apostles of death and violence lead us? To no end, I say, worthy of human consideration."[32]

In his Dublin speech—an amplification of his decision to join with O'Neill, Kennedy, and Moynihan in calling for the peaceful unification of the north and south of Ireland and for an end to enmity between Northern Ireland's warring Protestants and Catholics—he then continued, ". . . most conflicts that arise in the human experience lend themselves to the politics of accommodation, compromise, and ultimate peaceful settlement. Those that do not are readily apparent to the vast majority of informed opinion and call for different acts. But all of this is different from those who play at death and who seek to enhance themselves by these means in a society that has otherwise denied them respect and status. They, to me, are the leaders in the politics of death. They, to me, are the most reprehensible—and they must be stopped."

## Attica

Carey's deeply ingrained instinct to renounce vengefulness came to bear on another question of justice denied, which his administration inherited on day one: the state's one-sided prosecutions in the wake of the infamous Attica State Correctional Facility uprising of September, 1971, a bloody episode in which nearly half of the upstate prison's twenty-two hundred inmates rioted and seized control of the facility, taking hostage thirty-three correction officers. During the protracted incident, negotiations over prisoners' demands for better conditions collapsed and Governor Rockefeller ordered the state police to retake the facility by force, with some troopers mustering private arms. More than forty people were killed in the mayhem, both inmates and officers. But of the scores of individuals indicted in subsequent months, not a single one was a state trooper or a guard—all were prisoners. Many people felt that this judicial result was unbalanced, unfair, and a justifiable source of cynicism about the state's law enforcement and judicial system.

Malcolm Bell, an assistant to the special prosecutor on Attica appointed under Governor Rockefeller, took it largely upon himself to investigate the uprising, and he handed the incoming Carey administration a hefty, confidential document concluding that Rockefeller's special prosecutor on Attica had ignored evidence of the use of excessive force by state police and guards. S. Michael Nadel, first assistant counsel to the governor, assessed the report's integrity and soon reported his findings to Gribetz. They brought in Alfred J. Scotti, once a special assistant to former Manhattan district attorney Frank Hogan, to review Bell's assessment and to go back over the now-yellowing evidence from the cases. Scotti concluded that disciplinary action—where the standard of proof was less than that which was required in a criminal trial—was now warranted against at least a dozen state troopers and prison guards. Still another review was conducted at the governor's request by state Supreme Court justice Bernard Meyer.

In late 1976, nearly five years after the notorious incident that for many Americans had symbolized everything that was wrong with the nation's correctional system, Carey moved to put a bandage on the still-raw wound. Saying he confronted "the real possibility that the law itself may well fall into disrepute," the governor commuted the charges against the eight inmates who had been sentenced, one of them accused of killing a prison guard and who, because of Carey's actions, would become eligible for parole soon. To balance his decision, Carey ruled out prosecuting any guards and troopers, saying the evidence was old and poorly organized. He requested instead only disciplinary proceedings.

The date of Carey's announcement, December 30, 1976, a day before the massive festivities of New Year's Eve centered in Times Square, suggested that he may have wanted to minimize public attention to his pardons and that he expected to be assailed for being "soft" on crime at a time when public appetite for judicial retribution and the death penalty was rising. His decision was derided by the state law enforcement unions. Yet his prudently wrought actions succeeded in closing the book on the incident. "I have the responsibility to bring this tragic affair to a conclusion, which, however unsatisfactory, will foster respect for our system of justice as one capable of recognizing and correcting its wrong," he said.[33]

## Judicial Reform

Carey's desire to improve public confidence in the courts also led him to propose a state constitutional amendment that provided for the gubernatorial appointment of justices to the state's Court of Appeals from a list of candidates prepared by a commission on judicial nomination, rather than through the election process. While not an issue that captivated the public imagination, the governor took court reform seriously, as did many editorial writers, civic groups, and bar associations. He unveiled his proposal, shaped greatly by Gribetz, in May, 1976, saying it was aimed at reducing the role of partisan politics in the composition of the state's highest court. At that time, the Court of Appeals consisted of politically elected judges nominated by party leaders and elected after having run unopposed.

During the debate, Cyrus Vance, whom Carey appointed to head a blue-ribbon committee of lay people, issued a report recommending that judges of all state courts be similarly appointed. While the idea generated by Vance was supported by Carey, the goal of merit selection of judges rested uncomfortably with many state legislators, who would be denied the hoary tradition of influencing which judges would appear on the ballot. Even so, the governor's reform of the Court of Appeals judicial selection process won approval in two successive legislative sessions, as legally required, in part as a result of his agreeing to have the state pick up municipalities' local court system costs on a permanent basis.

By a 2-to-1 margin, voters approved the desired constitutional amendment in November, 1977, marking the first significant court reform in New York State of the modern era.[34]

## Juvenile Justice

In keeping with his skepticism about the efficacy of harsh, if politically popular, laws, Carey appointed Peter Edelman, formerly a legislative assistant to Senator Robert Kennedy and law clerk to U.S. Supreme Court justice Arthur Goldberg, as the director of the state's Division for Youth. The division operated juvenile reformatories. The addition of the liberal Edelman marked a departure from the law-and-order policies of Nelson Rockefeller, whose reputation for toughness was cemented in 1973, when he proposed, for adult offenders, the most severe drug laws in the nation, and to much public acclaim—Rockefeller's constituent mail ran 10-to-1 in his favor after he introduced the legislation.[35] The "Rockefeller Drug Laws" made the sale of a small amount of illegal drugs such as heroin, cocaine, and marijuana an offense comparable to that of second-degree murder, with a minimum sentence of fifteen years and a maximum sentence of twenty-five years to life.

But not long after Carey became governor, the focus of several hair-raising studies and front-page headlines helped shift the debate from the issue of rampant drug addiction by adult offenders to the scourge of youth crime; much research and press coverage stated that underage offenders rarely served a full term in the state's reformatories—just three years if they were fifteen, and half as long if they were younger. As cries rang out for tougher sentences for violent young people and for putting fourteen- and fifteen-year-olds on trial as adults, Carey and Edelman avoided the easy, popular path. They chose to place the emphasis on rehabilitation rather than on severe punishment. An administration bill based largely on Edelman's recommendations called for mandatory minimum sentences for young people found guilty of crimes entailing the use of force, along with slightly longer maximum sentences. It rejected the idea of allowing fourteen- and fifteen-year-olds convicted of dangerous acts to be tried as adults and sentenced to prisons, and called for a Bill of Rights for all institutionalized children. Despite the scuttling of a children's Bill of Rights portion of the bill, and a compromise allowing for an increase in the mandatory minimum sentence, set at two years, and the maximum term, set at five, the resulting Juvenile Justice Reform Act of 1976 encompassed many of Edelman's ideas, penalizing so-called incorrigible youth yet providing them with opportunities to set themselves straight.[36] In the face of much opposition, Carey stood with Edelman, motivated, in part, by his religious beliefs, which taught him to believe in the possibility of every human being, no matter how reprobate, to redeem himself. At the same time, he was a Kennedy man at heart.

## The Politics

But politics, of course, continued to intervene. As Easter Sunday neared in 1977, Carey encouraged his secretary of state, Mario Cuomo, to enter the New York City mayor's race. The governor had already offered Cuomo the chairmanship of the state Democratic organization, which he had turned down. Cuomo did not see himself as a politician—his objectives were loftier, his ambitions greater, than filling the shoes of Patrick Cunningham, who had departed in the wake of Maurice Nadjari's scrutiny. Carey, with David Burke at his side, pushed Cuomo to run for mayor as the governor's favorite candidate and retire the incumbent, Abe Beame.

Carey appealed cannily, perhaps mischievously, to Cuomo's religious faith.

"This is a fateful day, Mario," Carey told him, according to his own recollection. "Mario, after Holy Thursday, Good Friday came next, and the Savior had a vision of his crucifixion and he said, Oh my Father, please let this cup pass from me. In other words, He begged his Father to relieve him of the pain of crucifixion, but then He thought about it, and He went through with it. Now Mario, you can let this cup pass from you, or you can try to become mayor, and you do know that the city can use your leadership. I'm not going to push you, but by Easter morning I want you to let Dave here know if you'll let this cup pass from you."

And with that, Carey and Burke walked out.

"You son of a bitch," Burke snapped, according to Carey. "You trapped him. Now he's going to go around thinking he's Jesus Christ."[37]

Cuomo did enter the race, with Carey's support. And he intended to stay in the race on the Liberal line if he failed to win the Democratic primary, believing Carey would stick with him.

All through the summer of 1977, many New Yorkers reached the conclusion that their troubled, unruly city was faltering badly. Just a year after New York had welcomed the magnificent tall ships of the American bicentennial, the city wore a hard, edgy demeanor. A citywide loss of electricity plunged the metropolis into darkness one mid-July evening, setting the stage for commercial vandalism and looting so intense, widespread, and even gleeful that police, already demoralized by cuts in jobs and overtime, were unable and in some cases unwilling to do much to stop it.

New York City may have been saved from bankruptcy, but it was still strapped for revenue and slashing its way toward a balanced budget under the constraints of the Emergency Financial Control Board. Public services were being cut to the bone, enraging local activists who had resisted the temptation to flee to the suburbs and instead stayed to fight for their besieged schools, parks, firehouses, and police precincts. Bridges and roads decayed as capital spending on infrastructure came to a screeching halt, and an epidemic of arson-for-insurance reduced poor neighborhoods of the Bronx and Brooklyn to smoldering, rubble-strewn landscapes. Even in affluent sections of Manhattan, real estate development all but ceased. And to add to the growingly pervasive sense of defeatism and dread, a chubby-faced serial killer dubbed the "Son of Sam" and the ".44-caliber Killer" trolled lover's lanes in Queens, the Bronx, and Brooklyn, killing and maiming innocents, young men and women, and terrifying the entire city. He was finally captured in August, 1977, in the middle of the hard-fought Democratic mayoral primary, and more than a year after his murder spree had begun. Mayor Beame hoped to capitalize on his arrest, but instead only narrowly avoided a public relations disaster: waiting at Gracie Mansion shortly after being awakened with word of David Berkowitz's arrest, Beame tried to shake hands with the suspect, whom he somehow mistook for the arresting officer in the case. Luckily, Beame press aide Sid Frigand jumped in, heading off what would have been "the photo op from hell," as Frigand put it years later.[38]

With one potential PR nightmare avoided, Beame quickly faced yet another in his bid to win a second term. The many Democrats vying to succeed him could not have been happier when, less than two weeks before the Democratic primary, the U.S. Securities and Exchange Commission released a nervously anticipated, 962-page report on the factors that had produced the city's near-bankruptcy, about which the front page headline in publisher

Rupert Murdoch's *Post* shrieked (coming shortly after the paper's endorsement of Koch for mayor): "BEAME CONNED THE CITY."[39] The SEC report criticized Beame's "deceptive practices masking the city's true and disastrous condition," while assigning blame as well—as was less loudly noted in much of the coverage—to nearly all the city's major banks. The findings and their timing signaled the impending fall of Beame, who, having declared that it was his tough decisions that had saved the city from ruin, assailed the SEC report as a "hatchet job."

When the primary date arrived, Cuomo, like Carey a strong opponent of the death penalty, fought his way to a close second in the large field of contenders, just behind Koch. The two leading vote-getters then went toe-to-toe in a bitter run-off primary two weeks later. When the votes of the runoff were tallied, Koch was on top, having been backed by bosses Meade Esposito, Donald Manes, and Stanley Friedman (the latter had been the city's lobbyist in Albany during the fiscal crisis) and managed by David Garth. Carey, in turn, endorsed Koch in the general election. While Carey would have been cutting his own throat, politically, if he had stiff-armed the Democratic nominee, Cuomo viewed Carey's decision as an almost unforgiv-able breach of faith—a broken promise to continue supporting him on the Liberal line even if he lost the Democratic primary.

In November, Cuomo came up short against Koch. Still, Cuomo's 8 percentage point margin of defeat was impressive for a minor party candidate, positioning him for bigger things to come.

Carey had more difficulty staying in control of his party once the fiscal crisis had relaxed its grip on the political dynamics of the state. If Cuomo sought to be his own man vis-a-vis Carey, the same was true of Beame, and the mayor became the first Democrat in the state to endorse Jimmy Carter for president, a month after the former governor of Georgia came in fourth in the 1976 New York presidential primary (far behind "Uncommitted"). Though Carey was the leader of New York's Democrats, and the presiden-tial endorsement therefore should have been his trophy to deliver, Carter needed the support of a big-city mayor in the Northeast and Beame was only too happy to oblige him.[40] Even so, Beame did call Carey from Gracie Mansion late that night to tell him of the unilateral endorsement; Carey, who was then trying to arrange increased state aid for the beleaguered City University of New York, was bad-tempered in response, all to little effect. For with Beame having come out for Carter (of whom Carey was no great fan), the New York delegation to the Democratic National Convention, which the mayor co-chaired, shifted its bloc of delegates from Washington senator Henry Jackson to the Georgia peanut farmer. With New York's help, then, but hardly with Carey's enthusiastic support, Carter in turn secured the Democratic presidential nomination. Carter did begin speaking more sympathetically than he had previously about the prospect of continued federal aid for New York City (his ads in New York City included the line, "I'll never tell the people of the City of New York to drop dead"), though he was careful to avoid making such assertions in more conservative states, or to offer explicit promises of support.

As for Carey, although he didn't reveal it until years later (at a Hofstra University conference on the fiscal crisis), he cast his vote that November for his old Washington colleague, Gerald Ford.[41]

Carey sidled up to his own reelection campaign in 1978, with media consultant David Garth once again firmly in charge of the operation. The governor had hoped to have an easy run and to go unchallenged in the primary, but then his own lieutenant governor, Mary Ann Krupsak, of upstate Amsterdam, made a surprise announcement that she would run against him, as did Brooklyn state senator Jeremiah Bloom, who had once bucked the will of Brooklyn political boss Meade Esposito in supporting Carey at the 1974 state Democratic convention. These displays of defiance against the sitting governor were striking; Krupsak threatened to take away upstate support, while Bloom was popular among Orthodox Jewish voters in the city. But the challenges propelled Carey back out on the hustings, forcing him to kick up much of the brio he had brought to his 1974 run. Carey's competitive juices thus activated, he set out to win, bowing to Garth's insistence that Cuomo, a respected figure known statewide, be chosen as his running mate.

Few could have doubted Carey's will to succeed when the governor, upon reading on the front page of the *Daily News* about a public furor over the imposition of a mere five-year sentence for Willie Bosket, a fifteen-year-old New York City boy found guilty of killing two subway riders just two months after his release from a state reformatory, voiced immediate public support for allowing state judges to try juveniles accused of serious crimes in adult courts. Carey offered a bill, quickly passed by the state legislature, which provided for longer sentences for young adults who committed two or more violent felonies, undercutting Peter Edelman and the progress he had led with Carey's support toward a more humane and rehabilitative juvenile detention system. It all went to show, unsurprisingly, that Carey did not operate in a bubble, and was hardly immune from the successful politician's need to make adjustments to his positions in an election year.

Carey won the primary handily and then, using his political skills and the timeless advantages of incumbency, pounded his Republican opponent, Perry Duryea, the assembly minority leader from eastern Long Island, over his reluctance to release his tax returns, and ultimately defeated him. At one point during the race, Carey, ever the showman, slammed a sledgehammer against a toll plaza to dramatize his plan to end tolls on the Southern State Parkway in Duryea's home county. The reverse ribbon-cutting, along with billboards reading "Welcome to Toll-Free Long Island," prompted the Duryea campaign to assail what it called an election-year stunt, inadvertently highlighting the incumbent's desire to end the despised tolls and therefore making him seem heaven-sent in the eyes of Long Island motorists, and voters, of both parties.[42]

At another point, Carey's administration learned that President Carter planned to cut the F-14 Tomcat Fighter Jet, threatening a contract held by Long Island's Grumman Corporation to produce thirty-six of them. With as many as twenty thousand new jobs at stake, Carey sent John Dyson, now his commerce commissioner, to talk with Vice President Walter Mondale, but Mondale's efforts to reverse the policy through back channels were unavailing. With Mondale's help, Dyson landed a meeting with Secretary of Defense Harold Brown and pleaded the case for Grumman to produce a pared-back twenty-four planes. It was rigorous science, not politics, Brown declared, that formed the basis of such decisions. Carey, advised of Brown's seemingly high-minded pronouncement, sent Dyson back to the Capitol to see New York representative Sam Stratton, calling ahead to let his old friend—No. 3 on the House Armed Services Appropriations Committee—know. Stratton escorted Dyson to see the chairman, Mendel Rivers of South Carolina. "Hell Sam," offered Rivers, after hearing Dyson's pleas, "if we're going to help Hughie, let's put the entire thirty-six planes back in." And they did.[43]

Though Duryea, a businessman and death penalty supporter, started the race as much as twenty points ahead of Carey, the city that Carey rescued in 1975 didn't forget his gesture, and returned the favor, casting ballots for the Carey-Cuomo ticket in such disproportionately large numbers that their votes offset Duryea's closer victories in many suburban and upstate counties.[44] It all amounted to a decisive but less than sweeping victory, and well-deserved clinch of a second term.

Carey's problems keeping peace in his own party during the election were mirrored by his increasingly strained relationship with the state legislature, which, in contrast, he had managed commandingly during the fiscal crisis. Upstate and suburban legislators in both parties reacted against the governor's city-centric focus born of the fiscal crisis, and many reasserted their independence from the executive branch and its cantankerous, at times glib, leader. Many especially resented Carey's attempts to wave the banner of fiscal responsibility vigorously over the state budget, including his effort to reject proposals to raise taxes to balance the budget and to push instead for cuts in aid to localities. One assemblyman even rose and labeled him a "son of a bitch" in the chamber, and the majority of lawmakers at one point overrode a governor's veto—the first time such a thing had happened in Albany in 104 years. Carey did not always conceal his disgust for the statehouse denizens, labeling them "small boys."[45]

## The Budget

In struggling to exert control over state spending, Carey vetoed a record 160 budget items during the 1980 legislative session. He limited annual state spending increases to less than 3 percent, in striking contrast to the average state growth rate of 11 percent that had taken place during the early 1970s. A big reason was his success in slowing the growth of Medicaid funding of nursing homes, physicians, and hospitals. Those cuts were achieved not by curtailing critical services for poor patients but by limiting the Medicaid reimbursements that health care providers could seek from the state. His governorship offers the only example of significant containment of crippling Medicaid expenditures in New York State.[46]

Carey indeed came to be recognized as a stubborn and frugal manager of the state's financial resources and as a tax-cutter, loathed by some, applauded by others. Whatever the cost to his popularity in the statehouse, when the state finally had shaken off the brutal 1970s recession, it was in a far better position to regain its footing and attract people, industry, and jobs.

At a historically and financially important ceremony on the steps of New York's City Hall, the city and state got a huge lift when Jimmy Carter signed a hard-fought congressional bill providing $1.5 billion in bond-repayment guarantees to further support the city's progress toward financial stability. In the previous months, Governor Carey, Mayor Koch, and many other state and city officials had paraded a battery of witnesses before the Senate Finance, Banking, and Urban Affairs Committee in an attempt to mollify its chairman, the once-helpful and now-parsimonious Senator William Proxmire of Wisconsin. The battle for federal guarantees represented a reprise, of sorts, of the 1975 "Battle of Washington," with a new mayor, new president, and new key names in Washington. Carter, and congressional leaders, stepped up to help the city at the moment when the Ford administration's seasonal loans were set to expire at the end of June, 1978—the repayment terms all having been satisfied by an intensely frugal city lorded over by the Emergency Financial Control Board. The infusion of the federal bond-repayment guarantees approved by Congress and signed into law by Carter allowed the city to restructure its debt, the annual cost of which could have kept the city from keeping up with its ongoing bills. The treasury's backing of city bond deals, like former President Ford's earlier treasury loans, came with little risk and no cost to U.S. taxpayers.

Thankfully, the financial services industry of Wall Street began to grow, generating new tax revenues, and interest rates turned favorable to the city's long term prospects. The once-suspect MAC bonds began selling at a premium, and during 1980, the Koch administration, waxing tough on unions and assisted by financial whizzes drawn from the business world, helped reorder the city's archaic books, balance the city's budget ahead of schedule, and establish long-term financial planning. This included a master schedule for debt service payments, which had not previously existed. The Koch administration's major objectives included restoring corporate confidence in New York City. Indeed, the only recent major commercial real estate project had been Donald Trump's Grand Hyatt in Manhattan, in 1976.[47] The city was still stalled, but turning a corner.

## Economic Development

In helping reestablish the foundations for economic growth, the Carey administration enlarged the mission of the state Urban Development Corporation, turning it into a broad economic development dealmaker under Richard Kahan, and, through it, the state revived the flagging Radio City Music Hall, which had come close to closing for lack of funds. In addition, the governor cleared the way for the construction of long-delayed Battery Park City, a riverfront residential development built on earth excavated during the construction of the World Trade Center, and whose operating authority is now named for Governor Carey. Work on the South Street Seaport and Jacob K. Javits Convention Center. These developments marked the first large-scale state capital projects since 1975.

Additionally, early blueprints for a reimagined Times Square, while not realized until the 1990s, took shape during Carey's tenure with the creation of the Times Square Redevelopment Project at the UDC, along with the restoration of hotels in Albany and Syracuse, making those cities more appealing to visitors and residents.

Carey was also responsible for the legislative passage of the Farm Winery Act of 1976, which allowed farmers to set up their own wineries, something they had found difficult since the days of Prohibition, and thereby stimulated growth of the now-thriving grape vineyards of eastern Long Island and the Hudson Valley. The state Commerce Department's "I Love New York" campaign, which helped reenergize tourism, was something of which Carey was justifiably proud, given its measurable success in overcoming the state's ramshackle reputation nationally.

The governor's desire to make the state more amenable to businesses and stem a population drain led him to propose an ambitious, $5.5 billion program to rebuild New York City's dilapidated mass transit system. Leading the effort for Carey was Richard Ravitch, whom he appointed in the fall of 1979 as the head of the Metropolitan Transportation Authority. The proposal came about after a citywide transit strike in April, 1980, which hamstrung the city for days and sent Mayor Koch to the Brooklyn Bridge with a bullhorn to congratulate commuters walking to work in defiance of the union pickets. In the wake of a union-MTA wage agreement, which Koch denounced as too high and the EFCB acceded to, the showdown finally ended. The transit fare, as a result, would be raised to sixty cents, in spite of Carey's earlier pledge to try to maintain it at fifty cents. The aging system, though, was desperate for capital investment.[48]

Republicans in Albany came through in the end with support for a major subway rebuilding program, apparently accepting Ravitch's promise that neither he nor Carey would seek to convert the MTA's selection of contractors, suppliers, bond counsel, and underwriters under the capital program into a rich source of campaign donations for their party. It became a huge economic development program, since the subways are crucial to the city's economic vitality, though they had long been neglected by their state and city overseers.

Carey also backed Ravitch's unpopular proposal for a slight sales tax increase across the metropolitan region served by the MTA, suburbs included, which, upon approval, provided the system with additional operating aid and offset the need to raise the fare yet again, possibly to an inexcusable and, for many lower-income New Yorkers, unaffordable $1.00.

Still, despite such efforts, many voters remained in a sullen mood, irritated by taxes, the declining condition of neighborhoods, and the fear of losing their jobs. The economic landscape was changing profoundly: women were entering the workforce en masse for the first time since World War II, manufacturing was disappearing as a way of life, and a college degree was fast becoming a necessity for achieving a middle-class life.

## Obstacles

Like most public figures serving in tough times, Carey took his lumps in the press. As the second term was winding down, he was described by some as becoming aloof and detached. The *Economist* termed him "the sometimes governor." The city tabloids focused on his personal life, with one columnist calling him "Society Carey"[49] amid his courtship and marriage, in 1981, to Chicago heiress Evangeline Gouletas, whom he met at Ronald Reagan's inauguration. The marriage was annulled shortly thereafter.

Another problem arose when he tried to prevent a neighbor from building a two-and-a-half-story house on the property next door to his family's Shelter Island vacation home. *Newsday* found out about it in the fall of 1980, and the governor soon conceded he had gone too far due to what he described as "security concerns," and reversed course.[50]

Carey also clashed publicly with some of his commissioners—unusual for him. Major environmental controversies provided the occasion. In one case, the governor sought a settlement that would not be too onerous for General Electric after two of its factories, which employed two thousand people, were found to have discharged five hundred thousand pounds of PCBs (polychlorinated biphenyls) into the Hudson River north of Albany as part of their operations. Carey's environmental commissioner, Ogden Reid, was gone before the end of the controversy, as the governor felt he had tilted unfairly toward environmentalists even after GE developed a plan to use a safer chemical as an alternative. A 1976 agreement, worked out under Reid's successor, environmentalist Peter Berle, set the stage for a gradual cleanup effort, GE's installation of a treatment facility at its plants, and, with the administration's help in a recession, no state requirement that the company, a major employer, acknowledge liability. Berle, too, didn't last, as Carey felt he failed to reconcile environmental concerns with the need to retain the corporation as a major employer in the state. Berle also upset Carey when he denied an air-quality permit needed for the construction of Westway, an ill-fated Manhattan waterfront highway and park strongly supported by Carey for its economic development potential.[51]

However, Carey's record in a state majestic with natural beauty could hardly be termed antienvironment. During his tenure, an enduring and nationally influential state law was passed, requiring that all proposals for large projects, whether private or public, include an environmental impact statement. In 1980, he also convinced the federal government to partner with the state in purchasing eleven hundred homes in the vicinity of the Love Canal toxic chemical dump in the city of Niagara Falls. The Love Canal crisis helped spark the federal Superfund Law that year, which addressed thousands of toxic waste sites around the country. The Carey team prevailed separately on Congress in late 1980 to pick up most of the cost for cleaning up a nuclear rod recycling facility called West Valley in Cattaraugus County.[52]

## The Center Holds

In January of 1982, Carey announced he would not seek a third term. "I needed to make a living," he recalled years later, noting the growing gap that then existed between his $80,000-a-year gubernatorial salary and his ability to pay his many children's college tuition bills. As a result of the decision, he was forced to choose, again, between Cuomo and Koch in the year's Democratic gubernatorial primary. Carey remained neutral for as long as possible, only to endorse the then favored Mayor Koch several days before the primary election. This time, however, Cuomo defeated Koch, helped by heavy labor support across the state. Carey made an awkward peace with his lieutenant governor three weeks before the general election, and Cuomo went on to defeat Republican businessman Lewis Lehrman in November.

Carey had become a national political figure. He had led the rescue of New York City; he had kept the aftershocks of that crisis from staggering the entire state; he had, too, participated in a drive for an "open convention" at the Democratic National Convention in New York in an unsuccessful maneuver to allow Ted Kennedy to undo Jimmy Carter's delegate victories from the primaries; and he had, starting in early 1981, delivered an early and forceful denunciation of Reaganomics for its deleterious effects on the poor and on states' finances. But now it was clearly Mario Cuomo's time, and two years after his election, Cuomo electrified Democrats across the country with his speech at the 1984 Democratic National Convention in San Francisco, delivering his own, forceful retort to President Ronald Reagan's "Social Darwinism" and "trickle down" economic policies. By then, of course, the operatic Koch-Cuomo and Carey-Cuomo tensions mattered little, except perhaps to them. Koch was the undisputed king of the city, and Cuomo could no longer be dismissed by critics as Carey's puppet. He would serve three terms in Albany. Finally, like Carey, Cuomo—the Queens attorney with the golden tongue and philosophical bent, the "Hamlet on the Hudson" as the press dubbed him—would be promoted for the presidency by pundits, though he too would choose not to run.

## Beyond the Governorship

"Governor Carey's shortcomings were dwarfed by his stature as a leader, his weight of character," the *New York Times* stated in a farewell editorial entitled "A Governor For Hard Winters." It added, "He brought greatness to the office."

Indeed he did, in many ways.

Just weeks after leaving office, Carey spoke to fellow St. John's Law School alumni at an annual school event, and he was in rare form, recalled one participant, Joseph Bellacosa, who served as chief clerk of the state Court of Appeals during the 1976 "Moratorium Act" case and, in 1987, was named a justice on the high court; after his retirement from the bench, he served as dean of the St. John's Law School.

Carey offered brief remarks about his days at the law school, and then someone asked how it felt to walk away from all the influence, attention, pageantry, and entourage that were part of being the governor of the Empire State.

For the appreciative listeners, including Bellacosa, Carey's response was reminiscent of a common Latin catchphrase, *Sic transit gloria mundi*, or

"Thus passes the glory of the world." The meaning of the phrase has also been described as "Worldly things are fleeting." But the former governor's comment typified the way he tended to imbue his quips with the values of Irish wit and wisdom, as his parents had done.

"I knew it was gone," Carey said, referring to democratically conferred power, "when I took my jacket off and, with no one standing behind anymore to catch it, it just fell on the floor."[53]

Freed from the pressures and responsibilities of public life, Carey remained busy in key positions at several law firms and as the chair and executive vice president of H.R. Grace & Co., with headquarters in Washington, D.C. At one point, too, the New York State Department of Education and the New York State Catholic Conference asked Carey to chair a blue-ribbon panel on the future of Catholic schools, which provided a well-regarded road map to improve Catholic education.

Although none of his post-governorship endeavors could possibly offer Carey the same drama, purpose, and enjoyment he had experienced as an elected official, he did not run for office again. In 2001, he and his family suffered another tragedy when his seventh son, Paul, who had worked as White House special assistant to President Bill Clinton and then as a commissioner of the Securities and Exchange Commission, lost his battle with a rare form of cancer at age thirty-eight.

The former governor had eleven thriving sons and daughters, along with twenty-four grandchildren, and four great-grandchildren, and remained active in the political scene, offering endorsements to both Republicans and Democrats in various city, state, and national races and ultimately watching with interest as a young senator, Barack Obama of Illinois (whom he would endorse) rose to power.

"I take the liberty of comparing my situation with that of my candidate, Senator Obama," Carey said at his Manhattan apartment one sun-splashed day in October, 2008, when he anticipated, correctly, that Obama would win. The young president-to-be faced a financial crisis that was causing American businesses to collapse, joblessness and housing foreclosures to soar, credit to be sharply and abruptly tightened, and many states, New York included, to suffer revenue meltdowns—much of it depressingly reminiscent of 1975. "He's walking into a maelstrom," concluded Carey.[54]

Few Americans were in a better position to know.

Hugh Carey brought into government the best and brightest of people, many of whom he had never known before, who went on to excel in their future achievements but never forgot that he gave them their opening to service. He was one of New York's greatest governors and a national figure of major significance. He deserves the honor of posterity.

Like other Irish-American politicians of his era, he closed more than a few speeches by quoting William Butler Yeats. It was the great poet and dramatist, and two-term Irish senator, who wrote: "Things fall apart; the center cannot hold: / mere anarchy is loosed upon the world." Yet Yeats's dark vision was not fulfilled in the Carey years. By force of will, wit, intellect, and experience, Carey navigated New York through one of the most difficult periods imaginable, the worst time since the Great Depression of the 1930s, and notably and remarkably enabled it to emerge from the terrible ordeal on a strong footing.

Largely because of him, the center held.

# Notes

## Notes to Chapter 1

1. Sidney Schanberg, "They Applauded Life," *New York Times,* April 24, 1982, 23.

2. Clarence Sundram, telephone interview, May 6, 2008.

3. Felix Rohatyn, interview by Charlie Rose, *Charlie Rose Show,* December 21, 2000.

4. These and other family and personal recollections are from ten interviews, each three to four hours in duration, that Robert Polner conducted with Hugh Carey in Manhattan from late October, 2008, to late February, 2009.

5. Here we have been aided by *Timberwolf Tracks: The History of the 104th Infantry Division, 1942–1945,* by Leo A. Hoegh and Howard J. Doyle (Infantry Journal, Inc.: 1946).

6. Hugh Carey, interview by Robert Polner, December 9, 2008.

7. Ibid.

8. Oral history interview with Ken Hechler, World War II army combat historian, by Betty Lewis ("The Bridge at Remagen," www.appalachiacoal.com, July 14, 2001.). See, too, oral history interview with Ken Hechler at http://www.truman-library.org/oralhist/hechler.htm.

9. Ibid.

10. *Timberwolf Tracks* by Hoegh and Doyle contains soldiers' remembrances of Nordhausen, 327–38, as does "Remembrance of Things Past" from Ben Giladi's *A Tale of One City* (New York: Shengold, 1976), 296; and Martin Gilbert's *The Day The War Ended: May 8, 1945—Victory in Europe* (New York: Henry Holt, 1995), 10–11.

11. Mialet's and Farris's remembrances were drawn from the website www.jewishgen.org/forgottencamps and "Mittelbau-Dora Concentration Camp," www.104infdiv.org/concamp.htm.

12. Carey's recollections of Nordhausen are in Giladi's *A Tale of One City,* 296, and are cited as well in Gilbert's *The Day The War Ended,* 10–11.

13. Menachem Shayovich, interview by Seymour Lachman, August 6, 2008.

14. David Garth, interview by Robert Polner, June 23, 2008.

15. Hugh Carey, interview by Robert Polner, December 9, 2008.

16. Bruce Jackson, SUNY Distinguished Professor and Samuel Capen Professor of American Culture, University at Buffalo (see http://www.acsu.buffalo.edu/~bjackson/buffalocouncilcappun.html).


## Notes to Chapter 2

1. William V. Shannon, *The American Irish: A Political and Social Portrait*, (New York; Macmillan, 1963), 64.

2. For Irish-Black relations during the Civil War, see Leslie M. Harris, *In The Shadow of Slavery: African Americans in New York* (Chicago: University of Chicago Press, 2003), 263–88; and Susannah Ural Brace, *The Harp and the Eagle: Irish American Volunteers and the Union Army, 1861–1865* (New York: Carroll & Graf, 2006), 233–44. In *The American Irish,* William V. Shannon notes that before and during the Civil War "Irish opinion was almost unanimously opposed to abolition" despite a Papal bull opposing slavery, and that the anti-black attacks and attitudes were "a classic example of the poor in their misery venting their fury on other poor who were even worse off" (55–57).

3. Shannon, ibid., 72.

4. For *Rerum Novarum,* see www.newadvent.org/cathen/12783a.htm, as well as Joshua M. Zeitz, *White Ethnic New York: Jews, Catholics, and The Shaping of Postwar Politics* (Chapel Hill: University of North Carolina Press, 2007), 117–118.

5. See this online account in PoliticsNYC at http://www.politicsnyc.com/meetthenewbossb.shtml.

6. See Shannon, *The American Irish,* 78–84.

7. Seymour P. Lachman with Robert Polner, *Three Men in a Room: The Inside Story of Power and Betrayal in an American Statehouse* (New York: New Press, 2007), 67–74, for Frances Perkins's comments at Smith's funeral.

8. Hugh Carey, interview by Robert Polner, October 30, 2008.

9. Ibid.

10. Ibid.

11. Ibid.

12. Edward C. Carey, interview by Robert Polner, May 22, 2009.

13. Hugh Carey, interview by Robert Polner, November 19, 2008.

14. Nicholas Pileggi, "Cash and Carey," *New York,* May 1975, 46–52. (the article quotes a *New York Post* interview with Edward M. Carey). On Edward M. Carey, see also "The Other Carey," *Time,* July 21, 1975, and Paul Lewis's obituary, "Edward Carey, 85, Oil Executive and Brother's Campaign Backer," *New York Times,* May 14, 2002. See, too, John Corry's "Portrait of the Politician as a Private Man," *New York Times Magazine,* June 11, 1978, p. 27.

15. Hugh Carey, interview by Robert Polner, October 30, 2008.

16. Ibid.

17. Al Lewis, telephone interview, May 14, 2008.

18. For more on the Carey campaign style, see William V. Shannon, "The Last Hurrah," *New York Times Magazine,* May 14, 1976, 3. Hugh Carey's recollec-

tions are also in Anna Quinlan's "About New York," *New York Times*, November 3, 1982, B5

19. Hugh Carey, interview by Robert Polner, October 30, 2008.

20. Ibid.

21. The reference is to coauthor Seymour Lachman, who attended the rally.

22. Al Lewis, interview, May 14, 2008.

23. Ibid.

24. Shannon, "The Last Hurrah."

25. Dale Van Atta, "Cloud Riders," in *With Honor: Melvin Laird in War, Peace, and Politics* (Madison: The University of Wisconsin Press, 2008).

26. Hugh Carey, interview by Robert Polner, January 20, 2009.

27. Ibid.

28. Van Atta, *With Honor*, 82.

29. Ibid., 80–87.

30. See Irwin Unger, *The Best of Intentions: The Triumph and Failure of the Great Society Under Kennedy, Johnson, and Nixon* (New York: Doubleday, 1996).

31. Guian McKee, "Prelude to Faith-Based Initiatives?" The Johnson Presidential Recordings and the Debate over Parochial Schools in the War on Poverty, *Presidential Recordings Project*, Winter 2003, 21–27. Another of Congressman Carey's major contributions in Congress included a bill to provide for the education and training of the handicapped, which Carey introduced on August 4, 1966 (HR 16847), "to provide for the education and training of the handicapped." It became known as the Handicapped Child Benefit and Education Act.

32. Ibid., "Prelude to Faith-Based Initiatives?"

33. Ibid.

34. See Lester Sobel, ed., *New York and the Urban Dilemma* (New York: Facts on File, 1976), 82–84.

35. Carey, interview by Robert Polner, October 30, 2008.

36. Michael Long, Conservative Party chairman, telephone interview by Robert Polner, May 6, 2009.

37. Hugh Carey and David Burke, interview by Robert Polner, February 25, 2009.

38. Ibid.

39. Vincent J. Cannato, *The Ungovernable City: John Lindsay and His Struggle to Save New York* (New York: Basic Books, 2001), 413.

40. Editorial, *New York Times*, June 25, 1969.

41. Tom Regan, telephone interview by Robert Polner, May 12, 2009.

42. Ibid.

43. The authors were influenced by Hugh Carey's account of this episode in an interview with Robert Polner on October 30, 2008. For a somewhat different account, see Thomas P. O'Neill with William Novak in *Man of the House: The Life and Political Memoirs of Speaker Tip O'Neill* (New York: Random House, 1987), 218–20. Further insight into Carey's congressional experience was provided by Larry L. King's "Case of Pig-Shit Irish: The Road to Power in Congress: The Education of Mo Udall and What it Cost," *Harper's*, June 1971, 61. See, too, Martin Nolan, "New York's Congressmen: The House is Not a Home," *New York*, March 22, 1971.

44. Hugh Carey, interview by Robert Polner, October 30, 2008.
45. Hugh Carey, interview by Robert Polner, December 9, 2008.
46. Hugh Carey and Tom Regan, interview by Robert Polner, December 18, 2008.

## Notes to Chapter 3

1. The authors were aided by the recollections of Ken Auletta in a telephone interview with Robert Polner on July 31, 2008.
2. Daniel C. Kramer. *The Days of Wine and Roses Are Over: Governor Hugh Carey and New York State* (Lanham, MD: University Press of America, 1997), 20. The book is an excellent source on the Carey administration.
3. Hugh L. Carey, interview by Robert Polner, December 18, 2008.
4. Tom Regan, interview by Robert Polner, December 18, 2008.
5. Ken Auletta, telephone interview by Robert Polner, July 31, 2008.
6. Ibid.
7. David Garth, interview by Robert Polner, June 23, 2008.
8. Ibid.
9. Tom Regan, telephone interview by Robert Polner, March 12, 2009.
10. Jerry Cummins, telephone interview by Robert Polner, May 21, 2009.
11. Ibid.
12. Frank Lynn, "Carey, Starting Drive, Calls Wilson 'Nixon's Man.'" *New York Times*, March 27, 1974, 22.
13. Carol Opton, interview by Robert Polner, June 18, 2008.
14. Jeff Greenfield, conversation with Robert Polner, April 18, 2009.
15. David Garth generously provided authors Seymour P. Lachman and Robert Polner access to his archive of Carey campaign commercials.
16. Jerry Cummins, telephone interview by Robert Polner, May 21, 2009.
17. Andy Logan, "Around City Hall: Numbers Game," *The New Yorker*, July 8, 1974, 52–60.
18. Hugh Carey, interview by Robert Polner, December 11, 2008.
19. Ibid.
20. Jerry Cummins, telephone interview by Robert Polner, May 21, 2009.
21. The authors benefitted from the *New York Daily News*'s and *New York Post*'s coverage of the 1974 convention, available on microfilm at the New York Public Library.
22. Ken Auletta, telephone interview by Robert Polner, July 31, 2008.
23. Pileggi, "Cash and Carey" (see ch. 2, n. 14).
24. Jerry Cummins, telephone interview by Robert Polner, May 21, 2009.
25. Andy Logan in "Around City Hall: The Woodman and the Tiger," *The New Yorker*, August 26, 1974, 66–69.
26. Linda Greenhouse, interview by Seymour P. Lachman, June 30, 2008, and telephone interview by Robert Polner, December 8, 2008.
27. Ibid.
28. Logan, "The Woodman and the Tiger."

29. The authors relied on the campaign reporting of numerous reporters from the *New York Post* and *New York Daily News*.

30. Richard Reeves in "Carey vs. Wilson: And in Each Corner, Nelson Rockefeller," *New York Times Magazine*, October 27, 1974.

31. See Fred Ferretti, "Before The Year," in *The Year the Big Apple Went Bust: The Intimate, Blow-by-Blow Account of New York's Financial Follies* (New York: G. P. Putnam's Sons, 1976), 23–83. Ferretti's book is an especially a valuable source.

32. Kramer, *The Days of Wine and Roses Are Over*, 19.

33. Ibid., 33.

34. Frank Lynn, "Wilson and Carey Debate State and National Issues" and accompanying "Excerpts for the Wilson-Carey debate," *New York Times*, October 15, 1974.

35. Editorial, *New York Times*, November 4, 1974.

36. Abraham Beame and Harrison J. Goldin, letter to the editor, *New York Times*, November 11, 1974, cited in Robert W. Bailey, *The Crisis Regime: The New York City Financial Crisis* (Albany: State University of New York Press, 1984), 18.

37. Christopher Carey and Hugh Carey, interview by Robert Polner, November 19, 2008.

## Notes to Chapter 4

1. See Robert P. Kerker's *The Executive Budget in New York State: A Half-Century Perspective* (New York: New York State Division of the Budget), 144–48.

2. Hugh Carey, interview by Robert Polner, November 19, 2008. Carey also referred to Rockefeller's comments, speaking at a conference on the Carey years held in New York City on Apr. 20, 1995 (cited in Kramer, *The Days of Wine and Roses Are Over*, 34).

3. Kerker, *The Executive Budget in New York State*, 148.

4. Hugh Carey discusses the transition in an interview he gave for *Making Experience Count: Managing Modern New York in the Carey Era*, edited by Gerald Benjamin and T. Norman Hurd (Albany: Nelson A. Rockefeller Institute of Government, 1985), 1–15.

5. John Dyson, interview by Seymour Lachman and Robert Polner, July 29, 2009.

6. Ibid.

7. According to Cummins, Carey, in addition to having a steel-trap memory, possessed the ability to read someone else's position paper and "fifteen minutes later sound as if he had written it himself."

8. Benjamin and Hurd, *Making Experience Count*, 1–15.

9. Ferretti, *The Year the Big Apple Went Bust*, 99.

10. See Sam Roberts, "Democratic Infighting, Old-Time Party Bosses and Gridlock that Lasted Weeks, in 1965," *New York Times*, June 22, 2009, A21

11. Hugh Carey, interview by Robert Polner, November 19, 2008.

12. See Jewel Bellush and Bernard Bellush, *Union Power and New York: Victor Gotbaum and District Council 37* (New York: Praeger, 1984).

13. Robert A. Caro, *The Power Broker: Robert Moses and the Fall of New York* (New York: Alfred Knopf, 1974), 734.

14. Ibid., 734–56. There are those, however, who believe even Robert Moses's power had its limits. See, for example, Henry T. Fetter, "Revising the Revisionists: Walter O'Malley, Robert Moses, and the End of the Brooklyn Dodgers," *New York History*, Winter 2008, especially p. 60 and his citation of the introduction by Hilary Ballon and Kenneth T. Jackson to their coedited volume, *Robert Moses and the Modern City: The Transformation of New York* (W. W. Norton, 2007), 66. See, too, Leonard Wallock, "The Myth of the Master Builder," *Journal of Urban History* (August 1991), 339–62.

15. Adam Simms, "New York's 'Secret Government': Public Authorities are Out of Control and Threatening the State's Fiscal Health" (Staten Island, NY: Hugh L. Carey Center for Government Reform, Wagner College, 2008).

16. Ibid, Simms. See also *Restoring Credit and Confidence: A Reform Program for New York State and Its Public Authorities: A Report to the Governor by the New York State Moreland Act Commission on the Urban Development Corporation and Other State Financing Agencies,* March 31, 1976.

17. Jack Newfield and Paul DuBrul, *The Abuse of Power: The Permanent Government and the Fall of New York* (New York: Viking, 1977), 28.

18. Hugh Carey, interview by Robert Polner, November 19, 2008.

19. Carol Opton, interview by Robert Polner, June 18, 2008.

20. After a series of positions serving the Carey campaign and the Carey administration,Opton was named deputy secretary to the governor and remained so throughout his second term.

21. Hugh Carey, interview by Robert Polner, January 16, 2009.

22. See Benjamin and Hurd, *Making Experience Count*, 7–8.

23. Jeff Greenfield, conversation with Robert Polner, April 18, 2009.

24. Francis X. Clines, interview by Seymour Lachman and Robert Polner, August 19, 2008.

25. Hugh Carey, interview by Robert Polner, November 19, 2008.

26. See *Restoring Credit and Confidence.*

27. Simms, "New York's 'Secret Government'"

28. Benjamin and Hurd, *Making Experience Count*, 4–5.

29. Kramer, *The Days of Wine and Roses Are Over,* 46.

30. See *Restoring Credit and Confidence.*

31. Kramer, *The Days of Wine and Roses Are Over,* 45–47

32. Richard Ravitch, interview by Seymour Lachman and Robert Polner, June 27, 2008.

33. Ibid.

34. Ibid.

35. Ibid.

36. Ibid.

37. Simms, "New York's 'Secret Government.'"

38. Ibid.

39. Hugh Carey, interview by Robert Polner, January 16, 2009.

40. Stephen Berger, interview by Seymour Lachman and Robert Polner, May 30, 2008.

41. Hugh Carey, interview by Robert Polner, November 19, 2008.

42. A copy of the memo was made available by Peter Goldmark.

43. Peter Goldmark, interview by Seymour Lachman and Robert Polner, March 2, 2009.

44. The authors' account of the growth of contemporary New York City was greatly aided by Thomas Kessner, *Fiorello H. LaGuardia and the Making of Modern New York* (New York: Penguin, 1989); Roger E. Alcalay and David Mermelstein, eds., *The Fiscal Crisis of American Cities: Essays on the Political Economy of Urban America with Special Reference to New York* (New York: Random House, 1977); Roger Sanjek, *The Future of Us All: Race and Neighborhood Politics in New York City* (Ithaca, NY: Cornell University Press, 1989); Joshua B. Freeman, *Working Class New York: Life and Labor Since World War II* (New York: New Press, 2000); and William K. Tabb, *The Long Default: New York City and the Urban Fiscal Crisis* (New York: Monthly Review Press, 1982). In addition, see "New York City's Fiscal Problem: Its Origins, Potential Repercussions, and Some Alternative Policy Responses," Background Paper No. 1. (Washington, DC: Congressional Budget Office, October 10, 1975), and Rona B. Stein, "The New York City Budget: Anatomy of a Fiscal Crisis," *FRBNY Quarterly Review* (Winter 1976).

45. See Congressional Budget Office, "New York City's Fiscal Problem."

46. In the introduction to his invaluable book on the MAC, the EFCB, and the political impact of the New York City financial crisis, *The Crisis Regime*, Bailey aptly writes, "There is always pressure to spend in New York because there is so much to be done" (4).

47. See Kessner, "New York City Before LaGuardia," *Fiorello H. LaGuardia and the Making of Modern New York,* 208.

48. Ibid.

49. See Charles R. Morris, "Wagner and Lindsay," in *The Cost of Good Intentions: New York City and the Liberal Experiment, 1960–1975* (New York: McGraw Hill, 1980), 21–22.

## Notes to Chapter 5

1. Hugh Carey interview by Robert Polner, November 19, 2008.

2. See "The ITT Affair," *Time,* March 13, 1972.

3. Ibid. See also "Dita Beard on Dita Beard," *Time,* April 3, 1972.

4. "The ITT Affair" and "Dita Beard on Dita Beard."

5. See "Investment: Felix the Fixer," *Time,* June 17, 1974.

6. Hugh Carey, interview by Robert Polner, November 19, 2008.

7. Felix Rohatyn, interview by Seymour Lachman and Robert Polner, July 13, 2008.

8. Ibid.

9. Ibid.

10. David Burke and Hugh Carey, interview by Robert Polner, February 25, 2009.

11. Felix Rohatyn, interview by Seymour Lachman and Robert Polner, July 13, 2008.

12. Tom Regan and Hugh Carey, interview by Robert Polner, December 18, 2008. John Dyson separately recalled the staff discussions, including the moment of Carey's decisive declaration.

13. Paul Gioia, telephone interview by Robert Polner, December 30, 2008.

14. The descriptive "unthinkable" appears in Carey's September 5, 1975, address to the state legislature calling for passage of the Emergency Financial Act and, under it, an Emergency Financial Control Board to enforce city spending limits.

15. Steven R. Weisman, telephone interview by Robert Polner, August 3, 2009.

16. Morris, *The Cost of Good Intentions*, 223.

17. "The tradition in New York," Dick Netzer, then dean of the Graduate School of Public Administration at New York University (now the Robert F. Wagner Graduate School of Public Service) told the *Times*'s Steven Weisman, "is that the budget is a fake piece of paper from the start of the fiscal year. There's confusion, lack of knowledge, obscurity and use of stealth." See Weisman's "How New York Became a Fiscal Junkie," *New York Times Magazine*, August 17, 1975.

18. See Morris, *The Cost of Good Intentions*, 223.

19. Ibid.

20. Congressional Budget Office, "New York City's Fiscal Problem," 6 (see chap. 4, n. 44)

21. See Sanjek, *The Future of Us All*, 83–93, and Freeman, *Working Class New York*, 256–58. See, too, Congressional Budget Office, "New York City's Fiscal Problem."

22. See Ferretti, *The Year the Big Apple Went Bust*, 105–12.

23. Ibid., 107

24. Ibid., 108.

25. Ibid., 133.

26. Paul Hoffman, *Lions of the Eighties: The Inside Story of the Powerhouse Law Firms* (New York: Doubleday, 1982), 238–40.

27. Ibid.

28. Edward I. Koch, interview by Seymour Lachman and Robert Polner, June 26, 2008.

29. See Ferretti, *The Year the Big Apple Went Bust*, 152.

30. Ibid., 53.

31. See Morris, *The Cost of Good Intentions*, 228–31.

32. See Bailey, *The Crisis Regime*, 24

33. The speech is excerpted in Ferretti, *The Year the Big Apple Went Bust*, 157–61.

34. Ibid., 161.

35. Ibid., 167.

36. See Congressional Budget Office, "New York City's Fiscal Problem," 5.

37. See Charles J. Orlebeke, "Saving New York: The Ford Administration and the New York City Fiscal Crisis," in *Gerald R. Ford and the Politics of Post-Watergate America*, vol. 2, ed. Bernard J. Firestone and Alexej Ugrinsky (Westport, CT: Greenwood, 1992), 361.

38. Hugh Carey, interview by Robert Polner, November 19, 2008.

39. President Ford's "Dear Abe" letter is excerpted in Ferretti, *The Year The Big Apple Went Bust*, 187–88.

40. William E. Simon, *A Time For Truth*, (New York: Readers Digest Press, 1978), 165.

41. Ferretti, *The Year the Big Apple Went Bust*, 189–90.

42. Ibid., 191.

43. Orlebeke, "Saving New York," 366.

44. Beame's speech is excerpted in Ferretti, *The Year the Big Apple Went Bust*, starting on p. 199.

45. Ibid., 209–11.

46. George Arzt, interview by Robert Polner, July 8, 2008.

47. Hugh Carey, interview by Robert Polner, December 18, 2008.

48. Ferretti, *The Year the Big Apple Went Bust*, 214.

49. Ibid., 216.

50. Ibid.

51. The statutory powers of MAC are well described in Bailey, *The Crisis Regime*, 27–33.

52 Ibid., 30.

53. Ferretti, *The Year the Big Apple Went Bust*, 221–22.

54. Ibid., 235

55. Ibid., 236–37.

56. Bailey, *The Crisis Regime*, 30–31.

57. Felix Rohatyn, interview by Seymour Lachman and Robert Polner, July 13, 2008.

58. The letter is included in Ferretti, *The Year the Big Apple Went Bust*, 255–58.

59. Ibid., 259.

60. Ibid., 260.

61. Ibid., 265.

62. Felix Rohatyn, interview by Seymour Lachman and Robert Polner, July 13, 2008.

63. William Ellinghaus, telephone interview by Robert Polner, April 29, 2009.

64. Felix Rohatyn, interview by Seymour Lachman and Robert Polner, July 13, 2008.

65. Ferretti, *The Year the Big Apple Went Bust*, 268–73

66. Ibid., 273–79. Ferretti includes Beame's entire address before the city council.

67. Howard Rubenstein, interview by Seymour Lachman and Robert Polner, May 10, 2008.


## Notes to Chapter 6

1. The authors' account of the city's near-default and the "Bankers' Agreement" during the Great Depression was aided by Thomas Kessner's chapter "Now We Have a Mayor" (257-91) in his biography of Fiorello H. LaGuardia, and Robert Caro's chapter "New York City Before Robert Moses" (323–46) in *The Power Broker*.

2. See Kessner, *Fiorello H. La Guardia and the Making of Modern New York*, 263.

3. Richard Ravitch, interview by Seymour Lachman and Robert Polner, February 4, 2009.

4. Orlebke, "Saving New York: The Ford Administration and the New York City Fiscal Crisis," in *Gerald R. Ford and the Politics of Post-Watergate America*, vol. 2, ed. Bernard J. Firestone and Alexej Ugrinsky (Westport, CT: Greenwood, 1992), 365.

5. Ibid., 367.

6. See Ferretti, *The Year the Big Apple Went Bust*, 298–99, in which the Ellinghaus letter is reprinted.

7. Ibid., 299–301

8. The September 4, 1975, editorial in the *Wall Street Journal* entitled "The Last Recourse" began this way: "The fiscal agony of New York has gone on so long that the only hope for a responsible and reasonably straightforward resolution is a voluntary bankruptcy," and quickly added, "Voluntary bankruptcy is to be preferred to involuntary bankruptcy," as the city "desperately needs a rearrangement of its debts and obligations, including labor contracts and pension plans."

9. Felix Rohatyn, interview by Seymour Lachman and Robert Polner, July 13, 2008.

10. For a transcript of the Carey address, see Ferretti, *The Year the Big Apple Went Bust*, 314–18.

11. Ibid., 316.

12. Peter Goldmark, interview by Seymour Lachman and Robert Polner, July 15, 2008.

13. Al Viani, telephone interview by Robert Polner, February 18, 2009.

14. Jack Bigel and Edward Rogowsky, interview of Gedale D. Horowitz (videotaped), Graduate School and University Center, CUNY, November 11, 1986.

15. Hugh Carey, interview by Robert Polner, January 16, 2009.

16. The authors are grateful for Bailey's insights and detailed account—in *The Crisis Regime*— of the Financial Emergency Act and the powers of the new EFCB (39–46).

17. Ferretti, *The Year the Big Apple Went Bust*, 318

18. Ibid., 319.

19. Ibid., 305.

20. Hugh Carey, interview by Robert Polner, January 16, 2009.

21. Richard D. Kahlenberg, *Tough Liberal: Albert Shanker and the Battles Over Schools, Unions, Race, and Democracy* ( New York: Columbia University Press, 2007), 182.

22. Ibid., 183.

23. Ibid.

24. Ferretti, *The Year the Big Apple Went Bust*, 336; the Beame speech is reprinted in its entirety.

25. Ibid., 340.

26. Richard Ravitch, interview by Seymour Lachman and Robert Polner, February 4, 2009.

27. Hugh Carey, interview by Robert Polner, November 19, 2008.

28. Richard Ravitch, interview by Seymour Lachman and Robert Polner, February 4, 2009.

29. See Hoffman, *Lions of the Eighties*, 250.

30. Ibid., 251.

31. Ibid., 251.

32. James Vlasto (former Carey press secretary, and a friend of Victor Gotbaum), telephone interview by Robert Polner, December 11, 2009.

33. Sidney Frigand, telephone interview by Robert Polner, August 19, 2009.

34. Richard Ravitch, interview by Seymour Lachman and Robert Polner, February 4, 2009.

35. Ibid.

36. Kahlenberg, *Tough Liberal*, 185–86

37. Richard Ravitch, interview by Seymour Lachman and Robert Polner, February 4, 2009.


## Notes to Chapter 7

1. See Orlebeke, "Saving New York: The Ford Administration and the New York City Fiscal Crisis," in *Gerald R. Ford and the Politics of Post-Watergate America,* vol. 2, ed. Bernard J. Firestone and Alexej Ugrinsky, 372. This section of Orlebeke's essay is entitled "Rocky Jumps Ship." Orlebeke later alludes to Rockefeller's view that key White House advisers urging Ford to rebuff New York City's plea for assistance were partly motivated by a desire to isolate the vice president and "knock me off" the Ford reelection ticket for 1976 (Rockefeller interview transcript dated October 31, 1977, 32–33, File NAR interview with Trevor Armblister, Box 35, James Cannon Papers, GRFL). Armblister was Ford's collaborator in the writing of Ford's *A Time to Heal: The Autobiography of Gerald R. Ford* (New York: Harper & Row, 1979).

2. As Martin Shefter notes in the introduction to his seminal *Political Crisis/Fiscal Crisis: The Collapse and Revival of New York City* (New York: Basic Books, 1985), "The threat of fiscal crisis distinguishes urban politics from national politics in the United States. The national government is not periodically threatened with bankruptcy, even though deficit spending has become a regular feature of federal fiscal policy. The national government can always acquire the cash to pay its bills, even if federal tax revenues fall behind federal expenditures, because it possesses the legal

authority to print money—that is, if its revenues will not cover its expenditures, the federal government can always inflate the currency." Prior to 1975, New York City fiscal crises occurred in 1856, 1871, 1907, 1914, and 1933, he added.

3. Orlebeke, "Saving New York," 368.

4. Ibid., 369.

5. Hugh Carey and David Burke, interview by Robert Polner, February 25, 2009.

6. Orlebeke, "Saving New York," 369–70.

7. The Carey group included Burke, Goldmark, Rohatyn, Rifkind, Ellinghaus, Levitt, first assistant counsel Michael Nadel, and John Heimann. Ford had with him eight aides, including, in part, Rumsfeld, Seidman, Greenspan, and Yeo.

8. Hugh Carey, interview by Robert Polner, November 19, 2008, and January 20, 2009.

9. Orlebeke, "Saving New York," 371.

10. The Laird golf game and Mayor Daley anecdotes are drawn from the Carey interviews with Robert Polner, a telephone interview that Laird gave to Polner on February 20, 2009, and Dale Van Atta's "A Second Career" in *With Honor: Melvin Laird in War, Peace, and Politics* (Madison: University of Wisconsin Press, 2008).

11. Melvin Laird, telephone interview by Robert Polner, February 20, 2008.

12. Hugh Carey, interview by Robert Polner, November 19, 2008.

13. See Lester Sobel, ed., *New York and the Urban Dilemma* (New York: Facts on File, 1976), 135.

14. Ibid., 134.

15. Ibid., 140.

16. Orlebeke, "Saving New York," 373.

17. Testimony by Governor Hugh L. Carey before the Senate Committee on Banking, Housing, and Urban Affairs, Dirksen Senate Office Building, Washington, D.C., October 10, 1975 (issued by Robert Laird, Press Secretary to the Governor), Georgetown University Library.

18. Orlebeke, "Saving New York," 373.

19. The Ford speech is reprinted in its entirely in Sobel, ed., *New York and the Urban Dilemma*, 144–47.

20. Felix Rohatyn, interview by Seymour Lachman and Robert Polner, July 13, 2008.

21. Cannon's comments are included in *Gerald R. Ford and the Politics of Post-Watergate America*, vol. 2, ed. Bernard J. Firestone and Alexej Ugrinsky, 396–97. Among the other discussants at the April, 1989, Hofstra University forum on the New York City fiscal crisis were Abraham Beame, Hugh Carey, Richard Ravitch, and Ken Auletta; their remarks are also included in the volume.

22. Melvin Laird, telephone interview by Robert Polner, February 20, 2009.

23. Hugh Carey, interview by Robert Polner, February 25, 2009, in which he stated his belief that Ford generously afforded him extra time to try to win congressional votes in favor of aiding the city, and that if he was successful, and only then, Ford would support federal assistance. Carey worried that the fallout from the *Daily News* headline might cancel out their understanding.

24. Sobel, ed., *New York and the Urban Dilemma*, 147.

25. Ibid., 147–48.

26. Ibid., 151.

27. Ibid., 149–50.

28. See Orlebeke, "Saving New York," 380–81.

29. Sobel, ed., *New York and the Urban Dilemma,* 151.

30. Tom Regan, telephone interview by Robert Polner, January 16, 2009.

31. Hugh Carey, interview by Robert Polner, November 19, 2008.

32. Ibid.

33. Ibid.

34. Felix Rohatyn, interview by Seymour Lachman and Robert Polner, July 13, 2008.

35. Sobel, ed.,. *New York and the Urban Dilemma,* 157–58

36. Ibid., 153–54.

37. Joseph Bellacosa, who served at the time as chief clerk to the Court of Appeals, recounted the case in an interview with Robert Polner in June, 2009.

38. John Connorton Jr., interview by Seymour Lachman and Robert Polner, May 19, 2008.

39. Peter Goldmark, interview by Seymour Lachman and Robert Polner, March 2, 2009.

## Notes to Chapter 8

1. The authors' account of the 1976 rescue of the state authorities was aided by "The Goldmark Buildout and the State Tax Hike" in Daniel C. Kramer's *The Days of Wine and Roses Are Over* (Lanham, MD: University Press of America, 1997); interviews with Peter Goldmark by the authors; and Ronald M. Joseph's "The 1976 New York State Fiscal Crisis," draft paper, unpublished (Boston University, School of Management Public Management Program, Curriculum Development Project, August, 1981); and Robert Kerker's *The Executive Budget in New York State: A Half-Century Perspective* (New York: New York State Division of the Budget) and the section entitled "The Build-out," 187–89.

2. See Lester Sobel, ed., *New York and the Urban Dilemma* (New York: Facts on File, 1976), 167. John Connorton Jr. also discussed the Yonkers near-default in an interview with the authors on May 19, 2008.

3. Peter Goldmark, interview by Seymour Lachman and Robert Polner, March 2, 2009. This type of encounter is also mentioned in Kramer's *The Days of Wine and Roses Are Over,* 96.

4. Peter Goldmark, interview by Seymour Lachman and Robert Polner, March 2, 2009.

5. See Kramer, *The Days of Wine and Roses Are Over,* 97.

6. Linda Greenhouse, "Roundup Time in Albany: Comic Opera," *New York Times,* March 13, 1976, 36.

7. Kerker, *The Executive Budget in New York State: A Half-Century Perspective,* 188.

8. Ibid., 189.

9. Thomas P. Ronan, *New York Times*, February 29, 1976, 1.

10. Anthony Lewis, "The Zeal of Maurice Nadjari," *New York Times Magazine*, Mar. 28, 1976, 188.

11. Jacob Grumet, New York State special deputy attorney general, and Nathan Skolnik, special assistant attorney general, "Report of an Investigation of Charges Made by Special Prosecutor Maurice H. Nadjari Concerning Governor Hugh L. Carey," June 21, 1976.

12. Ibid.

13. Ibid.

14. Ibid.

15. Ibid. This headline is cited in the report.

16. As it happened, the Carey-Lefkowitz meeting occurred December 29, the day a bomb linked to a Croatian "liberation" group exploded in a locker at LaGuardia Airport, killing eleven people and wounding seventy-five.

17. Hugh Carey, Judah Gribetz, and Michael Nadel; interview by Robert Polner. January 29, 2009.

18. See Grumet and Skolnik, "Report of an Investigation," 100.

19. Ibid., 100–101

20. Patrick Cunningham was sentenced in January, 1983, to three and a half years in prison for tax evasion and obstruction of justice in a separate case related to his law practice.

21. John Keenan, telephone interview by Robert Polner, September 8, 2009.

22. S. Michael Nadel with Hugh Carey and Judah Gribetz, interview by Robert Polner, January 29, 2009.

23. Kramer, *The Days of Wine and Roses Are Over*, 241–46

24. Clarence Sundram, "Willowbrook: The Community Challenge and The Role of Leadership," *AAMR News & Notes* 13: 4 (July–August 2000). The article deals with the twenty-fifth anniversary of the signing of the Willowbrook Consent Judgment, at an event held May 2, 2000, on the grounds of the former institution. See, too, Sundram, "Where has watchdog gone?" *Albany Times Union*, January 26, 2010.

25. David J. Rothman and Sheila M. Rothman, *The Willowbrook Wars: A Decade of Struggle for Social Justice* (New York: Harper & Row), 121, 365, and *passim.*

26. Celia W. Dugger, "Big Day for Ex-Residents of Center for the Retarded," *New York Times*, March 12.1993, 1.

27. In an interview in Manhattan with Robert Polner and Seymour Lachman on June 26, 2008, Edward I. Koch recalled telling an audience of senior citizens during the 1977 mayoral race about a liberal judge who refused to renounce his record of leniency toward violent criminals after he was mugged on the city's streets. A woman sitting in the audience shouted out: "Mug him again!" To Koch, such moments were further evidence that crime was the number one issue of the campaign.

28. Jonathan Mahler, *The Bronx is Burning; 1977, Baseball, Politics, and the Battle for the Soul of a City* (New York: Picador, 2005), 233.

29. Hugh Carey with S. Michael Nadel and Judah Gribetz, interview by Robert Polner, January 29, 2009.

30. Kramer, *The Days of Wine and Roses Are Over*, 257.

31. Ibid., 321–22.

32. Ibid., 255–56. In addition, Carey, Gribetz, and Nadel spoke at length about the Attica re-investigation in an interview with Robert Polner on January 29, 2009.

33. *New York Times*, November 27, 1977.

34. See Robert H. Connery and Gerald Benjamin, "The Governor and Urban Problems," in *Rockefeller of New York: Executive Power in the Statehouse* (New York: Cornell University, 1972).

35. Kramer, *The Days of Wine and Roses Are Over*, 262–64.

36. David Burke and Hugh Carey, interview by Robert Polner, February 25, 2009.

37. Sidney Frigand, interview by Robert Polner, July 14, 2008.

38. Mahler, *The Bronx is Burning*, 288.

39. Howard Rubenstein, interview by Seymour Lachman and Robert Polner, May 10, 2008.

40. The Hofstra conference on the Ford presidency was held over three days in April, 1989 and included a two-hour discussion on the fiscal crisis in which Carey, Beame, and former local, state and federal officials participated.

41. William T. Cunningham, telephone interview by Robert Polner, June 11, 2008.

42. John Dyson, interview by Seymour Lachman and Robert Polner, July 29, 2009.

43. Kramer, *The Days of Wine and Roses are Over*, 169–70.

44. See Kramer, "Carey, the Democratic party, and the State Legislature," in *The Days of Wine and Roses Are Over.*

45. Ibid.

46. James Brigham, interview by Robert Polner, July 10, 2008.

47. Richard Ravitch, interview by Seymour Lachman and Robert Polner. See also Kramer, "Carey and Ravitch Fix the Subways," in *The Days of Wine and Roses Are Over.*

48. The columnist was Jimmy Breslin.

49. His official statement (Press Release, November 12, 1980) stated in part: "I have directed the State Department of Transportation to rescind all legal action taken regarding the property . . . The title now will be re-conveyed . . . In light of this action, I have also asked the State Police to reassess the security questions originally raised relative to my residence on Shelter Island. I have been spending time on Shelter Island for 25 years. I regret if my position as Governor has in any way been a burden to my neighbors, and I trust my continued residence there will not cause them any inconvenience."

50. See Kramer, "Carey's Environmental Policy: A Balancing Act," in *The Days of Wine and Roses Are Over.*

51. Ibid.

52. Richard Ravitch, interview by Seymour Lachman and Robert Polner, February 4, 2009. See also Kramer, "Carey and Ravitch Fix the Subways" in *The Days of Wine and Roses Are Over.*

53 Joseph Bellacosa, interview by Robert Polner, June, 2009.

54. Hugh Carey, interview by Robert Polner, October 30, 2008.

# Selected Bibliography

Alcaly, Roger E., and David Mermelstein, eds. *The Fiscal Crisis of American Cities.* New York: Vintage, 1977.

Auletta, Ken. *The Streets Were Paved With Gold.* New York: Random House, 1979.

Bailey, Robert W. *The Crisis Regime: The M.A.C., the E.F.C.B., and the Political Impact of the New York City Financial Crisis.* Albany: State University of New York Press, 1984.

Bellush, Jewell, and Bernard Bellush. *Union Power and New York: Victor Gotbaum and District Council 37.* New York: Praeger, 1984.

Benjamin, Gerald, and T. Norman Hurd, eds. *Making Experience Count: Managing Modern New York in the Carey Era.* Albany, NY: Nelson A. Rockefeller Institute of Government, 1985.

Blum, Elizabeth D. *Love Canal Revisited: Race, Class, and Gender in Environmental Activism.* Lawrence: University Press of Kansas, 2008.

Brace, Susannah Ural. *The Harp and the Eagle: Irish American Volunteers and the Union Army, 1861–1865.* New York: Carroll & Graf, 2006.

Cannato, Vincent J. *The Ungovernable City: John Lindsay and His Struggle to Save New York.* New York: Perseus Books, 2001.

Caro, Robert. *The Power Broker: Robert Moses and the Fall of New York.* New York: Knopf, 1974.

Connery, Robert H., and Gerald Benjamin. *Rockefeller of New York: Executive Power in the Statehouse.* Ithaca, NY: Cornell University Press, 1979.

Egnal, Marc. *Clash of Extremes: The Economic Origins of the Civil War.* New York: Hill & Wang, 2009.

Elliot, Lawrence. *Little Flower: The Life and Times of Fiorello LaGuardia.* New York: Morrow, 1983.

Ferretti, Fred. *The Year the Big Apple Went Bust.* New York: Putnam, 1976.

Firestone, Bernard J., and Alexej Ugrinsky, eds. *Gerald R. Ford and the Politics of Post-Watergate America.* Vol. 2. Westport, CT: Greenwood Press, 1992.

Freeman, Joshua. *Working Class New York: Life and Labor Since World War II.* New York: The New Press, 2000.

Fuchs, Ester. *Mayors and Money: Fiscal Policy in New York and Chicago.* Chicago: University of Chicago Press, 1992.

Giladi, Ben. *A Tale of One City.* New York: Shengold, 1976.

Gilbert. Martin. *The Day The War Ended: May 8, 1945—Victory in Europe.* New York: Henry Holt, 1995.

Greenberg, Miriam. *Branding New York: How a City in Crisis Was Sold to the World.* New York: Routledge, 2008.

Harris, Leslie M. *In The Shadow of Slavery: African Americans in New York City, 1626–1863.* Chicago: University of Chicago Press, 2003.

Hoffman, Paul. *Lions of the Eighties: The Inside Story of the Powerhouse Law Firms.* New York: Signet, 1973.

Kahlenberg, Richard. *Tough Liberal: Albert Shanker and the Battle Over Schools, Unions, Race, and Democracy.* New York: Columbia University Press, 2007.

Kenny, Kevin. *The American Irish: A History.* New York, Longman, 2000.

Kerker, Robert P. *The Executive Budget in New York State: A Half Century Perspective.* Albany: New York State Division of the Budget, 1981.

Kessner, Thomas. *Fiorello H. LaGuardia and The Making of Modern New York.* New York: McGraw Hill, 1989.

Kosmin, Barry, and Seymour P. Lachman. *One Nation Under God: Religion in Contemporary America.* New York: Simon and Schuster, 1998.

Kramer, Daniel C. *The Days of Wine and Roses Are Over: Governor Hugh Carey and New York State.* Lanham, MD: University Press of America, 1997.

Kroeger, Brooke. *Nellie Bly: Daredevil, Reporter, Feminist.* New York: Times Books/Random House, 1994.

Lachman, Seymour P., with Robert A. Polner. *Three Men in a Room: The Inside Story of Power and Betrayal in an American Statehouse.* New York: The New Press, 2006.

Mahler, Jonathan. *Ladies and Gentlemen, The Bronx is Burning: 1977, Baseball, Politics, and the Battle for the Soul of the City.* New York: Picador, 2005.

McNickle, Chris. *To Be Mayor of New York: Ethnic Politics in the City.* New York: Columbia University Press, 1993.

Morris, Charles. R. *The Cost of Good Intentions: New York City and the Liberal Experiment, 1960–1975.* New York: McGraw-Hill, 1980.

Newfield, Jack, and Paul Du Brul. *The Abuse of Power: The Permanent Government and the Fall of New York.* New York: Viking, 1977.

O'Connor, James. *The Fiscal Crisis of the State New York.* New York: St. Martin's, 1973.

O'Neill, Thomas P., and William Novak, *Man of the House: The Life and Political Memoirs of Speaker Tip O'Neill.* New York: Random House, 1987.

Plotkin, Sidney, and William E. Scheuerman. *Private Interests/Public Spending: Balanced-Budget Conservatism and the Fiscal Crisis.* Boston: South End Press, 1994.

*Public Papers of Hugh L. Carey, Fifty-First Governor of the State of New York.* Albany, NY: New York Library Digital Image Project, 1982.

Rothman, David J., and Sheila M. Rothman, *The Willowbrook Wars: A Decade of Struggle for Social Justice.* New York: Harper & Row, 1984.

Sanjek, Roger. *The Future of Us All: Race and Neighborhood Politics in New York City.* Ithaca, NY: Cornell University Press, 1998.

Shannon, William V. *The American Irish: A Political and Social Portrait.* New York: Macmillan, 1963.

Shefter, Martin. *Political Crisis, Fiscal Crisis: The Collapse and Revival of New York City.* New York: Columbia University Press, 1992.

Simon, William. *Time for Truth.* New York: Berkeley, 1980.

Smith, Alfred E. *Up to Now: An Autobiography.* New York: Viking, 1929.

Snyder, William F. *The Carey Years: 1979–1982 and Epilogue: Selected Images from The New York State Archives.* Albany: New York State Archives, 2009.

Sobel, Lester A., ed. *New York and the Urban Dilemma.* New York: Facts on File, 1976.

Starr, Roger. *The Rise and Fall of New York.* New York: Basic Books, 1989.

Tabb, William K. *The Long Default: New York City and the Urban Fiscal Crisis.* New York: Monthly Review Press, 1982.

Taylor, Steven J. *Acts of Conscience: World War II, Mental Institutions, and Religious Objectors.* Syracuse, NY: Syracuse University Press, 2009.

Unger, Irwin. *The Best of Intentions: The Triumph and Failure of the Great Society Under Kennedy, Johnson, and Nixon.* New York: Doubleday, 1996.

Van Atta, Dale. *With Honor: Melvin Laird in War, Peace, and Politics.* Madison: University of Wisconsin Press, 2008.

Zeitz, Joshua M. *White Ethnic New York: Jews, Catholics, and the Shaping of Postwar Politics.* Chapel Hill: University of North Carolina Press, 2007.

Zinn, Howard, *LaGuardia in Congress.* New York: W. W. Norton, 1959.

# Index

215